8/95
9/15

ML

THE MARCH TO VICTORY

THE MARCH TO VICTORY

A GUIDE TO WORLD WAR II BATTLES AND
BATTLEFIELDS FROM LONDON TO THE RHINE

John T. Bookman and Stephen T. Powers

HARPER & ROW, PUBLISHERS, New York
Cambridge, Philadelphia, San Francisco, London
1817 *Mexico City, São Paulo, Singapore, Sydney*

We dedicate this book to our mothers,
Helen Turner Bookman
and
Mary Tallichet Powers
in memoriam, to our fathers,
John F. Bookman
and
John N. Powers

FIRST EDITION

Designer: Sidney Feinberg
Maps by George Colbert

Library of Congress Cataloging-in-Publication Data

Bookman, John T.
    The march to victory.

    Bibliography: p.
    Includes index.
    1. World War, 1939–1945—Battlefields—Europe—
Guide-books. I. Powers, Stephen T. II. Title.
D747.B65   1986   914'.04558   85-45181
ISBN 0-06-015506-X   86 87 88 89 90 HC 10 9 8 7 6 5 4 3 2 1
ISBN 0-06-096053-1 (pbk.)   86 87 88 89 90 HC 10 9 8 7 6 5 4 3 2 1

Contents

Preface

This guidebook is intended for the veteran of World War II, the student of military history, and any traveler to Europe, in fact or imagination, who has an interest in the Allied effort to defeat German military forces in Western Europe. We describe by both text and maps a series of tours over the principal World War II battlefields in northwestern Europe.

The tours described are arranged in geographical sequence, beginning in England, then to France, north to the Netherlands, and east through Belgium and Luxembourg to the Rhineland in western Germany. The tours describe the battlefields and the exploits of particular individuals and units, identify relics in the field, and locate monuments and museums. In the summer of 1984, we drove the roads, walked the ground, and visited the museums we describe. Each tour is preceded by an overview of the battle which establishes a context for, and allows a better understanding of, what you will see.

In our European travels, we have had many occasions to regret the absence of a guide like the one you now have in your hands. Too many times we have unknowingly passed by battlefields and arrived at museums closed for the day. There are, of course, many military histories of World War II, but these give scant assistance to someone who wants to visit the Normandy beaches or the battlefields around Bastogne. There are also many guidebooks for the European traveler on a variety of subjects, but none pays more than incidental attention to the sites and relics of the war. Our frustration at lost opportunities and lost time, and our keen interest in the events of the war, have inspired this book.

ACKNOWLEDGMENTS

Our debt is large to those historians who labored in the Office of the Chief of Military History, Department of the Army, and to other authors, many of whose names appear in the bibliography appended to this book. We are indebted as well to many nameless Europeans who made our visits to the sites described herein a provocative and informative experience.

We wish to thank Mr. M. S. Wyeth, our editor at Harper & Row, whose confidence in this book nearly matched our own; Mr. Hugh Mackay, who introduced us to Harper & Row; Professor Al Cornebise, our friend and colleague at the University of Northern Colorado, who provided unflagging encouragement; and Ms. Sandra Guest, who put our manuscript into readable form.

We also thank our friends Andra Schmidt and Millie Turner, who were forced to endure hot afternoons looking at weapons collections and wandering over weedy fields, and our children, Leah, Jessica, Rachel, and Greg, who were denied the attention of their fathers for long months. May this book be some repayment to them all.

Introduction: Using the Guide

To make the most effective use of this guide, we have several suggestions. Read the appropriate chapter, both "Overview" and "Tour" sections, before starting out on any given tour. More complete information about the museums which we mention can be found in Appendix A. We include maps in the "Tour" sections with places of interest keyed by numbers to the text. Our directions include approximate distances in kilometers on the Continent and in miles in England. You will need to estimate your travel time. Be generous. There is much else to be seen along the way. Know that in general it takes longer to get from one point to another in Europe than in the United States. The roads are often narrower, traffic is more congested, and built-up areas are more numerous. Furthermore, one must drive more slowly to see and read unfamiliar road signs.

This guide is too focused on military matters to be relied upon solely. Our maps are abstracts of more comprehensive maps of a particular region or city—not all towns and roads have been included. Therefore, you will need to acquire additional road maps. Those put out by Michelin are reliable and widely available. You will also need guides to hotels and restaurants. The popular American ones are most useful for the larger cities. During the peak tourist season, we recommend that you make hotel reservations in the larger cities. For this, the previously mentioned guides can help. Elsewhere you will find that reservations are less necessary, especially if you arrive at your destination by midafternoon. Local tourist offices usually have current lists of hotels and restaurants and their prices, and they can arrange accommodations for you. These offices can be found by following the "i" (for information) signs. In the Netherlands, look for "VVV." There are often English-speaking personnel at the tourist offices who can help you with any problem you encounter.

We have provided in Appendix B a short annotated bibliography which includes military histories and other guides to the battlefields. The latter are more sharply focused than this one and are not generally available in the United States.

Outside of London and Paris, we assume that you will be driving. While it is certainly possible to use public transportation to reach many of the sites we describe, travel by automobile is both simpler and quicker, although not necessarily cheaper. Gasoline prices in Europe are double those in the United States. Arrangements to rent, lease, or buy a car should be made in the United States. The names and addresses of those agencies that make such arrangements can be found in any of the general guides to travel in Europe. If you plan to tour in both England and on the Continent, it will be necessary to rent or lease one car in England and another for the Continent. We recommend that you cross the English Channel by Hovercraft. The comfort and speed are worth the small additional expense.

Those wishing assistance in visiting particular grave sites in military cemeteries contact:

American Battle Monuments Commission
Room 5127, Pulaski Building
20 Massachusetts Ave., N.W.
Washington, D.C.

Commonwealth War Graves Commission
2 Marlow Road
Maidenhead, Berks, UK

Volksbund Deutsche Kriegsgräbefürsorge
Postfach 103840
3500 Kassel, West Germany

Ministry of Anciens Combattants
rue de Berey
Paris 12, France

We have sought to be as accurate as possible in getting you to the World War II sites. Nevertheless, things change. New roads are built, old ones are closed, museums adopt different hours, and battlefield remains are moved to a new site. We also recognize that we have failed to mention some things, sometimes by design but sometimes inadvertently. In any event, we would like to hear your suggestions about how to make this a better book.

1

The Battle of Britain
and the Bomber Offensive

An Overview

"What General Weygand called the 'Battle of France' is over. I expect the 'Battle of Britain' to begin." So Prime Minister Winston Churchill declared to a hushed House of Commons on 18 June 1940. There was not long to wait. Toward the close of the month the Luftwaffe began to appear in increasing numbers over the English Channel.

It was not, however, until July that the German High Command began planning for a cross-Channel invasion. Hitler believed that after the fall of France Britain would sue for peace. When Churchill refused his peace offers, Hitler then had to make good on his threats to carry the battle to Britain itself. The German military had given little thought to a strategy or the tactics for a seaborne invasion. Development of the technical means—specialized landing craft, for example—had also been neglected. Nevertheless, throughout the summer the army assembled masses of troops on the Normandy coast and in the Pas-de-Calais, and the navy collected some three thousand barges and coasters from European waters in preparation for an invasion date of 15 September. If Operation Sea Lion (the code name for the invasion of Britain) was to have any prospect for success, command of the air over the Channel and the landing beaches was necessary. For this the German army and navy looked to the Luftwaffe.

Germany entered the war with the largest, best-trained air force in the world. By the summer of 1940, the Luftwaffe had available about 4,500 aircraft, including well over a thousand bombers and a thousand single-seat fighters. In the Messerschmitt Bf 109, the Messerschmitt Bf 110, and the Junkers 88, it had three of the most technically advanced fighting machines of the day. To pilot and crew these aircraft, the German training schools had been turning out airmen at the rate of eight hundred a month. The training program, moreover, was rigorous and long. German airmen had acquired even more valuable schooling in combat in Spain, Poland, and France. Success in those campaigns brought morale to a high pitch. German air commanders, from Reichsmarschall Hermann Goering on down, had every confidence that in a matter of weeks the Luftwaffe would win the Battle of Britain.

Triumph on the Continent also encouraged complacency about the readiness of the German air arm. The Battle of Britain initiated a years-long period of conflict in which strategic bombing at great distances was undertaken by both the Axis and the Allies. The Luftwaffe, however, had been designed to fight a short war in close connection with advancing ground forces. Both in the design and production of aircraft, emphasis had been given to the bomber. Only the Bf 109 was expressly intended for bomber support. This single-seat fighter would prove to be at least the equal of the Spitfire—the best British fighter. But production of the Bf 109 was permitted to fall to 140 per month by the summer of 1940. This rate was insufficient to keep pace with the losses taken during the Battle of Britain. Also significant was the failure to provide wing tanks for the German fighters. The Bf 109 had a flying time of about ninety minutes which brought London just within range of the squadrons based in northern France. German pilots could not long engage the intercepting Spitfires and Hurricanes. Those who failed to break off after ten minutes were often forced to ditch in the Channel.

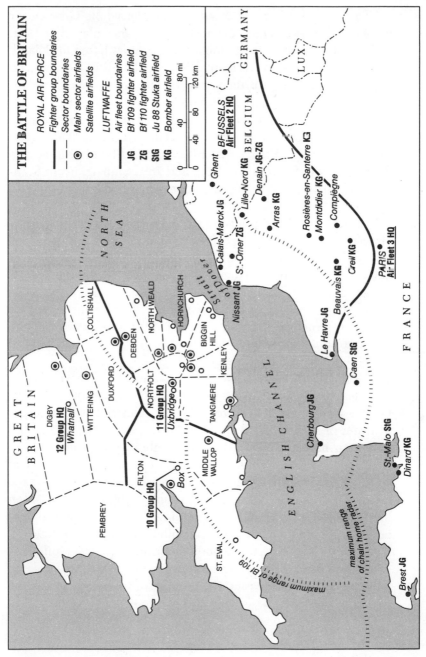

THE BATTLE OF BRITAIN

ROYAL AIR FORCE
- ⎯⎯ Fighter group boundaries
- ------ Sector boundaries
- ◉ Main sector airfields
- ○ Satellite airfields

LUFTWAFFE
- Air fleet boundaries
- **JG** Bf 109 fighter airfield
- **ZG** Bf 110 fighter airfield
- **StG** Ju 88 Stuka airfield
- **KG** Bomber airfield

Scale: 0 40 80 mi / 0 40 80 120 km

MAP 1

The Royal Air Force did not engage the whole German air force in the battle. Transport and liaison planes played no part. Nor did the squadrons of bombers and fighters based in Poland, Austria, and southern Germany. Bombers based in Norway and Denmark could reach Britain, but they had to fly unescorted, as the single-seat fighters had insufficient range. Nevertheless, it was a formidable force which Germany threw against the British defenders. On the eve of the battle, Germany had operational in northern France 656 Bf 109s, 168 Bf 110 twin-engine fighters, 248 Ju 87s (the "Stuka"), and 769 bombers. From Scandinavia, thirty-two Bf 110s and ninety-five bombers could also be committed.

The RAF had 1,200 pilots and a total of 591 serviceable fighters: 347 Hurricanes, 160 Spitfires, 25 Boulton Paul Defiants, and 59 Blenheims. Even fewer planes would have been available had not Air Chief Marshal Hugh Dowding resisted Churchill's attempt to send additional squadrons to France during the fighting in May. As it was, only sixty-six of the 261 Hurricanes sent to France returned to England. This left little more than half the fifty-two squadrons which the Air Ministry had earlier decided were necessary for the defense of Britain.

The initial British disadvantage in numbers of fighters proved to be less significant than the shortage of trained pilots. Newspaper magnate Lord Beaverbrook, whom Churchill appointed as Minister of Aircraft Production in May, spurred the aircraft industry to increase production. Throughout the summer more than four hundred fighters per month rolled off the lines. Despite all the losses from enemy action, the RAF concluded the Battle of Britain with more operational fighters—about seven hundred—than it had at the beginning. Not even Beaverbrook, however, could do anything about pilot casualties or fatigue.

In 1939, British flying schools continued to train pilots at peacetime rates. These rates soon proved to be too low to keep pace with losses. Increasing the number of trainees provided no immediate remedy. Basic pilot training took a year, and another year was required in operational training with a squadron. Soon after the outbreak of war, operational training time was reduced to six months. As the war progressed, and losses among pilots mounted, further reductions occurred: on 10 July to four weeks and a month later to two weeks. Pilots with as few as two hours in fighters—ten hours was about average—were committed to battle. Fatigue too decreased the combat effectiveness of Fighter Command. Some pilots flew as many as eight sorties a day. Even when the German raiders did not come, fliers had to be ready to scramble at a moment's notice.

Fortunately, many of the foreign nationals who volunteered for service in the RAF brought valuable experience with them. Twenty percent of the 2,500 pilots who flew fighters in the battle were foreigners. Most were from Commonwealth countries, but there were substantial numbers of Poles and Czechs and a small contingent of Americans—seven. Of the top ten pilots, five were foreigners. The top ace was a Czech, Sergeant Josef Frantisek, who shot down seventeen German aircraft.

Throughout the battle, Dowding husbanded his shrinking pool of pilots. Few understood as he did that so long as Fighter Command existed no invasion against Britain could be launched. He had already earned Churchill's displeasure by opposing the transfer of Hurricane squadrons to France in May. He then offended the Admiralty by balking at their insistence that Fighter Command fly standing cover over convoys moving through the Channel. Dowding also committed squadrons piecemeal and only when the raiders included bombers. Typically, the RAF fighters were greatly outnumbered by the attacking Germans. Thus was Fighter Command preserved in a battle of attrition. Ironically, the very tactics which permitted the RAF to win the Battle of Britain brought the dismissal of the commander of Fighter Command.

The Germans had no settled strategy for prosecuting the air war. They pursued a variety of ends, according priority first to one, then to another, and sometimes pursuing several at once.

Goering believed that Britain could be hammered into submission by bombing alone. But this strategy was at one time or another subordinated to others: paving the way for a seaborne invasion, denying air superiority to the RAF, and establishing German air superiority.

Four phases in the battle can be distinguished. The first began in early July and ran through early August. This phase was marked by attacks on British coastal convoys and air battles over the Channel. By 8 August, the Germans had sunk eighteen freighters and four Royal Navy destroyers; many more ships were damaged. So perilous had passage become through the Straits of Dover that destroyers were withdrawn from Dover. During this period, Luftwaffe losses in aircraft were twice as great as those of Fighter Command.

The first-line British fighters—the Spitfire and the Hurricane—had demonstrated their capabilities. The Spitfire was a match for the Messerschmitt Bf 109 except at altitudes above 20,000 feet, where the fuel injection of the German fighter gave it an advantage. The Hurricane did not match the Bf 109 in performance but, when flown by an experienced pilot, could fight successfully. By far the greater number of Fighter Command squadrons were equipped with Hurricanes during the Battle of Britain. These squadrons accounted for 80 percent of German aircraft shot down.

The other British fighters had not fared so well. The Defiants proved too slow and poorly gunned to survive. On 19 July, nine Defiants from the 141st Squadron took off from Hawkinge to intercept a force of Bf 109s. Only three returned to base. The Defiant squadrons withdrew to the north to shepherd convoys and to serve as inadequate night fighters. The Blenheim also suffered much in the early going. It was slower than the Defiant and unable to catch even the German bombers.

The second phase ran from 12 August to 19 August. Goering launched a major air offensive on Britain on 13 August (code-named Eagle Day). In preparation for this attack, German bombers struck coastal radar stations on the twelfth in an attempt to deny Fighter Command early warning of the assault planned for the next day. Of the four radar stations hit, three were back in operation within hours; the fourth, that at Ventnor on the Isle of Wight, would be transmitting again in four days. For the next week, the Luftwaffe subjected British ports, industrial sites, airfields, and radar stations to massive assault. German pilots mounted some 1,700 sorties a day.

At the week's end, both sides retreated to lick their wounds and regroup. The Luftwaffe had lost in excess of 280 aircraft; the RAF slightly less than half that number. The German raids had failed to achieve any decisive result. Goering did learn several lessons. The Junkers 87 dive-bomber, the celebrated Stuka of the campaigns in Poland and Western Europe, was too slow to compete against Spitfires and Hurricanes and was withdrawn from the battle. The bombers from Scandinavian bases carried out a raid on targets in Scotland and northern England on the fifteenth. Unescorted by fighters, they suffered considerable losses and were not again committed to the fight.

The third phase began on 24 August and continued until 6 September. In this two-week period, the Luftwaffe came closest to destroying Fighter Command. By concentrating his efforts on RAF airfields and aircraft plants, Goering forced Dowding to commit virtually his whole force in defense. On 30 August, Fighter Command flew over a thousand sorties—twice as many as flown on a single day in the previous month. The British fighters scored heavily, but their losses were also great. Both sides lost nearly three hundred planes.

Had the Germans persisted in this direct assault against Fighter Command, they might have won air superiority simply by exhausting the pool of British pilots. They did not persist, however, because Goering was impatient for a quick victory. When the desired results from bombing one set of objectives were not immediately realized, he switched to another. The events of 24 and 25 August also contributed to the change in focus of attack. In a night raid near London on the twenty-fourth, a German bomber overflew its target and mistakenly released its bomb load over the city—in violation of Hitler's prohibition. RAF Bomber Command retaliated the next night by hitting Berlin with eighty-one planes. The Germans vowed revenge.

A raid on London by over three hundred German bombers on 7 September marked the beginning of the fourth phase. Luftwaffe attacks now centered on London, at first by day and then by night. The city's suffering purchased relief for a beleaguered Fighter Command. Dowding was once again able to conserve his forces by piecemeal commitment against the German bombers.

The German bomber offensive against London and other cities in Britain continued through the fall and winter. The "Blitz" ended in May 1941, when the Luftwaffe moved to participate in the Russian and Mediterranean campaigns. The Battle of Britain had ended months earlier. The Ministry of Defense sets the official closing date as 31 October. By that time Goering had abandoned any attempt to destroy Fighter Command. However, as the Battle of Britain is connected with Operation Sea Lion, an earlier date may be assigned. From 7 to 15 September, the Luftwaffe lost 174 aircraft against RAF losses of 127. On 15 September, Fighter Command demonstrated decisively its continued vitality by shooting down fifty-six German planes. Two days later, Hitler postponed Sea Lion indefinitely.

The Battle of Britain, by later standards, was a small affair. Before the war's end, RAF Bomber Command would lose more airmen in one night than all Fighter Command losses during the battle; and the Luftwaffe in a day's combat would lose as many planes as it had in the whole summer of 1940. Nevertheless, the Battle of Britain had great significance. By their efforts, the "few," as Churchill called the RAF fighter pilots, had cast in doubt the invincibility of German arms. Many Americans began to believe that the British, with help, could contend against Germany. The RAF, by thwarting German invasion plans, also preserved Britain as a base of operations for prosecuting the war.

The Battle of Britain and the Blitz cast doubt on the doctrine which then reigned among many air commanders in Britain and, to a lesser extent, in the United States. The central tenets of this doctrine were three. First, the air force had a strategic role of its own, above and beyond any tactical role in support of naval and ground forces. Second, the application of air power in this strategic role could itself bring victory. And third, the bomber would always get through. For all the efforts of the Luftwaffe in its bomber offensive against Britain, British industrial production was not much affected and British morale, civilian and military, remained high. Furthermore, the hundreds of German bombers shot down by Fighter Command demonstrated that the bomber will not always get through.

These facts did not deter the British, or later the Americans, from mounting a bomber offensive of their own. Moreover, the aspirations of the Allied strategic air forces remained large despite evidence accumulated during the war that the results of bombing, while far from negligible, fell far short of the claims made by its proponents.

Neither Britain nor the United States entered the war with the aircraft, bombs, or target-locating devices which would permit realization of their aspirations. The provisions made for protecting the bombers against anti-aircraft fire and intercepting fighters were also inadequate. Throughout the war, RAF Bomber Command and the U.S. Army Air Force sought to make good these deficiencies.

It was a small force which set out from England on 4 September 1939 to begin Bomber Command's campaign against the Reich. Ten Blenheims and nine Wellingtons attacked two German warships at anchor in the Heligoland Bight. It was not an auspicious beginning for British daylight bombing. The enemy cruisers suffered only superficial damage; they shot down five Blenheims and two Wellingtons.

RAF bombers, in the first four months of the war, had a loss rate of 9.5 percent—higher than it would be for any subsequent period of similar length. Bomber Command discovered, as had the Luftwaffe, that bombers unescorted by fighters could get to their targets in daylight only at great cost. The bombers with which Britain went to war in 1939—the Wellington, the Hampden, and the Whitley—were slow, had little defensive armament, and did not have self-sealing fuel tanks. The comment of one pilot about the Whitley—"not the sort of vehicle in which one should go to pursue the King's enemies"—applied with only somewhat lesser force to the others. The advantage clearly lay with the defense as the British sought to bomb by day. The new year, 1940, saw more and more raids at night. By fall 1940, night bombing had become the established pattern, although occasional daytime missions were undertaken.

Another significant change in bombing strategy occurred in May 1940. Theretofore, the RAF had not bombed targets where German civilians would be endangered, for fear of provoking German attacks on Britain. Following the massive Luftwaffe raid on Rotterdam, Churchill lifted this ban. That night, Bomber Command dispatched ninety-nine planes to bomb the Ruhr. With this raid, the bomber offensive began.

Over the next fourteen months, Bomber Command mounted sporadic and varied attacks on the enemy. In response to the threat of Sea Lion, the over-age Battle and Blenheim squadrons were committed to daylight bombing of invasion barges and troop concentrations. Although effective in this role, these half-dozen or so squadrons suffered grievously and were largely used up in this way. The longer-range aircraft bombed targets in Germany at night. Rarely did more than one hundred planes participate in a raid, and raids were infrequent, averaging about four a month. Loss rates dropped sharply from those experienced at the beginning of the war. Nevertheless, over five hundred planes were lost to all causes from May 1940 to July 1941.

During this period the night air defense of Germany lay almost wholly with the flak arm of the Luftwaffe. Some 450 anti-aircraft guns and 100 searchlights were clustered around the major industrial centers. Without a precise radar system for tracking the British bombers, the flak batteries enjoyed scant success. In order to firm up the night air defenses, Goering began to expand the night fighter force. Here too, really effective fighter interception would await the introduction of more sophisticated radar.

The very difficulties which plagued the defenders of the German homeland in the early years of the war also affected the attacking British bombers. As night hid the bombers from the fighters and flak guns, so it hid the factories and rail yards from the bombers. Depending on the "dead reckoning" navigation of the day, pilots did well to arrive within twenty miles of their targets at the end of a run. Once in the general area, they would have to grope in the dark for the target—all the while in the area of greatest danger. By mid–1941, the RAF was engaging in extensive photoreconnaissance over Germany. Analysis of photographs taken at the time of bomb release and after the attack revealed the marginal nature of the bomber offensive. Only a third of the crews who reported hitting the target had dropped their bombs within five miles of it. Over the Ruhr, with its industrial haze, the figures were far worse. Even those crews who were on target had caused little damage, owing to the small load-carrying capacity of their aircraft.

However sobering these facts for the RAF commanders at High Wycombe and the political leadership in Whitehall, RAF bombers continued their flights over the Reich. In order to boost the morale of blitzed British families and to persuade a neutral United States and an invaded Russia that Britain could attack, Churchill grasped the only offensive weapon he had—Bomber Command.

There were developments in train which held out some promise that the bomber offensive could be made to work or, at any rate, to work better than it had. At the close of 1941, Bomber

Command began to take delivery of a new generation of air-craft. These four-engined bombers had better performance and greater load-carrying capacity than their predecessors. The Lancaster, which first saw service in March 1942, would be the British workhorse for the rest of the war. New navigational aids were produced to better enable the crews to find their targets. Tactics were also revised. Up to this time, bomber crews had flown routes of their own choosing to the target. This permitted the tracking and interception of the bombers on an individual basis by the German defenders—a task for which they were specially fitted. Bomber Command began to concentrate the at-tacking force in a "bomber stream" in an effort to overwhelm the defense at a single point. This more than halved the duration of attack and thereby reduced the opportunities of the night fighters.

These developments coincided with the arrival of a new com-mander for Bomber Command—Air Chief Marshal Arthur "Bomber" Harris. A former bomber group commander, he brought to his new post strongly held views as to what his air-craft and crews could and could not do. They could not carry out precision bombing; they could bomb an area.

On 28 March 1942, Harris dispatched 234 bombers to show what area bombing could do. In the raid, Lübeck was heavily damaged. In the following month, four consecutive attacks on Rostock destroyed much of the city and severely damaged U-boat and aircraft factories. Still greater successes were needed, Harris thought, to prevent the diversion of Bomber Command to tactical missions and to support his demands for more re-sources. Therefore he staged a series of thousand-bomber raids. This force was four times larger than any previously assembled by the RAF. First Cologne in late May, then Essen, and finally, on 25 June, Bremen suffered under the hail of metal. Having demonstrated the destructive potential of Bomber Command, Harris returned half his bombers and crews to the operational training centers from which he had drawn them and renewed

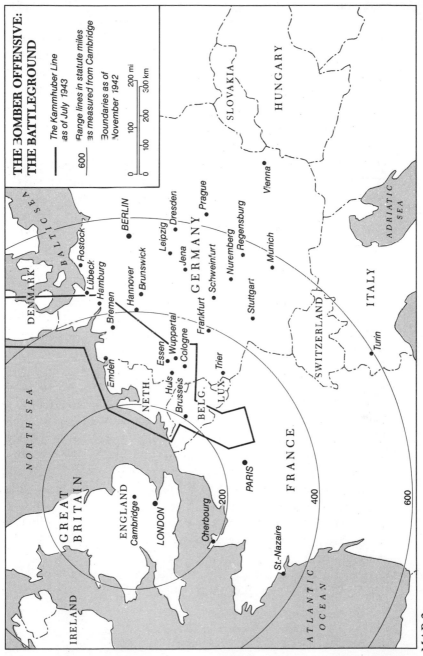

**THE BOMBER OFFENSIVE:
THE BATTLEGROUND**

— The Kammhuber Line
as of July 1943

600 Range lines in statute miles
as measured from Cambridge

— Boundaries as of
November 1942

0 100 200 300 km
0 100 200 mi

MAP 2

smaller-scale raids. There would be no more thousand-bomber attacks until 1944.

The increasing frequency and weight of the British attacks had stimulated a response from the Germans even before the thousand-bomber raids. In July 1940, Colonel Josef Kammhuber began organization of the night defenses. By the end of 1941, the "Kammhuber Line" was in place along the western frontiers of the Reich. The line consisted of early-warning radar and ground radar control of fighters, flak batteries, and searchlights. During 1942, the number of night interceptors increased from 180 to 350. This was a formidable barrier through or around which the RAF bombers had to fly. In the winter of 1941–42, Bomber Command's losses crept upward. Those losses might well have become prohibitive had the Germans devoted greater resources to defense of their air space. Other theaters, however, particularly the Russian, claimed the preponderance of the Luftwaffe's strength. And in May 1942, Hitler ordered the transfer of many searchlight and flak units out of the Kammhuber Line. As it was, Bomber Command just held its own by those innovations earlier mentioned. Britain, of course, had acquired a new, powerful ally months earlier, but the anticipated American bomber offensive had yet to materialize.

The United States Army Air Force entered the war with the conviction that it could succeed at unescorted daylight bombing where the British had failed. American air commanders were of course aware of the heavy losses incurred by the RAF in its daylight raids early in the war. But they were also aware that night bombing had thus far worked little damage on the Nazi war machine. They concluded that if German industry was to be destroyed it must be done by more precise attacks undertaken in the light of day.

American bombers would get through to their targets, it was believed, because they could defend themselves against German fighters and they would fly at altitudes above 20,000 feet, where fire from the ground would be less effective. Once over the target, bombardiers, peering through their Norden bombsights, could execute accurate drops. A comparison of the principal aircraft employed by the U.S. and British air forces indicates the difference in approach. Both the Lancaster and the B-17 Flying Fortress weighed about 60,000 pounds fully loaded. The average bomb load of the Lancaster ran a bit under 9,000 pounds and that of the Fortress about half that. The B-17, however, had some 12 percent of its weight in armor and defensive armament, while the Lancaster had just 6 percent. Flying in large formations, the American bombers would exact an unacceptable toll of intercepting fighters.

The execution of the American strategic bombing offensive against Germany rested with the Eighth Air Force based in Britain. It would later be joined by the Fifteenth Air Force based in Italy. Activated in January 1942 under Colonel Asa M. Duncan, the Eighth began preparations to move to England the following month. By June, aircraft, crews, and ground personnel under a new commander—General Carl "Tooey" Spaatz—began to arrive at their bases in southeastern England. At peak strength in mid-1944, the Eighth numbered about 200,000 men, 2,600 heavy bombers, and 1,100 fighters.

The missions flown by the Eighth Air Force in 1942 did little to test American confidence in the "self-defending formation." The rail-marshaling yards at Rouen and Sotteville were the targets of the first attack on German-occupied Europe. Twelve B-17s with Spitfire escort returned unscathed. Other escorted attacks against targets outside Germany were mounted with small loss. The scale of these operations increased throughout the year. On 9 October, 108 B-17s and B-24s bombed a steelworks in Belgium. On this raid German fighters shot down four bombers for a loss of two interceptors. These missions were flown against targets less heavily defended than those in Germany and almost always with fighter escort. When raids were made without escort, the bombers suffered. On 23 November, thirty-six B-17s unaccompanied by fighters attacked the U-boat pens at

St.-Nazaire. German interceptors shot down four bombers and severely damaged another—a harbinger of things to come in 1943.

As Bomber Command readied itself to deliver really wounding blows and the Eighth Air Force continued its buildup, the political and military leadership of the United States and Britain met in Casablanca in January 1943. From this conference came a directive expressing agreement that the Allies would undertake a combined bomber offensive in preparation for a cross-Channel invasion—Roundup—tentatively scheduled for the coming summer. The Casablanca Directive gave priority to the bombing of submarine construction yards, aircraft factories, transportation facilities, oil plants, and other industrial targets. In 1943, the German fighters would exact a high price from bombers over the Reich. The Pointblank Directive of June 1943 reaffirmed the Casablanca priorities but also acknowledged that "depletion of the German fighter strength must be accomplished first."

Bomber Command continued its area bombing of German cities for the remainder of the war despite Casablanca and Pointblank. Air Marshal Harris had grave doubts about the operational feasibility of precision bombing of industrial targets. Furthermore, he resented the ascendance of American ideas about how the air war should be conducted. After all, it would be largely a British effort for some months to come. He also had reservations about the underlying rationale of the Casablanca schedule of priorities. He was loath to contemplate an invasion in the teeth of a still formidable Germany; indeed, he believed that bombing by a sufficiently large force would bring Hitler to his knees. Many of his superiors shared, more or less, these ideas, and so Harris was permitted, with some exceptions, to go his own way.

In deference to the Casablanca Directive, Bomber Command attacked Lorient and St.-Nazaire. These raids accomplished, in Harris's words, the destruction of "two perfectly good French towns" but worked no damage to the U-boat pens buried under yards of concrete. Having demonstrated to his satisfaction the futility of such a policy, he initiated the "Battle of the Ruhr." From March through July, the British bombers wrought devastation on Essen, Düsseldorf, Dortmund, and other cities in the Ruhr. In the most successful of these raids, much of Wuppertal was laid waste. Most of the 657 raiders put their bombs within three miles of the aiming point. Seven hundred acres of the city were severely damaged—larger than the area blitzed in London through the whole war. There was also great loss of life—3,350 killed as well as thousands injured.

In the "Battle of the Ruhr," Mosquito fighter-bombers of the Pathfinder Force had guided the heavies to the target. Equipped with the newly developed radar, Oboe, and target-marking bombs, this elite group of carefully selected crews had begun to fulfill the promise held for it when first organized in August 1942. The Oboe radar, however, had an effective range of only 280 miles from the ground stations in England. But within this area, which took in the Ruhr, Bomber Command could now carry out more accurate attacks than had earlier been possible and could do so without ever seeing the target.

RAF bombers returned to a familiar target in late July—Hamburg. Loss rates over this heavily defended city had in earlier attacks run about 6 percent. On the night of 24 July, the raiders carried within their bomb bays a new weapon codenamed Window with which to confound the German radar. The release of 92 million strips of aluminum foil during the attack paralyzed the night defenses. Only twelve of the 746 bombers which had left England failed to return, for a loss rate of 1.5 percent. Hamburg was visited three more times in rapid succession, with staggering results—70 percent of the city gutted by fire-storms, in excess of 30,000 dead, and a million people in flight from their homes.

Emboldened by the success at Hamburg against the second most populous German city, Harris turned his attention to Berlin. This time the Luftwaffe was ready. After the initial confusion caused by Window, the Germans developed new tactics less reliant on radar. Hamburg also brought the withdrawal of fighter squadrons from the Mediterranean and Russian theaters to meet the threat to the homeland. In three attacks on Berlin in late August and early September, Bomber Command lost 123 aircraft, a loss rate of 7.5 percent.

The increased activity of the Eighth Air Force had also begun to concern German air commanders. In the winter and spring of 1943, the Eighth made infrequent penetrations into Germany. The Americans had first sent bombers over the Reich on 27 January 1943. Sixty-four B-17s and B-24s had attacked Wilhelmshaven. The arrival of good flying weather in the summer and the growth in strength of the Eighth allowed an increase in the pace and weight of the attacks. In June and July, between one and two hundred bombers mounted raids on German targets.

For the crews who participated in these raids and in those which followed, there was not much to distinguish one from another. Elmer Bendiner, a navigator on the B-17 *Tondelayo* of the 379th Bombardment Group, wrote that "if on a Wednesday one watches other men die and sees one's own death foreshadowed, it does not seem fitting to watch a similar deadly dance on Thursday and again on Friday and again on Saturday. Such a schedule can make the most awesome event a dull routine and turn battle into business."

On the days when a mission was to be flown, the call to wake came early. The small coal stoves did little to dispel the cold of the Nissen huts, so everyone hurried to dress and to get to breakfast. On these mornings there would be fresh rather than powdered eggs.

Following the briefing at, say, 0400, the crews dressed for the rigors of flying at 25,000 feet, where the temperatures might be thirty degrees below zero. The planes were not heated, and the slipstream of cold air rushing past at 175 mph pushed through every fissure in the airframe. The waist gunners got the worst of it standing in front of the open bays in the sides of the aircraft.

Once cleared for takeoff, and this usually followed a wait of as long as an hour and a half, the bombers took off at thirty-second intervals—one minute if the weather was bad. Depending on the size of the attacking force, assembly over England into squadrons, groups, wings, and task forces might take as much as two hours. The congestion of aircraft in such a small area was great, and near misses were frequent. Some three hundrod planes were lost by the Eighth, about 5 percent of all losses, because of collisions in the assembly stage.

Meanwhile, the escorting fighters were also forming up over their bases nearby. P-47 Thunderbolts accompanied the bombers across the North Sea. In a later stage of the war, the bombers had their "little friends" along to the German border, and still later all the way to the target.

Upon clearing the coast, eastward bound, several rounds were fired to test the machine guns. By this time the raiders were at an altitude so thin that the crews had oxygen masks in place. Frequent checks were made over the intercom to ensure that all were awake and alert. Should the connecting hoses linking the face masks with the oxygen supply become frozen or severed, unconsciousness and death came quickly.

Over the coast of Fortress Europe, the threat of death assumed another guise. The long-range German radar had long since picked up the assembly of the bomber formations over England. The defending flak batteries and fighter squadrons prepared a reception. As pilot Bert Stiles put it: "Travel by Flying Fortress is a hell of a way to go anywhere. . . . The welcome is so surly. No one is ever glad to see us."

On raids deep into Germany, the planes were over enemy-occupied territory for some four hours. The flak thrown up by the batteries on the coast and on the journey to and from the target could be terrifying, but it was usually not fatal. At the target it was another matter. Here was the site of greatest danger from flak as well as from enemy fighters. In order to provide a stable

platform for the bombardier, it was necessary to make a straight
and level run of from six to twenty minutes. During this period,
the bombers were like ducks in a shooting gallery.

Upon bomb release, the bombers headed for a designated
rally point to resume formation for the homeward flight. There
would be crippled planes now with wounded aboard. Their safe
return to base required that they stay within the protective confines of the formation. Over half the bombers lost in 1943 had
first dropped out of formation. Very few of these stragglers survived.

Enemy fighters accounted for most losses. The Luftwaffe
made Western Europe a gauntlet through which the Eighth had
to run. Fighter attacks might come from any direction but
straight-on from the front—twelve o'clock—was especially favored by the enemy. Against attacks from this direction, the
Fortresses and Liberators could bring to bear less well their ten
.50-caliber machine guns.

For those crews whose ships had taken hits or who were low
on fuel, the appearance of the North Sea in their windscreens
required a decision. Should they abandon the aircraft and risk
almost certain capture or attempt to make England and risk
ditching in the sea? Over four thousand crewmen of the Eighth
Air Force went down in the sea. Just 35 percent were rescued.

For those crews with fewer problems, it was simply a matter
now of finding their airfields and putting down. Aircraft with
wounded aboard or with severe mechanical problems fired two
red flares to secure priority for landing. Once on the ground, the
crews threw off their flying clothes, dragged out cigarettes, and
walked around their planes. There was usually much to see.
General Ira Eaker, who had taken over from Spaatz as commander of the Eighth in December 1942, reported at the close
of 1943 that "it is normal for from 25 to 50 percent of aircraft on
a deep-penetration mission into Germany to suffer some form of
battle damage."

The airmen could relax and celebrate their return from one

more mission in their assigned tour of duty of twenty-five. It would have to be done again, of course, and the prospects for survival were bleak. The average life of Eighth Air Force bombers and crews during 1943–44 was fifteen missions. Despite the odds, there were many crews who flew twenty-five missions and more and lived to talk about it.

On 17 August 1943, the Eighth mounted its most ambitious attack since joining the RAF in the bomber offensive. More than 350 bombers left England to strike at industrial targets deep in the German heartland. By this time, considerable improvements had been made in the German defenses. The Luftwaffe had operational four hundred single-seat Bf 109s and Focke-Wulf 190s and eighty twin-engine Bf 110s to fight the battle by day. All had been fitted with more armament. These modifications better enabled the German fighters to bring down the tough American bombers; they also markedly affected flying performance. This would tell later in dogfights with American fighters.

The Luftwaffe did not yet, however, have to contend with a fighter escort over Germany. American air commanders had begun to acknowledge a need for escort, but no suitable plane with sufficient range was available. It was only in late July that P-47s equipped with drop tanks began to provide cover as far as the German frontier. Beyond that point the bombers were on their own.

As soon as the American raiders entered Germany on 17 August, the Luftwaffe struck. For an hour and a half relays of German fighters attacked that part of the invading force making for the Messerschmitt aircraft factories at Regensburg. Twenty-four Fortresses fell. After dropping their bombs, the Regensburg raiders continued over the Alps to Italy and then to bases in North Africa. They were thus spared the ordeal of the return flight over heavily defended territory. The 230 bombers in the second wave got it on the flight to and from Schweinfurt. Twenty-one were shot down by fighters on the run in, another was downed by flak over the target, and fourteen more fell to fighters on the return to England. The costs mounted still higher when fifty-five of the aircraft which had landed in Africa had to be abandoned there beyond hope of immediate repair. A final three Fortresses were lost on the flight from Africa to England. Total losses were 118—almost a third of the attacking force. More than half of those bombers which made it back to England had suffered some damage.

A week later the Eighth could muster only 166 planes to hit targets in northern France. For the next several weeks, raids were confined to nearby targets under a protective umbrella of Thunderbolts and Spitfires. When replacement aircraft and crews accumulated, the eyes of air strategists turned again to the map of Germany. On 6 September, Stuttgart was the target of an attack by 338 B-17s. Forty-five did not survive the day. Once again the Eighth recoiled. The imperatives of Casablanca and Pointblank were not to be denied for too long however.

On 14 October, 291 Forts headed for Schweinfurt for another try at the ball-bearing plants. The Luftwaffe assembled fighters from northern France and throughout Germany to meet the raiding party. Flying some five hundred sorties over a three-hour period, the German fighters tore into the American formations. They shot down sixty planes, inflicted severe damage on seventeen and moderate damage on 121 others. The fall of Fortresses was heard all the way back in the United States. General Henry "Hap" Arnold, commander of the Army Air Force, felt it necessary to try to quiet the public outcry.

The Eighth did not again attempt a deep-penetration mission into Germany until February 1944. The cost of the fall campaign had been high, prohibitively high. Had there been comparatively great damage to German industry, the losses may have been justified. In retrospect, we know that German production increased during the period. American air commanders did not know this at the time. They did recognize that unescorted daylight attacks had proved to be too expensive. Some other way would have to be found to prosecute the air war against the Reich.

Only Bomber Command, flying by night, ventured beyond the cover of fighter escort during the winter months of 1943–44. The sole exception was a raid on 2 November by the newly formed Fifteenth U.S. Air Force. From temporary bases in North Africa—they would soon move to Italy—112 B-17s and B-24s attacked the Messerschmitt factories at Wiener-Neustadt. Losses were high, almost 10 percent, but the raid did succeed in drastically curtailing production for some time. The significance of this raid was not fully realized until the following spring. For a variety of reasons the Fifteenth flew no more missions into Germany until then. Nevertheless, the formation of an air arm in Italy exposed Germany to attack from another quarter. Against attacks from the south, moreover, Germany was less prepared to defend itself than in the north. The defender's problems were further compounded by the fact that more and more industrial facilities were being dispersed to areas less accessible to the Eighth Air Force and Bomber Command but now within the reach of the Fifteenth.

The losses suffered in the raids on Berlin in August and September did not dissuade Harris from writing to Churchill that "we can wreck Berlin from end to end if the USAAF will come in on it. It may cost us 400–500 aircraft. It will cost Germany the war." Although the Americans did not come in, Churchill gave his blessing to the "Battle of Berlin." Between 4 November 1943 and 24 March 1944, Bomber Command hit Berlin in strength on sixteen occasions. Loss rates fluctuated between 4.5 and 7 percent. Nearly five hundred bombers were lost, but Berlin, bloodied to be sure, continued to stand. In thirty-five major attacks on German cities from 18 November 1943 to 31 March 1944, Bomber Command lost 1,047 aircraft, and another 1,682 suffered damage. The German night fighters had demonstrated that they still possessed a lethal punch. Fortunately, April brought Harris's command under the direction of Eisenhower and an end to deep-penetration raids on Germany. Tactical targets in France were now to get priority as the Allies prepared for the Normandy invasion.

While Bomber Command was engaged in its winter campaign against Berlin, the Eighth Air Force sought to develop its fighter arm to stem any recurrence of the hemorrhaging experienced in the previous fall. By mid-December, the number of fighters available for escort duty had trebled. Most of these 550 fighters were P-38s and P-47s. Neither provided a wholly satisfactory solution. The P-38 was a good performer at low and medium altitudes but showed less well above 20,000 feet, where most of the action took place. The P-47 had the opposite problem. Modifications carried out on the Thunderbolt's engine in late 1943 increased its low-altitude performance.

The biggest problem, however, was range. The P-47, even with its hundred-gallon drop tank—initially made of papier-mâché—could fly only to the western German border. A larger drop tank of 165 gallons was fitted in the first months of 1944, which increased the range of the Thunderbolt to four hundred miles. The P-38, introduced in late autumn 1943, had a comparable range. Although the P-38 and the modified P-47 brought a larger part of Germany under the protective cover of fighter escort, Berlin and other important targets would have remained uncovered but for the arrival of the Mustang.

Designed and first produced early in the war, the P-51 Mustang had initially been a disappointment. Once fitted with a Packard-produced Merlin engine and additional fuel tanks, it acquired a performance and range which well satisfied the need for a long-range fighter. It could outperform all the German piston-engined planes and, with a range of six hundred miles, could fly to Berlin and back. The appearance over the Continent of large numbers of Mustangs shifted the balance of the contending forces in favor of the offense.

On 11 January 1944, the Eighth Air Force began a series of large escorted attacks on the German aircraft industry. The purpose of these attacks was not only to destroy the Luftwaffe at its source but to challenge the German fighters to give battle with the bombers and their escorts. These attacks reached a crescendo during "Big Week." The week began on 20 February with a deep-penetration raid into Germany—the first since "second" Schweinfurt. Over the next five days, the Eighth, sometimes joined by the Fifteenth, struck hard at aircraft factories as far away as western Poland. In all, the USAAF flew some 3,800 heavy bomber sorties over Germany. Two hundred twenty-six bombers were lost for a rate of 6 percent. The escorting fighter squadrons lost but twenty-eight of their number.

These raids and those which followed in the spring of 1944 did succeed in slowing German aircraft production. There were fewer planes delivered to the Luftwaffe than production schedules projected. Nevertheless, the number of single- and twin-engined fighters produced in May was 50 percent greater than in January: 2,200 as compared with 1,500. The attempt to defeat the Luftwaffe, then, by strategic bombing was not successful. It must be added, however, that Reichsminister Albert Speer, in charge of German industry, could work this recovery only by concentrating on the production of existing aircraft types. The Luftwaffe needed, and would increasingly need, new and superior planes with which to contend against a much more numerous foe. When Germany did introduce later in the war the first production jet fighter, the ME 262, it was a case of too little, too late.

In the destruction of the Luftwaffe in the air, the Eighth largely succeeded. During February alone, Germany lost 355 aircraft destroyed or missing. In the first six months of 1944, about two thousand day fighters were lost and another thousand damaged. These losses could be made good, but the losses in experienced pilots could not. German aces with scores of victories to their credit fell to the marauding Mustangs and Thunderbolts. Over the period January through June, the Luftwaffe lost over a thousand pilots, and almost another thousand were wounded. Into the breach the German training schools thrust replacements with far fewer hours than their American counterparts. They did not survive long.

By July, the Luftwaffe was rapidly becoming a spent force. Germany halted introductory flying training altogether during the summer, and heavy and medium bomber crews were largely disbanded for conversion to fighters. Single-engine fighter production rose to 3,800 in September, but no longer could a sustained defense be mounted for want of pilots to fly them and fuel to put in them. It is a measure of the demise of the German air force that during 1944–45 flak batteries shot down more day raiders than did the fighters. Masses of German fighters were encountered by Allied formations late in the war, but their appearance was occasional at best.

Earlier in 1944, the Luftwaffe had struck in force at every incursion into Germany. On 6 March, 730 B-17s and B-24s with an escort of 796 fighters headed for Berlin. Sixty-nine heavy bombers never returned, and more than a hundred were badly damaged. Losses of this magnitude, greater than those suffered in the raids on Schweinfurt, Regensburg, and Stuttgart, had been accounted staggering in the previous year. They were now regarded as acceptable, so large had the Eighth, and the USAAF, grown and so fecund the training schools and factories in supplying replacement crews and aircraft.

By June, Lieutenant General James Doolittle, who had taken over the Eighth from Eaker in January, had in his command over two thousand B-17s and B-24s and, by autumn, two complete crews for each plane. There were over 1,500 fighters to shepherd them. In Italy, Eaker, now commander of the Fifteenth, had another thousand heavies to send against the enemy. During the summer, the Eighth routinely dispatched a thousand bombers against Germany. It had mounted its first thousand-bomber raid in May, and in December would send two thousand bombers in relief of the beleaguered infantrymen in the Bulge.

After the break in the bomber offensive imposed by the need to support Overlord, Bomber Command renewed its strikes against German cities. The Eighth Air Force initiated a campaign against the German oil industry in which the Fifteenth figured prominently and Bomber Command rather less so. This must be counted as perhaps the only real victory for strategic air power in the war. In April 1944, the Germans produced 175,000 tons of aviation fuel. This figure had decreased to just 7,000 by September. Germany's production of all fuel supplies was reduced to 23 percent of what it had been in the spring.

The effects on the battlefield, both in the air and on the ground, were not immediate; Germany had accumulated large fuel reserves before the attacks began. Nevertheless, a fuel famine was not long averted. For the Luftwaffe, it meant fewer and fewer sorties, and at the end fighters stayed on the ground for want of fuel as German cities burned around them. The loss of France and Belgium in late 1944 added to the Luftwaffe's difficulties. Without early-warning radar stations and advance airfields, defense in depth became impossible.

In the autumn of 1944 and throughout the last months of the war, the strategy and tactics of the American and British air forces became increasingly similar. So clean had the Mustangs and Thunderbolts swept the skies of Luftwaffe day fighters that RAF bombers, bereft as they were of armor and armament, began daylight operations. The first such raid on 27 August saw all two hundred bombers return. Thereafter daylight attacks became increasingly frequent. For both the day and night raiders, Bomber Command provided fighter cover in the form of Spitfires with drop tanks and American-supplied Mustangs.

The Eighth Air Force adopted the British strategy of bombing cities and carried out such attacks with tactics devised in the night war, including pathfinder groups, radar guidance, and electronic devices for jamming German radar. By the end of the war, the Eighth had dropped more bombs on Berlin than any other target.

Tour of the Battle of Britain and the Bomber Offensive

This tour is divided into two parts: places that can be reached by means of the Underground in London and its environs, and sites outside London which must be reached by other means. The British rail and bus systems are quite good and can be

counted on to get you to, or close to, all of the places we identify—with a few exceptions. You may, of course, drive to them
all. In what follows, the directions given for reaching sites outside London assume that you are driving. Parenthetically, we
had no experience driving on the left until recently. The first
day was very hard on the nerves—absolutely complete concentration required. By the third day, we felt confident about getting on the road. Courage, you American visitors.

England was home base for the RAF Hurricanes and Spitfires
in the Battle of Britain and for British and American bombers
during the bomber offensive. It was also a giant supply depot
and staging area for ground operations on the Continent. The
tours described below identify sites associated with air and
ground operations.

The tour outside London begins in the southeast near Folkestone, swings just south of Greater London, drops down to Portsmouth, and has a western end near Dorchester. It picks up again
north of London around Cambridge and goes east into East
Anglia.

Imperial War Museum

In taking the Underground to the sites in London, remember that the stations served as air-raid shelters for thousands. During the Blitz, people would begin to take up places in
the early evening. At 2230 hours, the electricity was cut off and
the trains stopped running. Some people erected bunks on the
platforms, others stretched hammocks across the tracks, and still
others slept on the escalator stairs. Henry Moore, the English
sculptor, made a series of powerful drawings of these scenes
which can be seen in London's Tate Gallery.

Many of the stations are deep underground and were virtually
impervious to bomb blast. Those closer to the surface were vulnerable. Bank station suffered a direct hit in January 1941, with
the loss of one hundred lives. Another strike at Marble Arch station killed thirty.

Take the Bakerloo Line to Lambeth North station. Walk south on Kennington Road to Lambeth Road, then east to the Imperial War Museum.

The museum is open Monday through Saturday, 1000–1750, and Sunday, 1400–1750. Admission is free.

HMS *Belfast*

From the Imperial War Museum, walk east on Saint Georges Road to the intersection with London Road. Cross the street to the Elephant and Castle station.

The area around Elephant and Castle was among the worst hit in all of London during the Blitz. German bombers unable to find their targets to the north would head for home and, upon clearing the Thames, jettison their bomb loads.

Take the Underground on the Northern Line to London Bridge station. Walk east on Tooley Street to Vine Lane on the river side. Vine Lane gives access to HMS Belfast.

HMS *Belfast* has summer hours of 1100–1750 daily and 1100–1630 during the winter; closed holidays. Admission is charged.

Parliament Square

Take the Circle or District Line to Westminster station. Walk toward the Thames, turning north on Victoria Embankment. In a quarter mile, you will see on the river side of the road the RAF Memorial (1).*

The Memorial is dedicated to the Royal Air Force dead of both world wars.

* Bold numbers are keyed to Map 3.

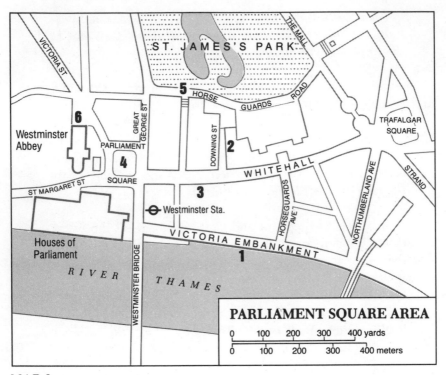

MAP 3

Walk west at the next intersection on Horse Guards Avenue to Whitehall. Proceed south on Whitehall to Downing Street. At Number 10 is the official residence of the Prime Minister (2).

Winston Churchill had his residence here during his tenure as Prime Minister from 1940 to 1945.

On the other side of Whitehall, a few steps to the south, is a full figure statue of General Montgomery standing on the lawn of a government building (3).

Continue down Whitehall to Parliament Square. Standing at the eastern end of the square is a monumental sculpture of Winston Churchill (4).

Turn west, along the square, on Great George Street. At Horse Guards Road, turn north. The entrance to the Cabinet War Rooms is at the side of Clive Steps (5).

These underground rooms were Churchill's command center during the Blitz. Some three hundred people worked here on a round-the-clock basis. The rooms are open Tuesday to Sunday, 1000–1750. There is an admission charge.

Return to Parliament Square. On the south side is Westminster Abbey (6)

Among the chapels in the Abbey is one dedicated to the RAF. The stained-glass windows of the chapel depict airmen in various attitudes and the crests of the fighter squadrons which took part in the Battle of Britain. In the floor are commemorative stones to Air Chief Marshal Hugh Dowding, commander of Fighter Command during the battle, and to Hugh Trenchard, Chief of the Air Staff from 1919 to 1929, and architect of an independent Royal Air Force.

The Abbey is open Monday through Friday, 0900–1645, and

Saturday, 0900–1445. There is an admission charge to all the royal chapels.

Central Church of the Royal Air Force

Take the Piccadilly Line to Aldwych station. Turn east on the Strand to the church, St. Clement Danes, which stands in the middle of the street.

This church was destroyed in 1941 during the Blitz. In 1958 it was reconsecrated as the Central Church of the RAF. Books along the perimeter of the interior record the names of American and RAF airmen who died in the war. U.S. Air Force members and their families and friends donated the church organ.

London Headquarters of Dwight Eisenhower and of Charles de Gaulle

Take the Piccadilly or Bakerloo Line to Piccadilly Circus station. Walk south on Regent Street to Charles II Street, where you should go west to St. James's Square. At Number 31 St. James's Square is Norfolk House.

Here Eisenhower had his London headquarters during Operations Torch and Overlord. A plaque mounted on the front exterior wall commemorates Ike's residence.

Leaving St. James's Square on the south, cross Pall Mall to Carlton Gardens. A half-block down is Carlton House Terrace. Walk west to Number 4 Carlton House Terrace.

This was De Gaulle's London headquarters, from which he departed for France after Overlord. Commemorative plaques are affixed to the exterior.

Hendon Air Museums

Take the Northern Line to Colindale station. The trip takes about thirty minutes from central London. Upon leaving the station, walk north on Colindale Avenue to the traffic circle, where you should proceed north on Grahame Park Way to the Hendon Air Museums. It is about a half-mile walk. Taxis are available locally.

The Hendon complex of three museums is open every day 1000–1800. There is an admission charge to each museum.

The rest of the tour devoted to the Battle of Britain and the bomber offensive must be made by automobile. From Folkestone to Dorchester is 210 miles. The return from Dorchester to London is 127 miles.

HAWKINGE

Drive north out of Folkestone on A 260 to Up Hill (5 miles). In the middle of the village, turn west on Aerodromme Road. Follow the signs 1 mile to the Battle of Britain Museum (1).*

Hawkinge was one of the satellite airfields in the Hornchurch sector. There were fields like this one, usually grass, scattered across southern England. Dowding rotated Fighter Command squadrons among these fields as strategy and casualties demanded. Squadrons 79, 245, and 615 all saw service here during the Battle of Britain. At the time, the typical squadron had twenty-two pilots, sixteen operational aircraft, and two more in reserve.

Because Hawkinge lay directly in the path of Luftwaffe bombers attacking England from their bases in the Pas-de-Calais, its resident squadron was often scrambled to intercept. On 12 August 1940, the Germans destroyed two hangars and damaged four fighters on the ground. The base recovered quickly.

* Bold numbers are keyed to Map 4.

34

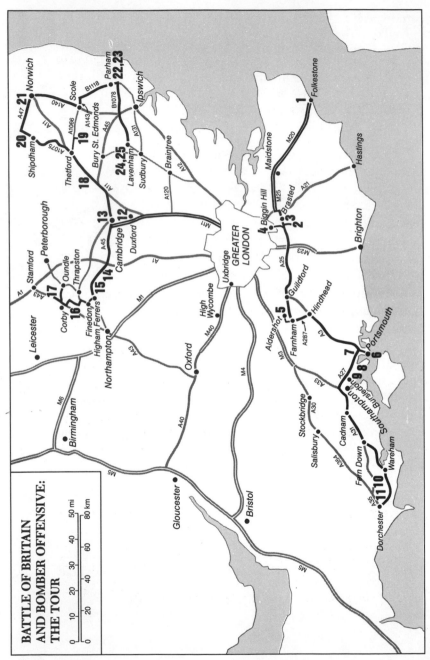

MAP 4

BATTLE OF BRITAIN
AND BOMBER OFFENSIVE:
THE TOUR

BIGGIN HILL

Reverse course. Take A 260 south to the divided highway M 20. Go west toward Ashford and Maidstone (35 miles). Take the M 25 west of Maidstone to A 21 south (18 miles). In less than a mile, you will intersect A 25. Turn west to Brasted. Stop at the White Hart on the south side of the road (2).

Fighter Command pilots from Biggin Hill frequented the bar in the White Hart. Still displayed is a ledger containing the names of Battle of Britain airmen.

The White Hart is a pleasant place to have lunch or dinner and to spend a night. Biggin Hill airfield and Chartwell, Churchill's home, are nearby. Brasted itself is full of antique stores.

Continue west on A 25 to Westerham. Turn south on B 2026, following the signs to Chartwell (3).

This was Churchill's home for most of his adult life. It is preserved as it was during his life. There are many Churchill memorabilia displayed here, including a model of the "Mulberry" artificial harbor at Arromanches. Chartwell is closed Mondays and Fridays. On other weekdays the hours are 1400–1730, weekends 1100–1730. There is a National Trust bookstore and crafts shop. Admission is charged.

Return to Westerham. Drive north on A 233 about 5 miles through the village of Biggin Hill. You will first pass on the east the Biggin Hill airfield, now devoted to civil aviation. A little farther on, occupying both sides of the road, is a group of brick buildings still in use by the RAF. Park and walk through the gate flanked by a Spitfire and a Hurricane. Before you is the St. George's Chapel of Remembrance (4).

The chapel was built in 1951 as a memorial to those who died in the Battle of Britain. Air Chief Marshal Dowding laid the foundation stone. The same artist who designed the stained-glass window for the RAF chapel in Westminster Abbey did those in this chapel. A Book of Remembrance records the names of all those airmen of the Biggin Hill sector who lost their lives. Permission may be sought across the road to visit the original officers' mess.

Biggin Hill was a sector station in 11 Group commanded by Air Vice-Marshal Keith Park during the Battle of Britain. Park had his headquarters at Hillingdon House, Uxbridge (closed to the public), in northwest London. From there he directed the squadrons at the sector stations on the basis of information received from Dowding's Fighter Command headquarters at Bentley Priory, Stanmore (also closed to the public). At Hendon's Battle of Britain Museum, there is a reconstruction of the 11 Group operations room complete with plotting table upon which members of the Women's Auxiliary Air Force pushed about counters with rakes to keep track of the fight overhead.

There were usually two squadrons at Biggin Hill, one Spitfire and one Hurricane. Squadrons 32, 79, 610, and 92 all served here at one time or another during the battle. The base received extensive damage from bombing attacks. On 30 August 1940, a German raid killed thirty-nine people and damaged physical facilities, which forced the transfer of sector control to Hornchurch for several days. No sooner had repairs been made than Biggin Hill was hit again. An attack on 1 September wrecked the sector operations room.

ALDERSHOT

Return to Westerham. Turn west on A 25 to Guildford (31 miles) where you should pick up A 31 west to Farnham (10 miles). At Farnham, turn north on A 325 toward Farnborough. Watch for the Allisons Road junction. Go east to

Queens Avenue in Aldershot. Park in the church lot on the northwest corner and walk south on Queens Avenue, past the parade ground, to the entrance beside the DC-3 (5).

The Museum of Airborne Forces is open 0900–1230 and 1400–1630 weekdays; on Saturday opening time is one-half hour later, and on Sunday one hour later. There is an admission charge.

Browning Barracks, of which the museum is a part, was named after Major General Frederick "Boy" Browning, appointed first commander of the 1st British Airborne Division in 1941. The barracks serves as a training base for British airborne forces.

There are no fewer than nine military museums in and around Aldershot, including those of the Royal Army Veterinary Corps and the Royal Army Dental Corps. Further information can be obtained at the Museum of Airborne Forces.

PORTSMOUTH

Drive back to Farnham. In the center of town, pick up A 287 south to Churt and Hindhead (8 miles). Turn south on A 3 toward Portsmouth. About 6 miles north of Portsmouth, the A 3 joins A 3(M). Stay on A 3 to Portsmouth. Follow the signs to Southsea and the D-Day Museum (6).

The D-Day Museum is open 1030–1900 weekdays and 1030–2100 weekends. Admission is charged.

Inquire at the museum about obtaining permission to visit Southwick House.

Retrace your route north to the suburb of Cosham. At the second roundabout in Cosham, turn west on Southwick Hill Road. Follow the signs to Southwick (7).

Southwick House was Eisenhower's headquarters during the days immediately preceding Overlord. It was here that he made the decision to go on 6 June. Southwick House is now part of HMS *Dryad*, a Royal Navy training facility normally closed to the public. If permission has been obtained, you can enter to see the wall map showing H Hour on the British beaches.

While in Southwick, visit the Golden Lion pub in the village. It served as an unofficial officers' mess in 1944. According to the plaque on the door, Eisenhower and Montgomery were frequent visitors in the spring of 1944. The barmaid remembers that Ike took a half-pint of bitter, while Monty as usual ordered grape juice.

PORTSMOUTH-BOVINGTON CAMP

Return to Cosham. Get on M 27 west. In about 10 miles, turn off M 27 at Exit 9 for Park Gate and A 27. Turn west on A 27. At Sarisbury, turn south on the secondary road to Warsash (8).

This hamlet on the River Hamble was the embarkation point for three thousand British commandos who landed on Normandy on D Day. A plaque outside the Rising Sun pub pays them honor.

Return to A 27. Stop at Burlesdon (9).

See the collection on the River Hamble of Operation Neptune landing craft used in Normandy.

Continue on A 27 for about 8 miles to A 336. Turn west to Totton and Cadnam. When you intersect A 31, turn south toward Bournemouth. Stay on A 31 to Fern Down, where the road branches. Take A 348, which joins A 35. Just west of Lytchett Minster, turn off A 35 onto A 351 south to Wareham. In Wareham, turn west on A 352 to Wool. Look

*for the signs to Bovington Camp, which lies slightly north
and west of Wool* (**10**).

Bovington camp is a training facility for British tank crews
and has served in that role since the First World War. It is possible to see tanks firing on the ranges of the gunnery school. Inquire at the museum for directions to the public viewing areas
and about firing times.

The Royal Armoured Corps Tank Museum is open daily. Admission is charged.

RAF STATION WARMWELL

*Drive back to A 352. Turn west toward Dorchester. In
about 6 miles, turn north on B 3390 to Warmwell* (**11**).
Walk back to the church which you just passed on the east.

In the cemetery a small plot has been set aside for those who
died while serving at Warmwell.

*Continue north about 1 mile to the second sign on the
west marked "Warmwell Holiday Village." Park at the side
of the store.*

This vacationers' encampment was once RAF Warmwell Station. It served as a satellite field for Fighter Command in the
Middle Wallop sector of 10 Group. Squadrons 238, 609, and 17
were here during the battle. Walk through the camp past the
swimming pool—once a pit for gun testing—to the fence at the
back. Before you is the grass runway and to your left the old
hangars, now storage buildings for farm machinery and produce.

*Return to A 352. Turn west to Dorchester. From there the
return trip to London can be easily made via Salisbury,
Stockbridge, and the M 3.*

The second part of the tour outside London takes you to the
bases of the Eighth Air Force and Bomber Command in East

Anglia and the Midlands. Most of them were built during the war. In 1942, work on a new airfield began, on average, every three days. Bulldozers leveled once pastoral ground, perhaps 40,000 acres for the Eighth's bases alone. Truckers arrived to pour 175,000 cubic yards of concrete and 32,000 square yards of tarmac, and still others came with the 4.5 million bricks required in the construction of each bomber base. There was considerable standardization. Each airfield had three intersecting runways. The main one had a minimum length of 6,000 feet and the other two were at least 4,200 feet. Encircling the runways ran a perimeter taxiway which averaged three miles in length. Along the taxiway were hardstands, known as "frying pans," where the aircraft parked. Repairs could be carried out in three hangars.

Living quarters for the crews, maintenance personnel, and others who made up the population of three thousand at the typical base were situated a half-mile or so from the field. Storage for bombs, ammunition, gasoline, and other explosive or flammable materials was at a distant part of the base. While any infantryman would have exchanged accommodations with an airman at any time, the living quarters were far from luxurious. For most, it was a Nissen hut—sixteen feet wide, eight feet high at the center, and twenty-four or thirty feet long—with a concrete floor and brick end walls. Officers slept on metal cots, twelve to a hut, and enlisted men in double-decker bunks. Each hut was heated, more or less, by a small coal stove. Toilets, showers, and the mess were in separate huts. The few groups which inherited RAF bases built before the war—five or so, like the 91st Bombardment Group at Bassingbourn and the 458th at Horsham St. Faith—enjoyed a rather higher standard. These bases had brick barracks, two-man rooms, toilets close by, and the mess downstairs.

The fighter groups of the Eighth Air Force were intended, like Fighter Command, to use bases with grass runways. A few of these were old RAF stations with good facilities. Others were newly constructed on ground with inadequate drainage. At these, steel matting had to be laid to prevent the heavier American fighters from churning the ground to mud. (The Spitfire had a gross weight of 7,900 pounds, the Mustang 11,600, and the Thunderbolt 17,600.)

By the spring of 1944, the Eighth occupied fifty-six bases. The B-17s and B-24s were on forty-two of these, and their fighter escorts on the other fourteen. Eighth Air Force headquarters, like that of Bomber Command, was at High Wycombe, northwest of London. The headquarters staff took over a girls' boarding school in Wycombe Abbey. In each room was a bell button labeled "Ring for mistress." There were no such buttons in the Nissen huts of the aircrews. They walked and bicycled to nearby villages in search of companionship.

After the war, Wycombe Abbey again became a girls' school, and the Eighth abandoned the fields to the peacetime pursuits which they had served before its arrival. Road builders have torn up the runways for rip-rap, and farmers have used the huts and hangars for storage. Neglect and decay have taken care of the rest.

There is not much left to be seen on most of the bases. Lavenham and Framlingham are the best preserved. There are some remains at a handful of others. In most cases, the bases have come under private ownership, and permission should be obtained before exploring. The directions given below will get you to the nearest village. You will have to inquire locally for directions to the base itself.

DUXFORD

From central London, take A 11 to the M 11 north toward Cambridge. In 48 miles, turn off at Exit 10 to Duxford. Follow the signs to the museum (12).

Duxford was built during the First World War and is among the oldest RAF stations. During the Battle of Britain it served as a sector station in 12 Group. In April 1943, the 78th Fighter

Group of the Eighth inherited the base for the remainder of the war. During the stay of the 78th, the first runway of steel matting was laid on the previously all-grass field. The concrete runway was built after the war.

The museum is open 1030–1730 daily from March to November. Admission is charged.

CAMBRIDGE (MADINGLEY)

> *Continue on M 11 toward Cambridge. At Exit 13, turn west on A 45. Almost immediately upon leaving the M 11, take the first road north to Madingley. Follow the signs to the American military cemetery. (13).*

The cemetery contains 3,811 burial sites. On the "Wall of the Missing" are recorded the names of 5,125 including that of Alton G. Miller, better known as Glenn Miller. Miller left RAF Station Twinwoods Farm near Bedford on 15 December 1944. On a flight to Paris to arrange a concert, he was never seen again. No trace of the single-engine Noorduyn C-64 has ever been found.

On an exterior wall of the memorial room at the entrance to the cemetery is a plaque presented by local residents to honor pilots who gave their lives to avoid hitting English homes.

KIMBOLTON–CHELVESTON–GRAFTON UNDERWOOD– DEENETHORPE

This loop from Cambridge to Deenethorpe and back to Cambridge covers a hundred miles.

> *Go west on A 45 for 22 miles to Kimbolton (14).*

Kimbolton was once an RAF fighter base. Remodeled in 1942 by the addition of longer, concrete runways, it became home to the 379th Bombardment Group. Bendiner's B-17 flew from here.

Continue on A 45 for seven miles to Chelveston (**15**).

The 305th Bombardment Group was based here. A J-type hangar still stands. There is a memorial on the wall of the nearby church.

Proceed on A 45 for 1 mile to Higham Ferrers. Turn north on A 6 for four miles to Finedon. Turn north on A 510 to the junction with A 604 (about 3 miles). Turn west to Cranford St. John. There take the secondary road north to Grafton Underwood (**16**).

A number of Nissen huts remain and a field defense pillbox. There is a memorial plaque to the 384th Bombardment Group, which served here.

Continue north on the secondary road for about 4 miles to Brigstock. Turn northwest on A 6116 to Stanion. Take A 43 north for 3 miles to the secondary road, near Deene Hall, which runs east to Deenethorpe (**17**).

This was home for the 401st Bombardment Group. The control tower and some Nissen huts still stand.

Return to A 43. Go south to A 427. Turn east and drive 8 miles to Oundle. (Polebrook, the base of the 351st Bombardment Group, lies some 3 miles east of here. Save for a small memorial, little remains; the control tower recently went under the wrecker's ball.) At Oundle, turn south on A 605 to Thrapston. Take A 604, 28 miles, to Cambridge.

MILDENHALL-KNETTISHALL-SHIPDHAM-NORWICH

This leg from Cambridge to Norwich is about ninety miles.

Take A 45 east toward Newmarket. In 13 miles, turn off on A 11 north to Barton Mills (6 miles). Turn west on B 1102 to Mildenhall (18).

This was an RAF station used by both Bomber Command and Fighter Command. Squadron 149, Bomber Command, flew from here early in the war. The basic unit in the RAF, as in the USAAF, was the squadron. Initially Bomber Command squadrons had sixteen aircraft. They were later expanded to thirty. Between ten and sixteen squadrons made up a group. USAAF squadrons comprised sixteen bombers; four squadrons of bombers made up a group.

Return to A 11. Turn north toward Thetford. After you cross over B 1106, notice, on the south side of the road, Elveden Hall, which was 3d U.S. Air Division headquarters. In Thetford, turn east on A 1066. In 7 miles, turn south on the secondary road to Knettishall (19). If you go as far as Garboldisham, you've gone too far.

The crew huts at Knettishall have readable slogans and instructions on the interior walls. Some "artwork" is also in evidence. The 388th Bombardment Group served here.

Retrace your steps to Thetford. Turn north on A 11. About 2 miles outside Thetford, take A 1075 north to Shipdham (20).

The runways, two hangars, and Nissen huts with drawings on the interior halls remain at this base, home to the 44th Bombardment Group.

Continue on A 1075 to A 47. Turn east for 20 miles to Norwich (21).

In the Norwich Central Library is the 2d Air Division Memorial Library. Many Eighth Air Force memorabilia are displayed. Memorial plaques to each of the division's fourteen groups are mounted on the walls.

FRAMLINGHAM–LAVENHAM

This leg from Norwich to Lavenham is about 70 miles long.

From Norwich, take A 140 south to Scole—about 20 miles. Turn east on A 143. In 4 miles, turn south on B 1118 to B 1116. Drive south on B 1116, through Framlingham to Parham (22).

Men from the air base often visited the Parham Free House.

Drive east out of Parham to the airfield (23).

Through the efforts of private parties, this is one of the best-preserved of the Eighth's bases. The 390th Bombardment Group was based here.

Return to Parham. Go south on B 1116 to the junction with B 1078. Turn west on B 1078 and proceed for 25 miles to the junction with B 1115. Go straight on B 1115 to Monks Eleigh. Turn north on A 1141 to Lavenham (24).

In the bar of the Swan Hotel are patches from the army and air force units, American and British, which served at nearby bases and camps. On the rear wall is a signed ledger. This bar and another in the village, the Horseshoes, were frequented by men of the 487th and the 94th based at Bury St. Edmunds.

In the village church there is a memory book dedicated to those from Lavenham who died in World Wars I and II.

Continue north on A 1141. Just after the water tower, turn west on the secondary road to the airfield (25).

There is a small pillbox at the turnoff to this base of the 487th Bombardment Group. The control tower is now a private home. Many of the buildings, including Nissen and Maycrete huts, and parts of the runways remain.

The easiest return to London can be made as follows. Go back to Lavenham on A 1141. Turn south on B 1071 to B 1115 and then southwest to Sudbury. Take A 131 south for 14 miles to Braintree. Leave Braintree on A 120. A 15-mile drive will get you to the M 11.

Fighter Command pilots scramble for their Hurricanes during the Battle of Britain. (*The Trustees of the Imperial War Museum, London*)

Aerial view of the 381st Bombardment Group airfield at Ridgewell, Essex County. (*U.S. Air Force—NASM*)

Members of the 379th Bombardment Group survey the damage suffered on a mission in May 1944. (*U.S. Air Force—NASM*)

Crew of the "Bonnie Donnie" examine battle damage after a raid over Frankfurt in January 1944. (*U.S. Air Force—NASM*)

A burning Fort holds formation in the skies over Berlin. (*U.S. Air Force—NASM*)

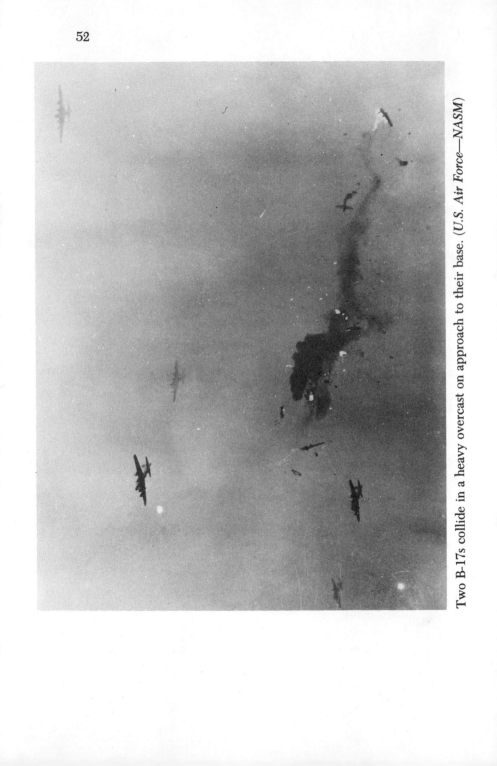

Two B-17s collide in a heavy overcast on approach to their base. (*U.S. Air Force—NASM*)

2

The Battle of Normandy

An Overview

In the years since 1945, it has become increasingly evident that the Grand Alliance forged between the British Commonwealth and the United States was often beset with disagreement over the correct strategy to insure the final defeat of the Axis powers. Early on, both British and American staffs could agree that Germany represented a greater military threat than Japan, but they did not often see eye to eye on the strategy that would most efficiently defeat the Reich.

The Americans were early and persistent advocates of a direct strategy—a cross-Channel attack that would first destroy German military power in the West, then drive deep into the heart of industrial Germany to end the war. The British, on the other hand, sobered by their disastrous experiences at Dunkirk and Dieppe, preferred to stage a number of small-scale attacks around the perimeter of fortress Europe. They thereby hoped to weaken German defenses before leaping precipitously across the Channel into the teeth of the still powerful Wehrmacht. The British simply could not afford the staggering losses entailed in a frontal assault on the northwest coast of Europe. "Memories of the Somme and Passchendaele," wrote Sir Winston Churchill years later, "were not to be blotted out by time or reflection."

British Lieutenant General Sir Frederick Morgan, Chief of Staff to the Supreme Allied Commander (COSSAC), put it more bluntly in his memoirs: "Certain British authorities instinctively recoiled from the whole affair, as well they might, for fear of the butcher bill." It is not surprising, then, that the harder the Americans pressed in 1942 and 1943 for a firm commitment on a cross-Channel attack, the more the British seemed to vacillate.

After a debate lasting through much of 1942, the Americans agreed to postpone any cross-Channel attack in favor of the November landings in North Africa—Operation Torch.

The strategic outcome of Torch was what American Chief of Staff General George C. Marshall had predicted. Success in Tunisia—the first the Allies had experienced against the Wehrmacht—inspired Churchill and his Chief of the Imperial Staff, Field Marshal Alan Brooke, to devise a Mediterranean strategy aimed at knocking Italy out of the war and at protecting British sea-lanes to the oil-rich Middle East. The July 1943 invasion of Sicily was followed by the landings at Salerno and Anzio, the collapse of Mussolini's government, and the beginning of the bitter and protracted fight up the Italian peninsula.

Thus it was not until the Teheran Conference in November of 1943 that the British, prodded by the Russians, reluctantly agreed to launch a cross-Channel attack, code-named Operation Overlord, in May of 1944 and to allow President Franklin D. Roosevelt to name a commander for the operation. Although both Marshall and Brooke coveted the appointment, had even been promised it, both were passed over. Instead, all concurred in the selection of General Dwight D. Eisenhower, then commanding United States forces in Europe. On 14 January 1944, Eisenhower, now titled Supreme Commander, Allied Expeditionary Force, arrived in London to begin work on the final invasion plan.

Months before Eisenhower's appointment as Supreme Commander, General Morgan and his COSSAC staff had produced a

preliminary plan for the seaborne invasion of Europe. Constrained by the range of fighters based in southern England and
by the availability of suitable landing beaches, COSSAC planners' options narrowed quickly to the Pas-de-Calais area and a
section of the Calvados coast on either side of the Norman town
of Arromanches-les-Bains. The Pas-de-Calais beaches, attractive
because of their closeness to England and the shortness of the
lines of advance to the German border, were rejected because of
their limited number, their remoteness from a major port, and
their highly developed defenses. Normandy, almost by default,
became the designated "lodgment area."

COSSAC planners proposed to land three divisions (two British and one American) abreast onto Normandy's sand and shingle beaches, followed immediately by two more and flanked on
the east, near Caen, by elements of a British parachute division.
Many details, including the exact landing date, were not specified by COSSAC in order to leave some flexibility to the Supreme Commander. However, the weather, tides, and light
conditions required for the landing were outlined and calculated
so that the precise calculations for H Hour on D Day could be
made in the future. The absence of an adequate port along the
Calvados coast led the planners in two directions. On one hand,
they specified the port of Cherbourg, located on the tip of the
Cotentin Peninsula, as an immediate post–D Day objective. On
the other, they began planning for the construction of two artificial ports (code-named Mulberries) to be towed from England
after the initial landings.

The Overlord plan also called for the pre-invasion strategic
bombing of selected targets in Germany and France in an effort
to destroy German tactical aircraft, "since only through air
power can we offset the many and great disabilities inherent in
the situation confronting the attacking surface forces." Later air
strikes would seek to interdict troop movements toward the
lodgment area. Bombing patterns were to be carefully designed
to avoid disclosing the actual landing sites. The landings them-

selves would be immediately preceded by massive air strikes at the beach fortifications.

Lastly, the Overlord plan called for feinted landings in southern France and in the Pas-de-Calais area, although the details of neither effort were spelled out. The Mediterranean feint ultimately became an actual landing, Operation Anvil, while the elaborate Pas-de-Calais deception—Operation Fortitude—was maintained until well after D Day.

On 3 January 1944, COSSAC staffer Brigadier Kenneth McLean briefed General Bernard Law Montgomery, recently appointed to command the Second British Army, and General Walter Bedell Smith, Eisenhower's chief of staff, on the various complicated elements of Overlord. Montgomery, as was his wont with plans not specifically his own, objected to various parts, specifically the weight of the initial assault landing. McLean later characterized Monty's position as simply "give me five divisions or get someone else to command." Backed by Eisenhower, he won his point—an additional American infantry division would now be landed at the base of the Cotentin Peninsula, covered by two airborne divisions dropped behind the landing beach. However, Monty's victory came at the expense of both Anvil, which had to be postponed until D Day plus 30, and the early May date for Neptune (as the assault landing phase of Overlord was now named) to allow for the production of a thousand additional landing craft.

Throughout the winter and spring months of 1944, the details of Neptune were settled and fitted into place. Planners at SHAEF (Supreme Headquarters, Allied Expeditionary Force) picked an early June date for D Day, with the landings coming over five beaches code-named, from east to west, Sword, Juno, Gold, Omaha, and Utah. Two American divisions, the 4th Infantry Division and the 1st Infantry Division (reinforced with the 116th Regiment of the 29th Infantry Division), were to land across Utah and Omaha beaches respectively. The veteran 82d Airborne Division was teamed with the green 101st to make the night drop on the Cotentin Peninsula behind Utah Beach. The 3d British Infantry Division, landing over Sword Beach, supported by the 6th Airborne Division to be dropped on the east bank of the Orne River, formed the east flank of the assault. Juno Beach was the D Day objective of the 3d Canadian Infantry Division. The 50th British Infantry Division was due ashore on Gold Beach, just east of Arromanches. The 3d British and Canadian divisions, with their reinforcements, formed I Corps, while the 50th Division was the spearhead of XXX Corps. Together, the two corps composed the Second British Army, commanded by Montgomery. The American assault divisions were the spearheads of two corps, V (1st Division) and VII (4th Division), organized into the First U.S. Army, commanded by Lieutenant General Omar N. Bradley. For the initial assault and the period through the breakout, both armies were designated as the 21 Army Group, under Montgomery's command.

While SHAEF planners fretted over their plans and schedules, thousands of American infantrymen were put through courses offered by the Assault Training Center at Woolacombe. The assault regiments were reorganized to reduce their overhead and increase their firepower. A tank battalion was assigned to each regiment to provide close-range artillery support. Some of these tanks were to be landed from LCT's (Landing Craft, Tank) in advance of the first wave of infantry; others, the duplex drive (DD) tanks (Shermans specially equipped with propellers and canvas water wings), were to "swim" themselves ashore. Landing close behind the tanks and infantry were the engineer demolition teams. Their dangerous job was to clear and mark gaps through the beach obstacles and minefields before the incoming tide covered them. The engineers were supported by naval demolition teams equipped with tank-dozers.

Two battalions of Rangers, the 2d and 5th, were attached to the 116th Infantry and given the specific task of destroying the six 155-mm guns thought to be dug in atop the Pointe du Hoc between the American beaches. Likewise, British forces included elite commando units—the 1st and 4th Special Service Brigades—assigned specific assault tasks on Sword, Gold, and Juno beaches.

Plans for air and naval bombardment in support of the attack were as thorough as those for the infantry. Air bombardment plans called for the shifting of Allied strategic bombing efforts from targets in Germany to the French rail system and then to the Atlantic Wall defenses. A final air strike was to occur minutes before H Hour, when medium and heavy bombers of the U.S. Ninth and Eighth Air Forces and the British Bomber Command would bomb fortifications on Utah and Omaha beaches. Each of the five landing forces was provided with its own naval escort and fire support. Of the nearly 5,000 ships of all types that would participate in the attack, 702 were classified as warships (including six battleships and twenty-two cruisers). Their fire would cover the landing craft during their hazardous passage to the beach and later be called in to destroy pockets of resistance. Neptune planners also placed a great deal of reliance on specially modified LCT's—some firing rockets, designated LCT(R)'s, and others carrying tanks or 105-mm self-propelled howitzers in firing positions—for gunnery support after the naval bombardment had lifted. On the whole, the air and naval bombardment plans were impressive, even if their execution on D Day was often flawed.

Twenty-First Army Group Headquarters scheduled a day-long review of Neptune on Good Friday, 7 April 1944, at St. Paul's School in Kensington, where a thirty-foot terrain board of the lodgment area had been constructed. It was Monty's show. Without notes, he held center stage for two hours while discussing the upcoming landing and his plans to fight a tank battle for Caen and Falaise on D Day. Admiral Bertram H. Ramsay and Air Chief Marshal Trafford Leigh-Mallory followed with their assessments of the naval and air facets of the operation, and in the afternoon army and corps commanders outlined the roles of their commands. By all accounts it was an impressive performance, although Churchill, looking somewhat old and tired, closed the meeting with the admonition that this was an invasion, "not the creation of a fortified beachhead."

SHAEF called the senior commanders together again at St. Paul's on 15 May for a final review. Eisenhower opened this meeting with some brief remarks, and Churchill again closed the day's proceedings—this time with words which somewhat startled the Americans: "Gentlemen, I am hardening to this enterprise." By this date two assault exercises had been held at Slapton Sands on the Devon coast, one of which resulted in the death of seven hundred Americans when a German E-boat sank two LST's and damaged a third. With their training virtually complete, the men of the assault units were cordoned off in camps, where they restlessly awaited orders to move to their embarkation areas.

Only the Supreme Commander could give those orders, and during the first days of June Eisenhower agonized over that decision. SHAEF planners had chosen 5, 6, and 7 June as the mornings, weather permitting, which met their requirements— a late-rising moon followed by a low tide at dawn—for a successful landing. Favorable tide conditions were not due to occur again until 18–20 June and not in phase with a full moon for another month. Eisenhower had chosen the earliest date, Monday, 5 June, for the assault, but adverse weather reports early in the morning of the fourth forced him to postpone the attempt. He decided that the high seas and overcast skies would jeopardize the success of any landing attempted that morning. Of his senior advisers, only Montgomery advised against postponement. As it was, Ike's order to delay Neptune turned back ships which had already sailed from ports in northern England.

At 2130 in the evening of the fourth, Eisenhower met with his staff in the library of Southwick House (his private trailer was parked on the grounds nearby) to learn that the stormy weather forecast for the Calvados coast had in fact materialized. However, Group Captain J. M. Stagg, the chief SHAEF meteorolo-

gist, proceeded to forecast a one- to two-day period of relatively
good weather, lasting through Tuesday, 6 June. Eisenhower was
faced with a cruel choice. If the ships sailed again, and were
again turned back, there could be no effort on the seventh, because they could not be refueled in time. A postponement until
the nineteenth would demoralize the troops on the crowded
ships and destroy the tight security hitherto maintained. Eisenhower weighed the consequences in silence for fifteen minutes,
then spoke: "I am quite positive we must give the order . . . I
don't like it, but there it is. . . . I don't see how we can do anything else." He met again with his staff in the early morning
hours of the following day to review his decision. After forty-
five minutes, he gave the order: "O.K., let's go." It was 0415,
Monday, 5 June.

Across the Channel, Wehrmacht troops manning the defenses
along the Atlantic Wall were lulled by the turn of the weather.
Naval patrols were canceled because the minimal weather conditions for an invasion (a sea state less than 4, wind speed under
24 knots, a visibility of 6,000 yards) were not met. Field Marshal
Erwin Rommel took the opportunity for a quick motor trip to
Germany to celebrate his wife's birthday. Seventh Army staff officers were away from their headquarters attending a map exer-
cise at Rennes. Their absence prompted the cancellation of a
Seventh Army alert scheduled for the night of 5 June. Although
caught off guard by their inability to forecast weather coming in
from the Atlantic, the German forces in France were nonetheless formidable.

By June 1944, the number of German divisions positioned in
Western Europe stood at fifty-eight, an increase of twelve since
the previous fall. Some were *bodenständige* (earth-rooted or
static) divisions without motorized transport, filled with men in
their late thirties and with former prisoners of war from the
Eastern Front who volunteered for service in the German army.
Others were training divisions, containing the underage and
unfit. That still left some thirty divisions of adequate strength in

France to oppose any Allied landing. Twelve of these divisions lined the Channel coast, backed by a reserve of ten panzer and panzer grenadier divisions. The size and tank strength of these divisions varied greatly, but all contained a nucleus of battle-experienced veterans.

Direct responsibility for the defense of the Channel coast fell to Field Marshal Erwin Rommel, commander of Army Group B (Armed Forces Netherlands, Fifteenth, and Seventh armies). The defense of southern France, both Atlantic and Mediterranean coasts, was the responsibility of Army Group G, commanded by General Johannes Blaskowitz. Both he and Rommel reported to sixty-eight-year-old Field Marshal Gerd von Rundstedt, Commander-in-Chief West (OB West). However, the chain of command between von Rundstedt and Rommel was muddled by the quasi-independent nature of Rommel's command and by their fundamental disagreement over the appropriate strategy to repel the expected invasion. Rommel, because of his disastrous North African experience with Allied air superiority, believed that the invasion would have to be turned back on the beaches, within forty-eight hours, if it was to be defeated at all. He therefore argued forcefully for personal command of all mobile reserves under OB West and for the positioning of those reserves well forward so that they could counterattack quickly. Von Rundstedt and his panzer group commander disagreed. They wished to hold the mobile panzer and panzer grenadier divisions in deep reserve, to be committed to battle only after the strength and axis of the invasion had been ascertained. In March 1944, a compromise was reached whereby Hitler gave Rommel control of three panzer divisions, the 2d, 21st, and 116th, while holding four others—Panzer Lehr, 1st SS Panzer, 12th SS Panzer, and 17th SS Panzer Grenadier—in reserve under the command of OKW, the Armed Forces High Command.

Despite these disagreements within the German High Command, Rommel, immediately after assuming command in December 1943, began to implement his strategy by strengthening beach defenses all along the Channel coast. To fortify the intervals between the already heavily defended ports, he ordered the laying of additional anti-personnel mines in a 100-meter-wide belt. By mid-May, some four to five million had been strewn behind likely landing beaches, and half a million beach and landing-zone obstacles had sprouted between tide marks and in open fields behind the coast. A network of trenches, firing pits, and resistance nests had been dug into the bluffs overlooking the beaches. They were supported by pillboxes and concrete bunkers covering the principal beach exits. The valleys of the Orne, Merderet, and Douve rivers, located on the flanks of the prospective Allied lodgment area, had been flooded to impede the mobility of any assaulting forces. Under Rommel's incessant prodding, the Atlantic Wall had begun to live up to its name.

On 1 June, the German Seventh Army had three static divisions (the 243d, 709th, and 716th) dug in along the Calvados coast and in the Cotentin Peninsula, backed by two attack infantry divisions (the 91st and 352d). Despite the vital information concerning the German order of battle gleaned from Ultra intercepts (the British top-secret code-breaking operation), the presence of the 352d Division behind Omaha Beach was not detected until it was too late to warn Bradley's V Corps commanders.

In fact, the probable location of the 352d Division was less of a concern to Eisenhower than was Air Chief Marshal Leigh-Mallory's pre–D Day warning that casualties in the American airborne divisions might run as high as 70 percent in the glider units and 50 percent among the paratroopers. On 30 May, Eisenhower agonizingly reappraised the airborne assault plans before deciding against cancellation. Possibly the gravity of that decision prompted him to draft a press release taking full responsibility if the invasion failed. It certainly drew him to the 101st Airborne's encampment in the evening of 5 June, where

63

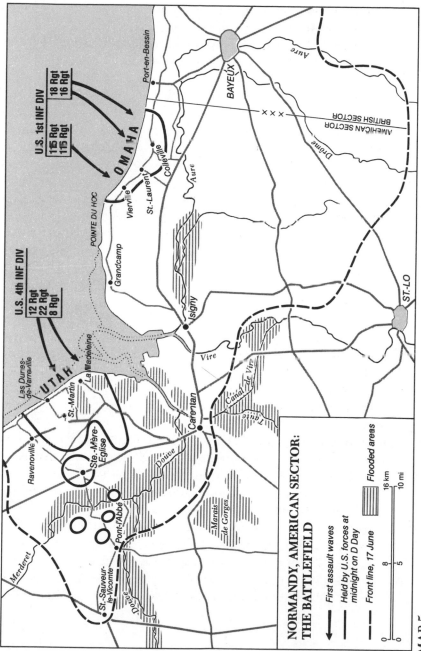

NORMANDY, AMERICAN SECTOR:
THE BATTLEFIELD

First assault waves

Held by U.S. forces at
midnight on D Day

Front line, 17 June

Flooded areas

MAP 5

U.S. 1st INF DIV — 18 Rgt / 16 Rgt — 115 Rgt / 116 Rgt

U.S. 4th INF DIV — 12 Rgt / 22 Rgt / 8 Rgt

OMAHA · UTAH

Port-en-Bessin · BAYEUX · Aure · Drôme · ST-LO

Colleville · St.-Laurent · Vierville · POINTE DU HOC · Grandcamp · Isigny · Vire · Canal de Vire · Taute · Carentan

La Madeleine · Les Dunes-de-Varreville · St.-Martin · Ste.-Mère-Église · Ravenoville · Douve · Pont-l'Abbé · Marais de Gorges · St.-Sauveur-le-Vicomte · Merderet

AMERICAN SECTOR / BRITISH SECTOR

he mingled with small groups of paratroopers as they waited to board their transports.

By midnight, the 822 C-47s carrying the assault units of the 82d and 101st Airborne divisions, some 13,000 men, were over the Channel in clear, moonlit skies. An unexpected cloud bank over the Cotentin, combined with heavy AA flak, scattered the tight formations, causing many paratroopers to land far from their designated drop zones. Despite the losses of "sticks" (the eighteen paratroopers carried by each plane) that came down in the Bay of the Seine, the flooded river bottoms, and far behind German lines, the D Day casualties came to only 15 percent. The scattered night drop seemed to confuse the Germans, who were unable to mount effective counterattacks against the often outnumbered and isolated paratroopers. After some hard fighting in the hedgerows and marshes around Ste.-Mère-Eglise, and with support from their glider infantry, the paratroopers were able to disrupt German efforts to reinforce their defenses behind Utah Beach, thereby greatly aiding the 4th Division's landing.

That effort had also been unexpectedly aided by the calmer seas in the lee of the Cotentin, which allowed twenty-eight of the thirty-two DD tanks assigned to Utah Beach to "swim" ashore, and by a strong current which swept the first wave of landing craft some 2,000 yards south to a less heavily defended front at La Grande Dune. Although German strong points held out for some time along the flanks of the landing zone, motorized units of the 8th and 22d Infantry pushed inland to link up with the 101st Airborne by nightfall. The 4th Division's D Day casualties were 197.

By contrast, the landing on Omaha Beach began and nearly ended in disaster. SHAEF miscalculations and errors became apparent early. Intelligence sources, including Ultra, failed to locate the 352d Division dug in behind the beach. Bradley's First Army staff had earlier rejected the use of specialized British tanks, Major General Percy C. S. Hobart's "funnies," which could have supported the infantry, because they would compli-

cate American logistics. These tanks included Shermans modified with mine-exploding chain flails (Crabs), Churchills mounting petards and carrying various bridging materials
(AVRE's—Armoured Vehicles, Royal Engineers), and Croco-
diles, Churchills fitted with a flamethrower. The saturation
bombing of the beach defenses by the heavy bombers of the U.S.
Eighth Air Force was ineffective because a late release—ordered by Eisenhower to protect the landing craft—meant that
most bombs fell well behind the beach, killing more dairy cows
than Germans. To cap these miscalculations, the LCVP's and
LCA's (Landing Craft, Vehicle, Personnel and Landing Craft,
Assault) carrying the two assaulting regiments, the 16th and
116th, were launched 10,000 yards offshore, greatly exposing the
seasick men to German fire. Many boats grounded on offshore
sandbars, forcing the infantrymen either to wade ashore or to
drift in with the advancing tide. Those ashore took shelter wher-
ever they found some scant protection from the hail of auto-
matic weapons fire sweeping the beach.

Much of the fire support planned for Omaha Beach never materialized. Twenty-seven of the thirty-two DD tanks assigned to
the 16th Infantry foundered on the run in. While LCT's brought
twenty-eight tanks ashore in the 116th Infantry's sector, many of
the DUKW's carrying the 105-mm howitzers foundered. Most of
the fire support that morning was provided by naval vessels
operating close inshore.

The failure of the first wave to silence or to suppress German
fire made the dangerous work of the engineer demolition teams
in clearing and marking paths through the beach obstacles almost impossible. Landing craft in the following waves milled
around beyond the rows of obstacles, some occasionally crashing
through, searching for a safe route to the beach. By noon, the
stalemate had become so critical that Bradley, waiting offshore
in the cruiser *Augusta*, considered diverting the follow-up
waves to the flanking beaches. The issue remained undecided
until midafternoon, when men from both regiments worked

their way up the bluffs and moved inland. The V Corps' assault across Omaha Beach cost two thousand casualties.

As dramatic as the American landings had been, it must not be forgotten that the first Allied soldiers to land in Normandy were British. At 0016, five gliders of the 6th British Airborne Division's glider infantry skidded to stops on the approaches to the bridges over the Orne River and the parallel Caen Canal. In short order both bridges were in British hands. Those six platoons of the 2d Battalion of the Oxfordshire and Buckinghamshire Light Infantry and the 249th Field Company, Royal Engineers, along with the sixty pathfinders (paratroopers equipped with beacons to mark the landing zones) who landed at the same time, were the vanguard of the British airborne assault on the eastern end of the lodgment area.

Before dawn, paratroopers and glider infantry from the 3d Brigade had captured the Merville Battery (a heavily fortified complex thought to contain 150-mm guns) in the most daringly conceived operation in the Neptune plan. Other men from the 3d Brigade destroyed bridges in the Dives valley in an effort to seal off the eastern approaches to the landing beaches.

High winds played havoc with both the pathfinders and paratroopers from the 5th Parachute Brigade, scattering them for miles along the Dives valley. Although concentration and movement were slow, units were able to reinforce the glider infantry holding the Orne bridges and to clear the landing zone near Ranville for the seventy-two gliders due to land at 0330.

Offshore, the ships of Naval Force "S" were preparing to launch the 8th Brigade of the 3d British Infantry Division against the three miles of sand due west of the mouth of the Orne, designated Sword Beach.

Preceded by the most intense naval bombardment of D Day, the landings on Sword were scheduled for 0730, an hour after sunrise, so that the incoming tide could cover offshore shoals. Supported by twenty-one DD tanks and numerous AVRE's, the 1st Battalion, South Lancashire Regiment, quickly neutralized the shore defenses and captured Hermanville, a mile inland. To the east, the 2d Battalion, East Yorkshire Regiment, found the initial going rougher. It was able to move inland only after the commandos of the 1st Special Service Brigade captured German positions in Ouistreham-Riva-Bella. Their sector of Sword, known as Queen Red, came under heavy artillery fire later in the morning. Only the quick release of the barrage balloons on which the German gunners had been ranging prevented the wholesale destruction of landing craft and vehicles now jamming the beachfront.

By afternoon, the 3d Division's drive inland began to falter short of its D Day objectives as troops dug in, anticipating a counterattack by the 21st Panzer Division. Nevertheless, commando units made contact with the paratroopers holding the Orne bridges at noon, and elements of the 3d Division relieved those in Bénouville that evening. For all their D Day successes, the British had failed to capture Caen, then only lightly held by the 21st Panzers.

To the west of Sword Beach, the 3d Canadian Division stormed ashore along the five miles of coast between La Rivière and St.-Aubin-sur-Mer. Neptune planners had timed the assault on Juno Beach so that the tide would be high enough to cover the offshore reef. Here, as elsewhere, both British and American bombers made their strikes too far inland to have much effect on the beach defenses. That left it to the navy to save the day. Fire support from the battleships *Warspite* and *Ramilles*, the monitor *Roberts*, and a host of lesser ships proved decisive.

Rough seas played havoc with the boats of the first assault waves. DD tanks and the other specialized armor arrived late on many parts of the beach, but with their help both the Regina Rifles and the Royal Winnipeg Rifles of the 7th Canadian Brigade quickly broke through the crust of German defenses. Nevertheless, Company B of the RWR suffered heavy losses when it landed ahead of its supporting armor. A similar situation developed on Nan sector when the tide swept the LCA's, carrying

68

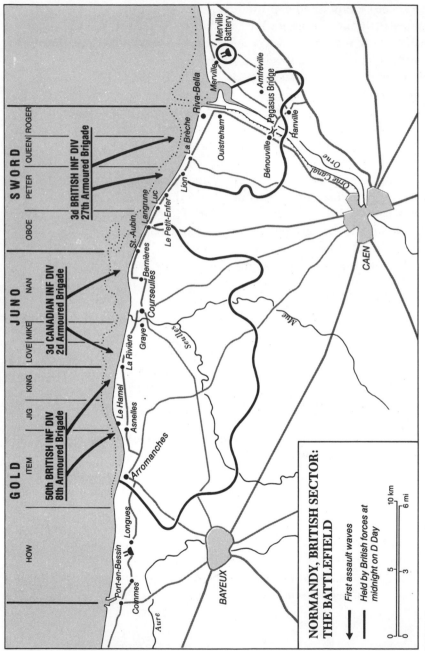

NORMANDY, BRITISH SECTOR: THE BATTLEFIELD

First assault waves

Held by British forces at midnight on D Day

| 0 | | 5 | | 10 km |
| 0 | 3 | | 6 mi | |

MAP 6

Company B of the Queen's Own Rifles two hundred yards from its assigned landing area. Company B lost sixty-five men on the sand between the water and the protective seawall. D Day casualties among the Canadians numbered a thousand. Yet that seems light when compared with the destruction of the 2d Canadian Division at Dieppe two years before. On that disastrous August day, the Canadians lost some 3,000 men (killed or taken prisoner) out of a landing force of around 5,000.

By dark, the Canadians had pushed to within three miles of Caen, withstood a counterattack from the 12th SS Panzers, and made contact with units of the 50th British Division moving inland from Gold Beach.

The experiences of the 50th Division were similar to those of the other Second Army forces that morning. The beach received the usual pounding from both air and sea, with the usual mixed results. Specialized tank units landed ahead of the infantry, playing a critical role in neutralizing the German strong points at Le Hamel and La Rivière. The preliminary bombardment had failed to silence the battery of casemated guns at Longues, west of the landing area, but after a twenty-minute duel, the cruiser *Ajax* settled the issue by knocking out three of the four casemates, two with direct hits through the embrasures. At the same time, Crabs, firing into blockhouses at point-blank range, subdued the defenses at Le Hamel and La Rivière long enough for the infantry to cross the beach. At the close of D Day, elements of the 65th Brigade had advanced to the outskirts of Bayeux. To the west, the 47th Royal Marine Commando had captured Arromanches (the future site of Mulberry B) and were almost to Port-en-Bessin, although they had failed to make contact with the Americans on Omaha Beach. The division's left flank rested firmly on the Canadians.

In all, the British and Canadian first waves had gotten ashore with fewer casualties than anticipated. The fact that the infantry landed at mid-tide meant that German weapons, sighted so as to provide enfilade fire on the forebeach, could not be brought to bear on the LCA's. By the time the infantrymen entered the killing zone, they were covered by fire from the specialized armor which, in most cases, beached just ahead of the LCA's.

As D Day drew to a close, the Allied forces were well short of planned objectives—beachheads six miles deep and control of Caen—but they were ashore and, however precarious their hold, determined to advance on the morrow. That evening Winston Churchill told an anxious House of Commons that the battle would be "pursued with the utmost resolution." Three thousand miles away Franklin Roosevelt asked for divine blessing: "Almighty God—Our sons, pride of our nation, this day have set upon a mighty endeavor."

Tours of the D Day Landing Areas

Because of the intense interest in the landing phase of the Overlord operation (Neptune), the Normandy coast is probably the most frequently visited of World War II battle sites. The entire area—from the mouth of the Orne River in the east to the dunes of Varreville in the west—abounds with museums, expositions, relics, monuments, and cemeteries associated with the Battle of Normandy. No fewer than four general guidebooks are currently available to the interested traveler. There is also a separate guide to the museums and expositions in the area, even a guide (in French) to the monuments and sites associated with the Norman resistance to the German occupation. These guides are listed in our annotated bibliography.

The Bayeux-based Comité du Débarquement (which we hereafter abbreviate as CD) has gone to great lengths to erect road signs directing the traveler to the principal sites and to provide first-rate information signs at the sites themselves. Especially impressive are the ten imposing stone commemorative monuments (CD monuments), often likened to the prows of ships, which have been erected at important sites all through the lodgment area. The CD's efforts and those of the Coastal Conservation Trust in acquiring historic sites—which now include Omaha and Utah beaches and the sites of the Merville, Longues-sur-Mer, St.-Marcouf, and Pointe du Hoc batteries— have converted the Normandy coastal area into the most accessible and best-marked of all World War II battlefields.

There is much to see in Normandy, almost too much for the traveler with limited time. Therefore, we have outlined two tours of the landing areas, both originating in Bayeux, which will take you to the most important and interesting sites. Our experience indicates that it is possible to tour the Second British Army landing areas in a long day. Another equally long day will be required to visit both American beaches and the Ste.-Mère Eglise area. Excursions to Caen or Cherbourg or around Bayeux will require additional time. For the traveler who plans a limited stay in Normandy, we recommend that you concentrate on the Bayeux, Omaha Beach, and Ste.-Mère-Eglise areas for the American landings, and the Arromanches, Bénouville–Pegasus Bridge areas in the British sectors.

Tour of the American Sector

The tour of the American landing areas begins in Bayeux and then proceeds through some of the thickest *bocage* country to the American cemetery overlooking Omaha Beach. From there it takes you west on D 514 to the Charlie and Dog sectors of Omaha and further along the coast to Pointe du Hoc.

The route follows D 514 past Grandcamp-les-Bains to its junction with N 13, then continues west through Isigny and Carentan to the intersection with D 913, which leads to Utah Beach. The flat terrain at the base of the Cotentin Peninsula contrasts sharply with the high, rugged bluffs to the east. Dunes, still studded with squat concrete bunkers, back Utah and the beaches extending northward.

As you follow the route inland toward the St.-Marcouf–Crisbecq Battery, Objective WXYZ, and Ste.-Mère-Eglise, the land gradually rises and the *bocage* reappears. From Ste.-Mère-Eglise you can either take N 13 north to Cherbourg to visit the Fort du Roule or return along it to Bayeux. In the latter case it will take you by the German military cemetery at La Cambe and the exposition at Surrain. The approximate distance of the tour from Bayeux to Ste.-Mère-Eglise is ninety kilometers.

BAYEUX

The ancient Norman town of Bayeux was liberated by elements of the 50th British Division on D Day without a fight; thus, it was spared the destruction visited on many of its less fortunate neighbors. Today, despite heavy automobile traffic and pizzerias, the town still retains much of its medieval Norman character.

Foremost among Bayeux's Battle of Normandy sites is the Musée Mémorial de la Bataille de Normandie (1)* located on the Boulevard Fabian Ware (actually part of the traffic loop which circles the town). Open April through June, September and October 1000–1230 and 1400–1830; open July and August 0930–1900; open November through March on weekends 1030–1230 and 1400–1830. Admission charge.

By driving northwest a short distance along the Boulevard Fabian Ware you will pass a British military cemetery and memorial (2).

Continuing north to the Rond-Point de Vaucelles (where N 13 branches off toward Cherbourg) you will pass a memorial (3) commemorating both the landing on 6 June and De Gaulle's arrival in France on the fourteenth.

There is a monument commemorating De Gaulle's first speech in liberated France (delivered in Bayeux on 14 June) in the Place Charles de Gaulle (4), two blocks east of the cathedral,

* Bold numbers are keyed to Maps 7, 8, and 9.

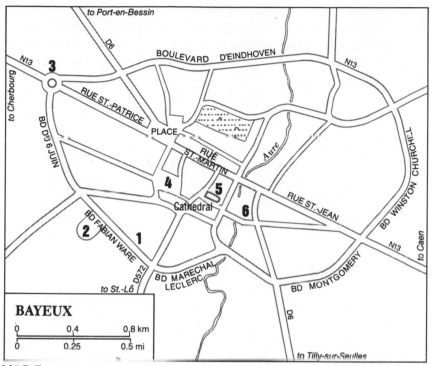

to Port-en-Bessin

BOULEVARD D'EINDHOVEN

N13

D6

N13

to Cherbourg

3

RUE ST.-PATRICE

BD DU 6 JUIN

PLACE

RUE ST.-MARTIN

Aure

4

5

Cathedral

6

RUE ST.-JEAN

BD WINSTON CHURCHILL

2

BD FABIAN WARE

1

D572

BD MARÉCHAL LECLERC

N13

to Caen

to St.-Lô

BD MONTGOMERY

D6

to Tilly-sur-Seulles

BAYEUX

| 0 | 0,4 | 0,8 km |
| 0 | 0.25 | 0.5 mi |

MAP 7

and a plaque to the 56th British Infantry Brigade inside the cathedral (5). Another plaque to the 50th Division is on the wall facing the cathedral's south side.

While in Bayeux, the traveler should not miss that relic of an earlier invasion: the Bayeux Tapestry. Since 1983, the 231-foot-long tapestry, depicting the events surrounding the Norman invasion of England in 1066, has been housed in a new museum on the Rue de Nesmond (6). Signs throughout the town will direct you to the museum. Open June through September 0900–1900; open October through March 0900–1200 and 1400–1800; open April through May 0900–1230 and 1400–1830. Admission charge.

OMAHA BEACH

The American Military Cemetery and Memorial

Omaha Beach can be most easily reached by taking D 6 out of Bayeux, then turning west on D 514 where the two roads intersect just outside of Port-en-Bessin (9 km). Follow D 514 west (signs mark the way) some 6 km to Colleville-sur-Mer, then turn north 1.5 km to the American Military Cemetery and Memorial (7). Park either in one of the outlying lots or in the small lot across from the visitors' center.

The cemetery occupies 172.5 beautifully landscaped acres on the bluff above Omaha Beach. The rows of white marble Latin crosses and Stars of David, some 9,386 in all, stand as silent witnesses to the bitter fighting Americans experienced in the Battle of Normandy. The cemetery is laid out in the form of a Latin cross, with a circular chapel at the intersection of the arms. The chapel is connected visually by a reflecting pool and mall to a semicircular colonnaded memorial. Loggias at each end of the memorial contain maps and accounts of the landings and of the subsequent campaign across northern Europe. In the center of the arc stands a bronze nude allegorical figure representing the

"Spirit of American Youth Rising from the Waves." The names of some 1,557 individuals whose bodies were never recovered are inscribed on the wall of the garden area behind the memorial. Well inside the cemetery entrance is a visitors' center containing a lounge and rest-room facilities. Open all year 0800–1800 (to 2000 on Sundays and holidays).

Walk to the seaward side of the cemetery, opposite the visitors' center, where an overlook commands an excellent view of the beach below.

An orientation table near the iron railing displays a map of the lodgment area indicating the location of the five landing beaches. From this position you are looking down at the Easy Red sector of Omaha Beach where Companies E and F, 2d Battalion, 16th Infantry, were to have landed in the first wave. They were to have been preceded by Company B of the 741st Tank Battalion (DD tanks) and followed by the 18th Regimental Combat Team at H Hour plus 195 minutes. Of the four DD tanks which made it ashore here, one was hit immediately. The remainder of Company B's tanks foundered offshore. Only one boat section from each infantry company waded ashore on Easy Red, losing much of their equipment in the neck-deep water. The tidal current swept the other boats to the east, to Fox Green sector (on your right). Two boat sections from the 116th Infantry, more than a mile east of their landing zone, also came in on Easy Red, fortunately taking only light casualties before finding cover against the shingle embankment at the high-tide mark.

Further to the east, the half-mile of beach facing the E-3 draw, designated Fox Green, was swept by crossing fire from German bunkers along the bluffs. It was along this sector of the beach that the majority of boat sections from Companies E and F landed. Casualties were heavy. After debarking in the neck-deep water, one section of Company F lost seventeen of its thirty-one men trying to reach the shingle. Other sections land-

76

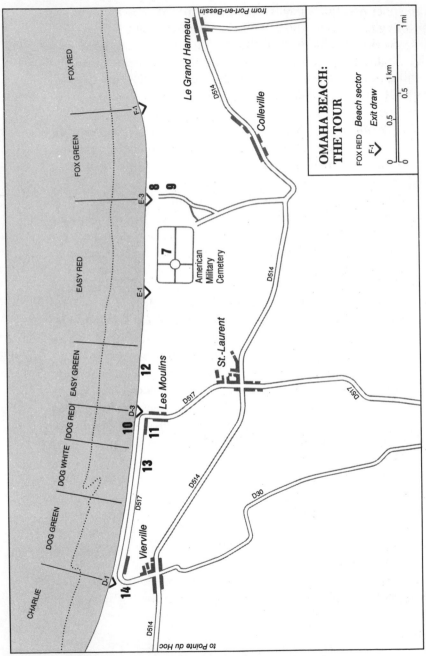

OMAHA BEACH:
THE TOUR

FOX RED *Beach sector*

F-1 *Exit draw*

MAP 8

ing further east lost a third of their strength. Seven men reached the shingle from one boat. Only two of Company F's officers survived the landing.

Company E fared little better. Scattered along a half-mile of Fox Green Beach, the boats came under fire as their ramps dropped. Many men were hit in the water; others tried to submerge themselves and drift in with the tide. Company E took most of its 105 D Day casualties in the water or on the tidal flat leading to the shingle bank. Only Company L of the 16th Infantry, landing still further to the east on Fox Red, came ashore in condition to fight up the bluffs.

Due to the offshore current and some bad navigation, four boat sections of Company E, 116th Infantry, also landed on Fox Green and were promptly shot to pieces. Three of the sections suffered over thirty casualties within a few minutes of debarking. Captain Laurence A. Madill, the company commander, hit while recrossing the beach, was heard to cry out before dying, "Senior noncom, take the men off the beach."

Some of the later companies landing on Easy Red and Fox Green sectors took equally heavy casualties, but others, notably those of the 1st Battalion, escaped the bloodbath.

By 0800, the situation in the Easy Red and Fox Green sectors was critical. Naval gunfire had been lifted to avoid hitting the infantry as they moved toward the bluffs. Vehicles, now beginning to reach the beach in large numbers, were unable to cross the shingle bank and were rapidly being destroyed by German fire. Most of the infantrymen who had managed to cross the tidal flat lay huddled against the shingle, unable or unwilling to move.

At this critical juncture, Colonel George A. Taylor, commander of the 16th Infantry, landing at 0815 with the surviving half of the command group, put it this way: "Two kinds of people are staying on this beach, the dead and those who are going to die—now let's get the hell out of here." Already, sections of Companies E and G had begun to work their way to the top of the bluffs between the E-1 and E-3 draws. Taylor quickly followed, setting up his command post just under the top of the bluff (not far from where you are standing). From there he continued to direct men inland. Just after 1000, first elements of the 18th Infantry landed on Easy Red, and by 1130 the E-1 draw was being opened by the various engineer units that had come ashore earlier.

At about this same time, further to the east, other bands of infantrymen were also penetrating German defenses in the less heavily defended areas between the draws. By midday it was becoming clear that the landing on Omaha Beach was not going to be defeated at the water's edge. However, the margin of victory was slim, provided by a few hundred courageous infantrymen, tank crews, and engineers.

From the overlook take the improved path down the bluff to a second orientation table (remembering that it is a steep climb back up) which describes the artificial harbor (Mulberry A) built here to supply the American forces ashore.

Mulberry A was largely destroyed by the "Great Storm" of 19–21 June. Parts were salvaged and used to repair Mulberry B at Arromanches. Other elements are visible today off Vierville-sur-Mer. Even before the storm, the Americans had begun the practice of "drying out" LST's—grounding them at high tide so that they could be unloaded directly on the beach, and then floating them off on the rising tide. So despite the loss of Mulberry A, the tonnage landed on Omaha and Utah beaches met projected schedules.

Continue down the path to the beach itself. You may return by the same route or take another path up the bluffs along the west side of the E-3 draw.

This path, which begins just past the beach house, leads to two monuments. The lower one (8), standing atop a German blockhouse, commemorates the D Day efforts of the 5th Engineer Special Brigade. Elements of this unit, landing from an LCI about an hour and a half after the first wave, were assigned the job of clearing paths through the beach mines and obstacles. Under fire, the engineers used their bulldozers to clear a path up the west side of the E-3 draw. For its heroic efforts, the unit was awarded the Croix de Guerre.

Further up the path stands an imposing obelisk (9) inscribed with the names of the men of the 1st Infantry Division who died on the beach below and during the advance inland (6 June to 24 July).

The path to the monuments can also be reached from the cemetery by walking through the garden east of the memorial to the service road. Turn right (south) along the road for 50 feet, then left (east) along a footpath leading to an iron gate. Once through the gate, you can see the 1st Division monument. It is also possible to drive from the outer parking lots along a service road skirting the east end of the cemetery to a small parking lot near the iron gate.

Dog Green and Charlie Sectors

To visit the western edge of Omaha Beach (Dog and Charlie sectors) return to D 514 and drive west to St.-Laurent sur-Mer, then follow the road (D 517) down to the beach at Les Moulins (5 km). CD signs mark the way.

Directly ahead on the seawall is a CD monument (10)—this one commemorates the landing on Omaha Beach. (Note the inscriptions to the 1st and 29th Infantry divisions on the flanks of the monument.) A monument (11) to the 6th Engineer Special Brigade is located at the end of the Rue du 116th RI US, a narrow lane which begins just behind the café facing the CD monument. By driving east along the beach road you can reach a memorial (12) commemorating both the 2d Infantry Division and the Provisional Engineers Special Brigade.

Drive west from Les Moulins to Vierville-sur-Mer.

The old beach road of forty years ago has been turned into an improved roadway lined with beach houses. As you drive west, you will pass a stele (13) on your left marking the site where the American dead were first buried after the landing.

Stop at the memorial (14) atop the blockhouse near the west end of the roadway.

You are now standing at the bottom of the Vierville (D-1) draw, exactly on the dividing line between the Charlie and Dog Green sectors (marked today by a sign on the seawall). This memorial fittingly commemorates the National Guardsmen who fought in France in both world wars; the mile of beach you have just driven encompasses most of the Dog sector of Omaha Beach, the D Day landing area of the 116th Regiment (Virginia National Guard), whose antecedent was the famous Stonewall Brigade of the Confederate States Army.

The initial assault on Dog Green was carried out by three units—Company B, 743d Tank Battalion (sixteen DD tanks); Company A, 116th Infantry (six boat sections in LCA's, followed by a command boat); and three LCM's (Landing Craft, Mechanized) carrying units of the 146th Special Engineer Task Force—all coming ashore a few minutes on either side of 0630. The collective stories of these units make one aware of how near defeat the landing on Omaha Beach hovered during its first hours.

The tankers of Company B suffered first. Because of the heavy seas, the DD's were not launched offshore. During the effort to bring them directly to the beach, one of the LCT's was sunk by German fire; half of the company's tanks and all but one of its officers were lost. The eight surviving Shermans began their fire mission at the water's edge.

Company A's turn came next. The boat sections took crippling losses before anyone set foot on the beach. LCA 5 foundered a thousand yards offshore; six soldiers drowned in the heavy seas. Boat 3 was hit a hundred yards from the beach; thirteen died. No one saw Boat 6 go down; there were no survivors, and only half the bodies were recovered later. As the remaining three boats grounded on the offshore sandbars (in front of you), they were swept by fire from flanking German positions. The heavily laden infantrymen, crouched behind the boats' bulwarks in three files, could hear machine-gun bullets ricocheting off the still raised ramps. Half the men from Boats 1 and 4 died in the water within fifteen feet of the ramps, either from wounds or by drowning. No unwounded officers or sergeants made the beach. The men who did struggle ashore lay at the water's edge until the incoming tide overtook them. Some took cover behind beach obstacles, only to be hit there. Others retreated back into the sea, lying on their backs, noses above water, hoping to drift in with the rising tide. Within minutes of touchdown, Company A no longer existed as a fighting unit. Most of its riflemen never fired their weapons. By H plus 30 minutes, two-thirds were dead.

Further to the west (to your left), two boat sections of Company C, 2d Rangers, coming in on Charlie sector, fared little better. One LCA was hit by an anti-tank shell, killing the company commander and a dozen men. Fifteen men from the second boat were hit as the ramp dropped. By the time the survivors managed to cross the 250 yards of sand to the base of the cliffs, thirty-five of the company's sixty-four men were casualties.

Landing to the east of Dog Green in the first wave, Company F took heavy losses. However, some sections of Company G, coming ashore at the same time on Easy Green, reached the low seawall above the high-tide mark intact. The companies landing after 0700 as part of the second wave had similar experiences. Covered by smoke from the grass fires on the bluffs, Company C found shelter along the seawall; but, preceding it by ten minutes, Company D was shot to pieces before the first man reached the sand. Fortunately, many companies in the later waves landed with lighter casualties. At 0730, the 116th Command Group, including Brigadier General Norman D. "Dutch" Cota, the assistant division commander, and Colonel Charles D. W. Canham, commanding the 116th, rode LCVP 71 in on Dog White. Urged on by these two officers, men of Company C and the 5th Ranger Battalion blew gaps in the wire along the beach road and crossed the 150 yards to the base of the bluffs. From there, still covered by smoke from the grass fires, they worked their way to the top. By 0830, they had overrun the German rifle pits and trenches along the crest.

Because of the east-setting current, few of the Army-Navy Special Engineer Task Force teams landed on their assigned sectors of Dog Beach. Despite their dispersal, the fast-rising tide (twenty-two feet on D Day), and enemy fire, they succeeded in clearing two paths through the obstacles on Dog White and Easy Green sectors before taking cover behind the seawall. Casualties ran as high as 41 percent among the engineers.

By the narrowest of margins, a few hundred men had managed to penetrate the German defenses on Omaha Beach. They made the difference between defeat and victory. General Omar N. Bradley summed up most people's feelings about those few when he wrote that "every man who set foot on Omaha Beach that day was a hero."

Before leaving this section of Omaha Beach, note the blockhouse and the remains of Mulberry A in Charlie sector.

As you drive through Vierville to rejoin D 514, you will pass a small private exposition, Exposition Omaha, 6 Juin 1944, housed in a Nissen hut.

POINTE DU HOC

Ranger Monument

To reach the Pointe du Hoc Ranger Monument (15) follow the CD direction signs west along D 514 to the car park outside the monument (8 km).

The Pointe du Hoc today retains much of its battlefield character because of the destruction left by the rain of bombs and shells the Allies unleashed to neutralize this rocky point. The much feared battery was bombed three times before D Day, then hit from the air again that morning. The battleships *Texas* and *Arkansas* battered the area with their 14- and 12-inch guns just after dawn. Later in the morning, the destroyer *Satterlee* saturated the position with her 5-inch guns in direct support of the Rangers. This concentration of fire left craters and ruined casemates which forty years have yet to erase.

From the barbed-wire fence along the cliff top, you can look down the hundred-foot cliff to the east beach where three companies of the 2d Ranger Battalion, commanded by Lieutenant Colonel James E. Rudder, landed on D Day. Their mission was to scale the cliff, then silence the six 155-mm howitzers thought to threaten the landing operations on both American beaches.

The Rangers came in forty minutes late in ten LCA's, trailed by four DUKW's and two supply boats. They lost one of each boat type on the run in. The LCA's were equipped with rocket-propelled grappling hooks which were fired as the boats grounded under the cliff. Despite small-arms fire, improvised mines, and grenades lobbed from above, the Rangers used their rope and aluminum ladders to scale the cliff within five minutes of landing. Ironically, they found the casemates empty of guns, which days before had been moved to new positions further inland. Later that morning, a patrol found the 155s unguarded and spiked them. Colonel Rudder then set up a defensive perimeter and waited for reinforcements. "Located Pointe du Hoc," he managed to signal V Corps that afternoon, "mission accomplished—need ammunition and reinforcement—many casualties." Those reinforcements were to have come from Rangers of the 2d and 5th battalions waiting offshore. Because Rudder's assault was late, the Rangers assumed that it had failed and landed instead on Omaha Beach. It took them two days to fight their

84

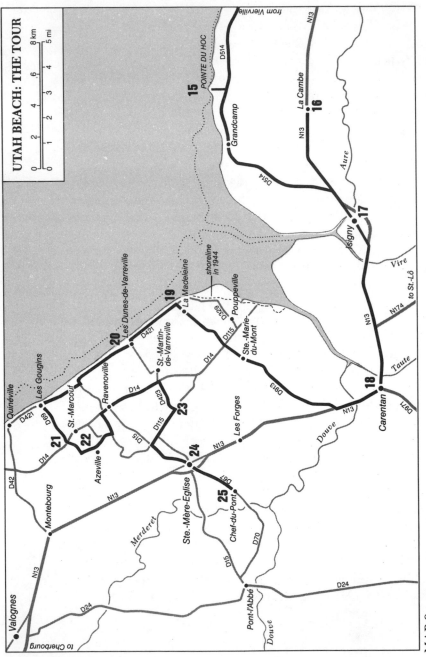

UTAH BEACH: THE TOUR

MAP 9

way overland to Rudder's relief. By then, his force had been reduced to about ninety effectives. Rudder received the Distinguished Service Cross for continuing to lead his men, although twice wounded.

The monument, standing on a German blockhouse which you can enter, consists of a rough granite obelisk flanked by tablets inscribed in French and English.

LA CAMBE

German Military Cemetery

To visit La Cambe (16), drive some 4.5 km east of the junction of N 13 and D 514. The cemetery lies south of N 13; there is limited parking near the entrance.

This site, originally an American cemetery, was given to the German government in 1948 after the American dead had been removed to the American cemetery overlooking Omaha Beach. The cemetery now contains over 21,000 German dead.

La Cambe stands in somber contrast to the American, British, and Canadian cemeteries in Normandy, with their open, gardenlike appearances. We recommend that you spend a few minutes visiting this cemetery.

ISIGNY AND CARENTAN

Continue on N 13 through Isigny and Carentan (19 km).

The Comité du Débarquement has erected monuments at both Isigny (17) and Carentan (18). The first commemorates De Gaulle's speech at Isigny on 14 June 1944. The Carentan monument stands outside the *mairie* (town hall). In 1973, the 101st Airborne Association placed a commemorative plaque inside the eighteenth-century building. Carentan also remembers the 82d Airborne Division with a summer flower display.

Utah Beach

To visit Utah Beach, either after touring Omaha Beach and the Pointe du Hoc Ranger Monument or directly from Caen or Bayeux, follow N 13 through Isigny-sur-Mer and Carentan to the D 913 turnoff (4 km past Carentan, just beyond the bridge over the Douve River). From the turnoff it is some 12 km through Ste.-Marie-du-Mont to La Madeleine on Utah Beach.

General Omar N. Bradley called the assault landing on Utah Beach "a piece of cake," and it was, compared to that on Omaha. The landing plan called for the 4th Infantry Division (Major General Raymond O. Barton) to land along 2,200 yards of sandy beach on a two-regiment front, two battalions abreast. Colonel James A. Van Fleet's 8th Infantry (including the 3d Battalion, 22d Infantry) was to land at 0630, followed by the 22d Infantry in eighty-five minutes and the 12th Infantry at 1030.

DD tanks were to lead the way in, preceded by an intense naval and air bombardment. Various engineer units were scheduled to land close behind the infantry to clear beach obstructions and to blow gaps in the low seawall paralleling the beach.

The landing of the thirty-two DD tanks was delayed when one of the control ships was sunk by a mine. Four of the tanks were lost when the LCT carrying them sank before they could be launched. In contrast to the heavy losses off Omaha, twenty-eight DD's made it to the beach able to provide fire support for the infantry already ashore.

The strong offshore current carried the first wave of infantry some 2,000 yards south, causing the boats to beach in front of the German strong point at La Grande Dune (a half-mile south of your present location). Fortunately, the defenses there were much weaker than those on the intended beach, due in part to visual bombing by the medium bombers of the IX Bomber Command and naval fire support.

Brigadier General Theodore Roosevelt, assistant division commander, landed with the first wave, the only general officer to do so on D Day. Shortly after coming ashore, Roosevelt, disregarding his personal safety, surveyed the beach before him and made two decisions that decisively influenced the course of the battle. Realizing that he and the first wave had landed a mile south of their assigned beach, he ordered the following waves to come in on this new beach. Emphasizing that decision for Colonel Eugene Caffey of the 1st Engineer Special Brigade, he said, "We're going to start the war from here." He then ordered the advance inland to begin immediately along the causeway leading to Beach Exit 2, directly to his front. For his heroism that morning, Roosevelt was awarded the Congressional Medal of Honor.

The 3d Battalion, 8th Infantry, quickly passed across the flooded area behind the beach to higher ground (along the road you have just driven to reach La Madeleine). The 2d Battalion moved along the beach to the south and opened up Exit 1 to Pouppeville and Ste.-Marie-du-Mont. Three battalions of the 22d Infantry moved north to clear opposition from Exit 4. Before dark, the 1st and 2d battalions of the 22d Infantry had linked up with the 502d Parachute Infantry west of St.-Germain-de-Varreville. Late afternoon also found the 2d and 3d battalions, 8th Infantry, astride route N 13 at Les Forges, but they had failed to link up with the 505th Parachute Infantry holding Ste.-Mère-Eglise two miles to the north. By then, the first elements of the 90th Infantry Division had come ashore. The landing on Utah Beach was becoming the big success story of D Day.

La Madeleine

In addition to a landing museum, La Madeleine (19) is the site of these monuments:

- A stone marker commemorating the 4th U.S. Infantry Division.
- A stone marker commemorating the 90th U.S. Infantry Division.
- A "milestone" marking 00 kilometers on the "liberation route." These stones, bearing the torch symbol of the Free French government, mark the triumphant routes of the 2d French Armored Division from Utah Beach across France. They are similar to the stones which line the Sacred Way (La Voie Sacrée), the road from Bar-le-Duc to Verdun along which hundreds of thousands of French soldiers moved in 1916.
- A monument to the 1st Engineer Special Brigade. This monument stands on top of a blockhouse which, complete with guns, has been converted into a crypt memorializing those who died on Utah Beach.

Nearby, the Musée du Débarquement à Utah Beach occupies a blockhouse known as W5. Open Easter to November 0900–1200 and 1400–1900; open in winter on Sundays and holidays 1000–1200 and 1400–1800. Admission charge.

Les Dunes-de-Varreville

Drive 4 km north of La Madeleine along D 421 to Les Dunes-de-Varreville (20), the original D Day landing objective of the 4th Division.

In 1944, it was a strongly defended position, and many of the original blockhouses still squat ominously amid the dunes. Today, the site is marked by a CD monument and a pair of armored vehicles with French insignia which commemorate the 1 August landing of the 2d French Armored Division.

St.-Marcouf–Crisbecq Battery

After leaving Les Dunes-de-Varreville, follow the CD road signs to the St.-Marcouf–Crisbecq Battery (21) located off D 69. The route inland to the battery is well marked, and there is a small parking space near the entrance to the battery. A CD information sign provides useful information about the battery and its capture by American infantry.

This fortified complex contained casemates housing 210-mm guns which easily reached Utah Beach. Despite shelling from large-caliber guns and repeated infantry assaults, the battery held out until 12 June, all the while harassing landing operations. It was the one major battery in the lodgment area which actually became a factor in the post–D Day battle.

On either side of D 420, less than two miles southwest from the St.-Marcouf–Crisbecq Battery, are the casemates of the Azeville Battery (22) which housed four French 105-mm guns.

After withstanding attacks from the 22d Infantry for two days, the battery surrendered after a flamethrower, triggered by Private Ralph G. Riley, set off ammunition inside one of the casemates. Riley was awarded the Silver Star for his single-handed attack.

Objective WXYZ

You may now follow the CD road signs from the St.-Marcouf–Crisbecq Battery to Ste.-Mère-Eglise or you may make a short detour to pass by "Objective WXYZ," a group of farmhouses and outbuildings that was the scene of a memorable D Day firefight.

To reach WXYZ (23), drive south on D 14 from St.-Marcouf until you reach the D 423 intersection (6 km), then turn west for 2 km to the intersection with D 115.

In 1944, the farm buildings you have just passed along D 423 had been pressed into service as a barracks complex for German artillerymen. On American maps they were simply given the designation "WXYZ." Today, there is nothing along this bucolic country road to recall for the traveler the events of 6 June. Yet here, Staff Sergeant Harrison Summers, 1st Battalion, 502d Parachute Infantry, fought almost single-handedly to capture the barracks.

Summers had been given fifteen men to accomplish his mission, one that really called for a battalion effort. Strangers to Summers and coming from different units, these men had little stomach for the firefight the sergeant was about to begin. Trusting that his example would inspire his men, Summers raced over to the first building, kicked in the door, and sprayed the room with his Thompson submachine gun. The handful of survivors burst out of the rear of the building, looking for cover further down the road. Summers, now covered by Private William Burt with a light machine gun, broke into a second house and shot its six defenders. And so it went from house to house. Two officers who joined him were taken out by German fire almost immediately. Private John Camien, carrying an M-1 carbine, pitched in later. The rest of Summers's squad provided some covering fire from the ditch paralleling the road. But it was largely Summers's fight. Building after building fell to the intrepid sergeant. The finale came after five hours of fighting, when Summers and Burt set the last barracks building on fire with bazooka rounds and tracers, flushing the eighty or so German defenders into an open field where fifty were killed. When asked how he felt, Summers, dragging on a cigarette, replied that he didn't feel "very good. It was all kind of crazy."

Ste.-Mère-Eglise

To reach Ste.-Mère-Eglise (24), turn north on D 115 to its junction with D 15 (3 km), then drive west on D 15 (3 km). Park in the town square (Place de 6 Juin).

One of the most disastrous drops (in a night filled with disasters) occurred in Ste.-Mère-Eglise. Around midnight, a stray incendiary bomb had set fire to the house of Monsieur Harion, located to the east of the square. Wakened by the mayor and the tolling of the church bell, the townspeople turned out in large numbers to form a bucket brigade supervised by members of the German garrison. (The hand pump used that night still sits on the east side of the square.) While the house continued to burn, the drone of planes could be heard over the tolling bell. The firefighters, looking skyward, saw ghostly silhouettes drifting down on them. Two sticks from the 1st and 2d battalions had gotten their green jump light directly over the village. Illuminated by light from the burning house and tracers from German AA guns, the paratroopers were easy targets for the Germans below. Few survived. One who did was Private John Steele, whose parachute caught on the steeple of the church in front of you. The wounded paratrooper hung there limply for two hours, pretending to be dead, before the Germans took him prisoner. The less fortunate hung from the trees all around the square where they had been shot. Once the fire in Monsieur Harion's house had burned itself out and the last of the paratroopers were killed or captured, the German garrison (a transportation company) quite inexplicably called it an evening and turned in.

A mile northeast of Ste.-Mère-Eglise, Lieutenant Colonel Edward Krause, commanding the 3d Battalion, assembled ninety men within an hour of landing and promptly ordered an advance on the village. Around dawn, the German garrison was again turned out, this time by the rattle of small-arms fire. Krause's men cleared the village in a rush, capturing thirty Germans and killing another eleven. With Ste.-Mère-Eglise in American hands, Krause ran a worn American flag to the top of the village flagpole, a flag that he had carried with him from Sicily.

North of Ste.-Mère-Eglise, the 505th's 2d Battalion, commanded by Lieutenant Colonel Benjamin Vandervoort, landed in its assigned drop zone and quickly assembled 575 of its 650 members. After some initial communications confusion (working radios were in short supply that morning), Vandervoort, who had broken his ankle landing, ordered the bulk of his men to fall back on Ste.-Mère-Eglise. He left Lieutenant Turner B. Turnbull and a platoon of forty-one to hold Neuville, two kilometers to the north.

Turnbull, a half-Cherokee known as the "Chief" to his men, had hardly deployed his troopers to either side of the road when they were attacked by a company of the 1058th Grenadier Regiment, 91st Division, supported by a self-propelled gun and a tank. German fire quickly killed Turnbull's one bazooka man, but the paratroopers used their 57-mm anti-tank gun, trailered up by Vandervoort behind his command jeep, to knock out both the self-propelled gun and the tank. By afternoon, the Germans had worked around both flanks of the American position and threatened to cut N 13. Turnbull ordered a fighting retreat—a move Vandervoort had tried to signal him earlier—and sixteen of the original forty-two troopers reached American lines. Turnbull and his men had bought eight hours, giving Colonel William Ekman, commanding the 505th, time to consolidate his position around St.-Mère-Eglise.

In the late morning, the enemy attacked along N 13 from the south, only to be driven back and counterattacked in turn by Company L, 2d Battalion. D Day ended with the Americans still in control of Ste.-Mère-Eglise, and further German attacks during the night failed to dislodge them. For their roles in the capture and defense of Ste.-Mère-Eglise, both Krause and Vandervoort received the Distinguished Service Cross.

All through 6 June, isolated groups of paratroopers were getting their first taste of hedgerow fighting within a few miles of Ste.-Mère-Eglise. One of the more confused fights took place west of the village at La Fière bridge, where uncoordinated groups from the 505th, 507th, and 508th regiments first captured, then lost this important crossing of the Merderet.

By the afternoon of the sixth, the paratroopers had made contact with elements of the 4th Division moving inland from Utah Beach. They had cut N 13 at Ste.-Mère-Eglise, thereby preventing the Germans from reinforcing the beach area. By their reduction of strong points at the beach exits, they greatly aided in the movement of the 4th Division off Utah Beach. Much hard fighting lay ahead to clear enemy resistance in the Carentan area, which was preventing a linkup between the two American beachheads. But it was apparent that Eisenhower's decision to go ahead with the night drop of the two American airborne divisions had been sound.

On one side of the square is the church (built between the eleventh and fifteenth centuries) on which Private John Steele landed. It contains two stained-glass windows commemorating the drop. There is a CD monument in front of the church. Next to it is a memorial to the 1944 mayor, Alexandre Renaud. The hand pump used to fight the fire on the night of 5–6 June still stands at the rear of the square behind the church. To the south of the square stands the Musée des Troupes Aéroportées. Open Easter through October 0900–1200 and 1400–1900 and on Sundays and bank holidays during the winter. Admission charge.

The Hôtel de Ville (Town Hall) is located just south of the square. In front stands a milestone marking "Kilometer O" on the "liberation route." Behind it is a stone honoring Generals Ridgway and Gavin. Inside the building is the American flag that Lieutenant Colonel Edward Krause raised over the liberated Ste.-Mère-Eglise. It had earlier flown over liberated Naples.

Before leaving Ste.-Mère-Eglise, you may wish to make a couple of short trips to nearby sites of interest.

Two kilometers east of the town on D 17 is La Londe Farm, the site of the first operational American air base in Normandy. A commemorative parachute drop is staged there each June 6, weather permitting.

Some three kilometers to the southwest on D 67, near Chef-du-Pont, is a memorial to the 508th Parachute Infantry (25).

CHERBOURG

The Fort du Roule

> *To visit the Fort du Roule, which is situated above the port of Cherbourg, drive north from Ste.-Mère-Eglise on N 13 some 37 km. (Two km north of Ste.-Mère-Eglise you will pass through Neuville-au-Plain where Lieutenant Turnbull fought his holding action.) As you enter Cherbourg turn right at the traffic light and follow the signs up the hill to the fort.*

The Fort du Roule, a classic star fort built in the nineteenth century, sits atop a rock spur which dominates Cherbourg from the south. In 1944 the Germans had turned the fort into a formidable strong point. Coastal artillery, facing the harbor, had been mounted in the lower level under the cliff edge. The upper ramparts were studded with concrete machine-gun and mortar emplacements and protected by an anti-tank ditch.

The task of reducing the fort fell to the 1st and 2d battalions of the 314th Infantry, 79th Division. Following earlier bombing attacks, their assault began in the morning of 25 June with an ineffective P-47 attack and an artillery barrage. The advance temporarily halted in a draw some seven hundred yards from the fort before resuming under covering fire. At this juncture Corporal John D. Kelly of E Company managed to take out a key pillbox with a pole charge and hand grenades, thereby allowing his platoon to penetrate the outer defenses. Meanwhile, Lieutenant Carlos C. Ogden of K Company, although twice wounded, used his rifle and hand grenades to knock out an 88-mm gun and two machine guns blocking his company's advance. Both men were awarded the Congressional Medal of Honor.

By noon, the 314th held the upper works of the fort. The German defenders continued to fire from the lower level until the next day, when fire from the town, demolition charges,

and an infantry assault along the cliff side smoked them out.
Today the fort is the site of the Musée de la Libération. Open
April through September 0900–1200 and 1400–1800; open October through March 0930–1200 and 1400–1730 (closed Tuesdays). Admission charge.

Tour of the British and Canadian Sectors

This tour of the British and Canadian landing areas begins in
Port-en-Bessin, a small seaport marking the western edge of
Gold Beach. By picking up D 514 there, it is possible to complete the tour by following that route to the Merville Battery (54
kilometers).

From Port-en-Bessin to Arromanches-les-Bains, high bluffs
studded with gun emplacements rise sharply above the narrow
beaches. For this reason the landings on Gold took place east of
Arromanches, between Le Hamel and La Rivière. There, the
bluffs give way to beaches. As you drive beyond Courseulles-
sur-Mer, marking the center of Juno Beach, these hills in turn
give way to the valleys of the Seulles and Orne rivers.

Once you reach the boundary between Juno and Sword
beaches at St.-Aubin-sur-Mer, D 514 takes you through an almost continuous strip of seaside resorts to Ouistreham-Riva-
Bella. Through this section, summer traffic can be heavy and
parking space difficult to find. Although the area around Bénouville is less congested, parking near the Pegasus Bridge is limited.

GOLD BEACH

Port-en-Bessin
*Port-en-Bessin can be reached from the Bayeux traffic
loop by driving some 9 km along D 6.*

This picturesque village was the objective of the 47th Royal
Marine Commando, which landed east of Le Hamel. The 47th

96

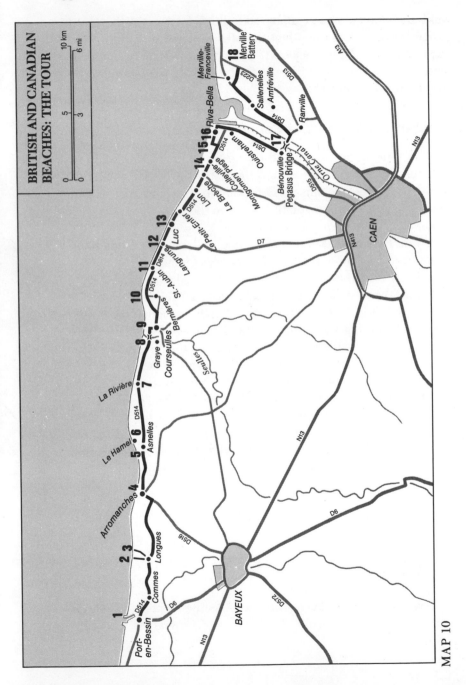

BRITISH AND CANADIAN
BEACHES: THE TOUR

MAP 10

was hard hit coming ashore, losing four LCA's (with nine others damaged) on the run in. Unexpected resistance delayed its advance westward, thus Port-en-Bessin was not liberated until the night of 7–8 June. Damage to the port was extensive; cargo would not begin to come ashore until 14 June.

A CD monument (1)* commemorating the landing stands on the jetty forming the outer breakwater. It is easily spotted from the shore because of the array of Allied flags flying above it. A well-preserved seventeenth-century defense tower, designed by the Marquis de Vauban, stands at the landward end of the jetty. Below it is a German blockhouse bearing a plaque to the 47th Royal Marine Commando.

Longues Battery

Continue east on D 514 through the village of Commes to Longues-sur-Mer. To visit a well-preserved Tobruk (2) (a small concrete bunker distinguished by a nipple on top out of which the defender could fire), turn north as you are leaving the village. The turn onto the farm road is marked by a red fire hydrant and a large stone barn. This road will take you to the cliff top just west of the Longues Battery. Turn west when you reach the concrete observation building and park where the road becomes unpassable. Continue west on foot to inspect the Tobruk.

Thousands of these small bunkers were built along the Atlantic Wall.

Return to D 514. Shortly you will pick up the CD direction signs pointing the way to the main battery (3).

Behind the cliffs overlooking the sea are the remains of a massive German battery consisting of four casemated 155-mm naval guns. They were controlled from a fortified bunker on the cliff's

* Bold numbers are keyed to Map 10.

edge. Despite repeated bombing and its incomplete state, the battery's fire managed to straddle HMS *Bulolo*, the XXX Corps command ship, on D Day morning. The battery was promptly silenced by fire from HMS *Ajax* and the French cruiser *George Leygues*. The garrison surrendered on 7 June.

Follow the CD signs to an orientation table on the cliff top.

From the orientation table you can see the command post which directed the battery's fire. The table also indicates the relative position of the bombardment ships.

Return to D 514 and continue east to Arromanches (6 km).

Arromanches-les-Bains

Arromanches was the site of the British Mulberry (Mulberry B), and today its remains dominate the seascape from this small port.

The artificial ports were the brainchild of Winston Churchill, who said he conceived the idea in 1917. Twenty-seven years later, two were actually constructed—Mulberry A at Omaha Beach (rendered unusable by the storm of 19–21 June) and Mulberry B at Arromanches. They were composed of several elements—floating breakwaters (Gooseberries) forming an outer protective circle, concrete caissons (Phoenix) and derelict ships sunk to form the perimeter of the harbor, pierheads which could rise and fall with the tide, and floating metal piers connecting the pierheads to the shore. All elements were constructed in England and towed across the Channel beginning on D Day plus 1. Some 500,000 tons of supplies had been off-loaded through Mulberry B by the end of August, when siltation and the opening of Cherbourg and lesser ports put an end to its usefulness. Whether or not the Mulberries were essential links in the supply chain is debatable, but as Chester Wilmot has pointed out, the fact that they were to be built gave Neptune planners the assurance that, failing all else, forces ashore could be adequately supplied. That assurance was worth a great deal in early 1944.

As you enter Arromanches, follow the CD direction signs to the Exposition Permanente du Débarquement (4), which is housed in a modern building near the seawall.

This museum is one of the best in Normandy. Open April through September 0900–1200 and 1400–1900; open October through March 0900–1200 and 1400–1800. Admission charge.

From the museum you can make a short but steep climb up the bluffs to the east of the town to see a Sherman tank, then continue to the top to the site of a German radar station. It is also possible to reach the radar station by driving east from Arromanches on D 514 and parking at the radar site (St.-Come-de-Fresne).

An orientation platform provides an excellent view of the port and the remains of Mulberry B. The bunkers visible from the cliff top were silenced by fire from HMS *Belfast,* which you can visit while in London.

Asnelles and Le Hamel

Continue along D 514 to Asnelles (2 km) where there is a monument to the 50th British Division (5). Just east of the village, turn toward the beach. Stop on the seawall by the huge blockhouse.

You are now at Le Hamel, on Jig sector, Gold Beach, which was assaulted by the 231st British Infantry Brigade (1st battalions of the Hampshire and Dorset regiments). The 1st Hampshire took the brunt of the fire from the 88-mm gun in this blockhouse. The attack was spearheaded by four Crabs which flailed their way through the minefields behind the beach. Three of the tanks were destroyed; the fourth made a wild charge through the village before it was knocked out. According to the plaque on the blockhouse (6), the Germans manning this 88-mm accounted for a total of six British tanks. Although certain German strong points held out through the afternoon, the Hampshires quickly worked their way around Le Hamel and began their advance inland.

The 1st Dorsets, landing further east, out of range of the fire from Le Hamel, had an easier time of it. Their specialized armor (8th Armoured Brigade) quickly opened three beach exits, and by afternoon they were fighting units of the 352d Division for control of the Arromanches ridge.

La Rivière
Continue along D 514 to the village of La Rivière, which marks the eastern end of Gold Beach (5 km).

At the crossroads marked by L'Eden, a "Bar Americain," there is a monument (7) to the 2d Battalion of the Hertfordshire Regiment.

Juno Beach

Graye-sur-Mer
From La Rivière, continue east along D 514 for 5 km. Some 250 meters before you reach the bridge over the Seulles, there is a road running down to the beach marked by a CD direction sign. Drive toward the beach and park near the tank (8).

Here, Prime Minister Churchill, with Generals Jan Christiaan Smuts and Alan Brooke, landed on 12 June for a tour of the beachhead. Four days later, George VI also came ashore here. A CD monument commemorates these events, as well as the assault landing.

The tank is a Churchill AVRE, which lay buried in the sand until its recovery in 1976.

Courseulles-sur-Mer

Return to D 514 and drive across the Seulles bridge into the port of Courseulles. Follow the CD direction signs to the port area and park near the DD Sherman tank (9).

This Sherman, belonging to the 1st Canadian Hussars, is one of the five (out of nineteen) whch foundered on the run in. It was recovered in 1971. Note the duplex-drive transmission (minus the screws) and the lip extending around the entire hull to which the canvas dam was attached. The DD's making it ashore provided vital fire support for Company A of the Regina Rifles, which encountered heavy fire both from German resistance nests in the harbor area and from artillery positioned further inland. Flanking the beach exit is a memorial plaque to the officers and men of the Regina Rifles who were casualties during the war. Nearby are plaques commemorating the 1st Canadian Scottish Regiment and De Gaulle's landing on 14 June.

Some three hundred yards east along the Avenue de la Combattante is a memorial to the Royal Winnipeg Rifles.

Bernières-sur-Mer

Continue east along D 514 to Bernières (3 km). Park near the CD monument in the town square (10).

You are now facing the Nan sector of Juno Beach, where the 8th Canadian Brigade (the Queen's Own Rifles and La Chaudière regiments) landed. The QOR was to have landed behind DD tanks, but the high seas breaking over the offshore reef meant that the tanks had to be brought into the beach well behind the infantry. As it was, the LCA's carrying the assault companies of the QOR were a half-hour late reaching the beach and some two hundred yards east of their designated landing area. The boats dropped their ramps among the beach obstacles. As many as one-fourth were damaged or sunk upon landing or when attempting to retract through the obstacle belt. One company of the QOR took sixty-five casualties crossing the hundred yards of sand to the seawall. Nevertheless, aided by fire from a flak ship just off the beach, the Canadians quickly overran the German resistance nests. When the Régiment de la Chaudière landed fifteen minutes later, much of the earlier fire had been suppressed.

An armored car near the monument bears a plaque to the Queen's Own Rifles. About two hundred yards away, near the beach exit, are plaques to both regiments of the 8th Brigade.

St.-Aubin-sur-Mer

Continue eastward on D 514 to St.-Aubin (2 km). Drive to the beach road (D 814) and proceed along it.

St.-Aubin was the landing site of the 48th Royal Marine Commando (4th Special Service Brigade), whose job it was to secure the east flank of the Canadians landing on Juno Beach. After a costly fight the commandos captured a resistance nest in the town. The next morning they moved east to Langrune, where they joined with the 41st Commando. The 41st had landed behind the British on Queen sector of Sword Beach, then moved west to capture Lion-sur-Mer in the morning of the seventh and to make contact with the men of the 48th Commando.

Near a blockhouse on the seawall is a memorial (11) to the North Shore (New Brunswick) Regiment and the 48th Royal Marine Commando. Some one hundred yards further on, by the Syndicate d'Initiative, is a monument to the Fort Garry Horse.

SWORD BEACH

Langrune-sur-Mer

Continue east on D 814 (the beach road) to Langrune (2 km) to see another monument (12) commemorating the 48th Royal Marine Commando.

Luc-sur-Mer

Continue east on the beach road to Luc (1.5 km). Drive past the casino and watch for a small park on the north side of the road.

The task of reducing the strong point at Le Petit-Enfer (near where you are parked) was assigned to the 46th Royal Marine Commando landing on 7 June. After taking the position, they moved inland to the village of La Delivrande.

About a half-mile east of the casino is a curious all-purpose stone monument (13) standing in a small square. One side bears inscriptions commemorating the raid by the 1st British Commando on 28 September 1941 and the liberation of Luc in June 1944. The opposite side carries an inscription commemorating French sailors and soldiers who died for their country.

Colleville–Montgomery Plage

Rejoin D 514 after leaving Luc. Continue east for six kilometers through Lion-sur-Mer (where the 41st Royal Marine Commando landed), past La Brèche d'Hermanville (where there are three monuments to the 3d British Infantry Division), to the Colleville–Montgomery Plage crossroad (14).

A sign at the crossroads marks the site of a temporary British cemetery and commemorates the landing on 6 June. A marker opposite it commemorates Number 4 Commando and Commandant Philippe Kieffer, who commanded two Free French troops of the 10 Commando. The commandos landed just after the first assault wave and quickly moved inland. They then fought their way through Riva-Bella until they were stopped by concentrated fire from the casino and its adjoining summer house. Only after a DD tank was called up from the beach were the commandos able to silence the defenders.

Ouistreham-Riva-Bella

Take the Avenue de Bruxelles toward the beach and continue east along the sea front until you reach a large dune with a steel turret on top (15). Park nearby.

This turret now serves as the base for a modernistic metal sculpture resembling a flame. As you climb the dune to the turret there are small stone markers inscribed with the names of commandos who fell on D Day.

The Musée du Commando No. 4 is located in a building just across the street from the turret. Open 0900–1200 and 1400–1830, June to 15 September; open weekends during the winter—hours may vary. Admission charge.

Further east along the Ouistreham-Riva-Bella sea front are the following items of interest (16):

- a memorial to Commandant Kieffer of 10 Commando;
- a CD monument;
- a steel cupola at the end of a jetty said to have been brought from the Maginot Line.

Bénouville and Pegasus Bridge

To visit the Pegasus Bridge after touring Sword Beach, return to D 514 and proceed south out of Ouistreham-Riva-Bella to Bénouville (4 km). Turn east at the crossroads and drive 200 yards to the swivel bridge, now known as the Pegasus Bridge after the insignia of the 6th British Airborne Division, which spans the Orne Canal (17).

The task of capturing the bridges over both the Orne River and Canal fell to a select force drawn from the 2d Battalion, Oxfordshire and Buckinghamshire Light Infantry, and the Royal Engineers, commanded by Major John Howard. The six gliders carrying this force were to land in the dark on the approaches to the bridges. In what was one of the great navigational feats of D Day morning, three of the gliders crash-landed (the most explicit term describing a glider's reunion with the earth) within fifty yards of the east end of the canal bridge. A lone German sentry who might have sounded the alarm did not do so because he assumed that an airplane had crashed nearby. His mistake was costly. While one of Howard's squads crossed the bridge in a rush, taking a single casualty, others overran nearby pillboxes and trenches before the surprised Germans could man their positions. Within minutes, the bridge and its defenses were in British hands.

The assault on the Orne River bridge went as smoothly, although one of the three gliders assigned to that operation missed the bridge area altogether, landing miles away in the flooded Dives valley. Only one of the remaining two gliders landed near the bridge. The twenty-odd men from that lone glider rushed the bridge despite the loss of surprise. Fortunately, the German guards did not know the odds; they scattered before the determined British charge.

Not only had the bridges been captured easily, but they were intact. Both structures had been wired for demolition, but the explosive charges had not been planted. Major Howard's men held their prizes throughout D Day while German pressure mounted. Around 1200 hours, some two and a half minutes after they were to have been reinforced, the beleaguered defenders were startled by the distant sound of bagpipes. The 6 Commando of the 1st Special Service Brigade, led by Brigadier Lord Lovat, had arrived with piper Bill Millin. The two forces joined ranks to the tune of "Blue Bonnets over the Border" and the crack of small-arms fire. Although the Orne bridges would not be truly secure until units of the 3d British Division arrived late

in the afternoon, the skirl of Millin's pipes had assured the men
of Howard's command that the seaborne invasion was in fact
ashore.

The Pegasus Bridge site is especially rich in D Day memorabilia. In addition to the original bridge itself (complete with
painted-over bullet marks and a bomb dent in the bridge coun-
terweight), the following monuments, memorials, and artifacts
are found nearby:

- A stone cross at the Bénouville crossroads commemorating the liberation.
- The Café Gondrée with its plaque proudly claiming it to
  be the first house liberated in France.
- The Musée des Troupes Aéroportées. Open April
  through September 1000–1230 and 1430–1700. Admission charge.
- A marker commemorating the linkup between the Ox
  and Bucks and the 6 Commando. In 1984, Bill Millin was
  photographed next to this marker which depicts him
  with pipes à la 1944.
- A CD monument commemorating the assault.
- Three orientation tables marking the spots where the
  Horsa gliders came to rest. They are located on the
  southwest side of the bridge, below the canal bank.
- A German pillbox complete with the 50-mm anti-tank
  gun used by Howard's men to silence a sniper in Bénouville.
- A Centaur version of the British Cruiser Mark VIII tank
  mounting a 95-mm gun. This tank belonged to the 5th
  Independent Battery, Royal Marine Armoured Support
  Regiment, which landed at La Brèche d'Hermanville.
  Three such regiments were organized a few months before D Day to provide additional fire support for the first
  waves of infantry. This Centaur IV was recovered in
  1975.
- A British cemetery in Ranville (some two kilometers

from the Pegasus Bridge). Among the 2,563 graves is that
of Lieutenant Den Brotheridge, who was killed in the attack on the bridge.
- Three memorials in Amfréville commemorating the 4
  and 6 commandos and the 1st Special Service Brigade of
  which they were a part.

Merville Battery

To visit the Merville Battery **(18)** *from the Pegasus Bridge
area, drive east from the bridge on D 514, cross the Orne
River (this bridge is new), and continue north through Sal-
lenelles. Turn right at the traffic light in Merville-Franceville and follow the CD direction signs to the battery, which
is located just off D 223.*

According to Allied intelligence, this battery contained four
casemated 150-mm guns sighted so that they could fire on ships
standing off Sword Beach. Neptune planners were obviously
worried about the damage these guns might inflict on the invasion fleet. The task of neutralizing the Merville Battery was
given to the seven-hundred-man 9th Battalion, 6th Airborne Di
vision, commanded by Lieutenant Colonel Terence Otway. The
plan Otway and his men had been rehearsing for months was
daring. Otway's main force would parachute in some distance
from the battery, gather their special equipment—including
flamethrowers, bangalore torpedoes, and anti-tank guns   then
assemble just outside the battery's defenses. This force, divided
into eleven teams, would lay the bangalores under the perimeter
wire, clear and mark the minefields, then take up covering positions to watch for the arrival of two tow planes with their gliders. On seeing Otway's signal (a star shell fired from a mortar),
the glider pilots were to land inside the battery's perimeter. The
garrison of some two hundred men would then be overrun by
this combined assault from air and ground. Otway was to signal
the fall of the battery with a flare before 0530, or ships of the
bombardment force would take it under fire.

This carefully rehearsed plan began to unravel before the first paratrooper touched ground. Instead of dropping in their assigned drop zone, Otway's men were scattered over a fifty-mile corridor. Some sticks took days to rejoin their outfit; of others no trace was ever found. Otway could assemble only 150 of his men by the time the attack was to begin. Most of the special equipment carried in by two of the battalion's gliders was likewise lost, including the mortar signal rounds. The frustrated men on the ground could only look skyward as the two assault gliders swooped low across the battery, and then, receiving no signal, landed outside the battery's perimeter. Otway gave no sign of the dismay he must have felt at that moment, for no sooner had the gliders come down and while the defenders' attention was still on the skies, he ordered the wire blown and his assault teams to attack through the gaps. The fight was over in ten minutes. Although half of the British force was dead or wounded, the Merville Battery had been silenced. Ironically, the much-feared 150-mm rifles turned out to be less formidable 75-mm guns.

The Comité du Débarquement has placed an excellent information sign at the entrance to the battery. Casemate Number 1 now houses a small museum. Open June through September 1030–1230 and 1400–1730; closed Tuesdays. Admission charge.

You may return to Caen via D 514 to Bénouville, then follow D 515 south into the city.

Rommel inspects the Atlantic Wall fortifications in April 1944. (*U.S. Army*)

110

SHAEF commanders at a press conference in London, 12 February 1944. Left to right: Bradley, Admiral Sir Bertram Ramsay, Air Chief Marshal Sir Arthur Tedder, Eisenhower, Montgomery, Air Chief Marshal Sir Trafford Leigh-Mallory, and Lieutenant General Walter Bedell Smith. (*U.S. Army*)

111

Troops of the 101st Airborne line up for chow in England in late May 1944. (*U.S. Army*)

Survivors from an LCVP are helped ashore on Omaha Beach, 6 June 1944. (*U.S. Army*)

As late as 11 June German artillery continues to pound Utah Beach. (*U.S. Army*)

The 3d Canadian Infantry Division disembarks on Juno Beach near Bernières-sur-Mer on D Day. (*The Trustees of the Imperial War Museum, London*)

3

The Breakout from Normandy

An Overview

Despite the Channel storm which broke over the beachheads two weeks after the landings, the Allied buildup continued with hardly a pause. By 29 July, SHAEF could count over a million and a half men ashore and tens of thousands more waiting in the staging areas in England. To support this burgeoning army, 1,602,976 tons of supplies had been landed through the Mulberries and lesser ports and across the beaches. The lines of communication linking all five beachheads were secure, although the British and Canadian armies had failed to capture Caen. Allied air and naval superiority remained complete; German efforts in both spheres had been sporadic and unsuccessful. Control of the Channel by Allied naval forces had prevented any interference with the movement of men and supplies, the towing of the Mulberry elements, or, later, the laying of PLUTO (Pipe Line under the Ocean) lines to carry fuel to the Cotentin. Allied air forces dominated the skies over France, flying thousands of sorties in the weeks following D Day. Aircraft attacked bridges and railroads hundreds of miles inland from the lodgment area, virtually halting German troop movement during daylight hours. By the end of July it was clear that the Allies were winning the race for numerical superiority on the Normandy battlefield. It remained uncertain, however, whether their armies could engineer a breakout from the difficult country in which they were fighting.

Overlord planners had seemingly given little thought to the terrain beyond the beaches. Their concerns had been so narrowly focused on the initial assault phase of the operation that they had made little effort to prepare the ground forces to fight in the confining river valleys and hedgerows that dominated the land—the terrible *bocage* of Normandy.

"Hedgerow" is a deceptive term, conjuring up long parallel, evenly spaced hedges separating the fields and apple orchards of the countryside. Rather, as any aerial photo of Normandy shows, the landscape was (and is) broken into countless boxlike fields, from a fraction of an acre to five acres. The sides of these fields were mounds of earth and stone five to six feet in height and covered with a tangle of trees and brush (often including a rank growth of nettles—let the adventurous traveler beware!). Small openings in the hedges led only into other enclosed fields, creating a gigantic maze. Visibility was rarely more than a few hundred feet, generally less. Roads, where they existed, were unimproved, often sunken or concealed by the hedges. The *bocage*, crisscrossed in the spring of 1944 with flooded river valleys, was ideal defensive ground, providing optimum cover for the German soldiers who extracted a price for every field they surrendered to the advancing Allies. Conversely, tanks were of marginal use in the *bocage*. Lacking maneuvering room and often blocked by steep stream beds, they were unable to push through the dense hedges, and as they climbed over the top, they exposed their thin bellies to German anti-tank gunners. To compound these difficulties, the limitations on British manpower (they were fully mobilized by 1944 and had no further reserves on which to draw) and the design of the American army (equipped and trained for a war of mobility, not of attrition) meant that the Allied armies would have a difficult task punching through the heavily defended *bocage*. The great fear of the

117

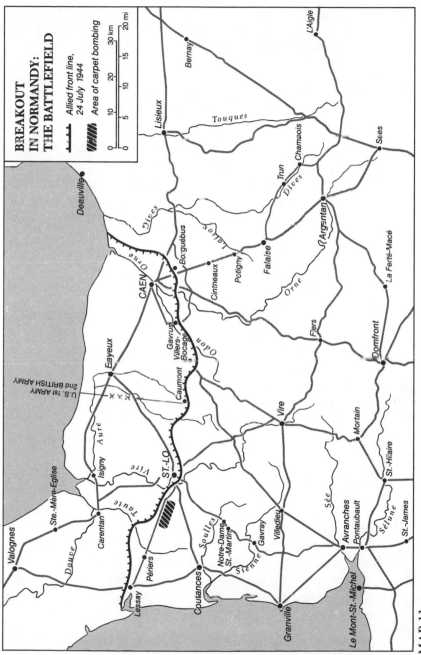

MAP 11

Overlord planners had been that the German defensive advan-
tages would offset the Allied superiority on the ground and in
the air to produce a stalemate, as had happened earlier at
Anzio.

Beyond these tactical difficulties that the *bocage* presented
lay the larger concern of how the battle of the breakout was
to be conducted. There has been much controversy among the
generals and the historians over this issue ever since the
war. Did the battle unfold according to the master plan outlined by Montgomery in his St. Paul's School briefing or was
it played by ear after the British failure to capture Caen? Was
there initially to have been a breakout from the British sector,
where the terrain was less difficult, or was it to have come
from the Americans pushing slowly through the *bocage* in the
west?

By coincidence, the American position on the right side of the
invasion force was not premeditated. Rather, it came about because of the natural decision to locate American camps along
the southwestern coast of England. It then followed that the
American armies would land on the westernmost Normandy
beaches, and that in turn placed them on the longer arc to the
German border. Much of the argument over Allied strategy in
the months ahead can be attributed to the fact that the American armies, with their superior mobility and greater manpower
reserves, were less well positioned than the British to strike a
mortal blow at the Reich. Montgomery's 21 Army Group, although able to move on a shorter arc, simply lacked the sustained combat power to punch through to the West Wall and
beyond.

But these strategic factors were not obvious in the days immediately following 6 June, as the First U.S. Army struggled to consolidate its toehold on the Calvados coast and capture the port
of Cherbourg. Overlord planners considered the early opening
of that port to be essential if the Allied buildup was to keep pace
with German reinforcement of the Normandy front. General

Bradley assigned the tasks of isolating the Cotentin Peninsula and capturing Cherbourg to Major General J. Lawton Collins, the dynamic VII Corps commander. Collins soon pushed the green 90th Division into the *bocage* west of Ste.-Mère-Eglise, where its attack stalled in the face of the veteran German 91st Division. Collins's first solution was to relieve the commanders of the division and two of its regiments; his second was to use elements of the 9th and 82d divisions, along with the maligned 90th, in a steady push across the peninsula, first to St.-Sauveur, then to the sea at Barneville. That stage completed, Collins realigned his corps to face northward (Manton Eddy's 9th Division completed the maneuver in a record twenty-four hours), ready to begin the drive on Cherbourg. Time had become even more critical because Ultra now revealed that Hitler had rescinded his "no retreat" order. Furthermore, no one knew how much longer the Fortitude deception would pin German divisions in the Pas-de-Calais area or how long the Mulberries would be out of commission.

"Lightning Joe" Collins, who received his nickname while commanding the 25th Division (code-named Lightning) on Guadalcanal, understood the unforgiving minute as well as any American commander. He opened his attack with a quick right-hand jab north from Ste.-Mère-Eglise by the 4th Division. In his center, the 79th Division's attack met with resistance, but on the left, Eddy's 9th quickly pushed aside the weak defenses barring its advance. The VII Corps was in position to begin the assault on Cherbourg's outer defenses by 21 June. Preceded by a massive aerial bombardment, during which regiments of the 9th and 4th divisions were accidentally strafed, the attack began in the afternoon of the twenty-second. The German defenders fought fanatically, especially those occupying the Fort du Roule, but the worst was over by the twenty-fifth. Scattered German units held out until the end of the month.

The port of Cherbourg had been thoroughly demolished by its defenders. Mined, most of its cargo-handling facilities totally ruined, the deep basin filled with debris, the work of making the port fully operational would go on for months.

While the VII Corps swiftly isolated and captured Cherbourg, the other Allied armies had carried the attack to the German forces ringing the lodgment area. Lieutenant General Leonard T. Gerow's V Corps, finding light resistance on its front, cautiously probed inland toward the village of Caumont. Sensing some weakness in the German deployment, Montgomery, who meanwhile had been battering unsuccessfully at the gates of Caen, unleashed his XXX Corps in an effort to outflank the western end of Caen's defenses. Led by the 7th Armoured, the "Desert Rats" of North African fame, the British advance swung west of Tilly-sur-Seulles and halted just outside Villers-Bocage. There, two tank squadrons of the 22d Armoured Brigade, with supporting infantry, were badly mauled by a German Mark VI (Tiger) tank commanded by SS Lieutenant Michael Wittmann. Taking council of their fears concerning further armored counterattacks, both Gerow and Lieutenant General G. C. Bucknall, XXX Corps commander, halted their divisions, when an aggressive push through the Caumont Gap might have broken through the thin German defenses.

Throughout the remainder of June and into July, the First U.S. Army fought a bloody and demoralizing battle down the Cotentin plain to clear the *bocage* and flooded bottomland before launching the armored breakout which Bradley hoped would unhinge the Seventh Army. The American advance from their positions south of Carentan and Isigny to the St.-Lô–Périers road (some twenty to thirty kilometers), which was reached on 18 July, cost 40,000 casualties, 90 percent of whom were infantrymen.

Meanwhile, Montgomery initiated a series of battles around Caen which he hoped would produce a breakout or at least pin down a significant number of German divisions on that front. He scheduled the first of his offensives, code-named Epsom, for 26 June; and despite rain and fog, the 15th Scottish Division, supported by the 31st Armoured Brigade, began its advance west of Caen on schedule. Slowed by the weather and minefields, the Scots halted a mile short of the Odon River, but the next day captured the bridges over the river. The 11th Armoured Division was quickly passed through the 15th's positions to exploit the gains.

But the German defenses, consisting of defensive lines several miles deep, were not so easily breached. Even when the suicide of the Seventh Army's commander, General Friedrich Dollmann, left a temporary void in the German command structure (von Rundstedt and Rommel were in Germany to confer with Hitler), panzer units that had been assembled for a counterattack against Bayeux were ordered to attack the flanks of the "Scottish Corridor." Their attack on the western flank of the corridor carried them just short of Cheux by the afternoon of the twenty-ninth. All the while, advance elements of the 11th Armoured continued to hold the crest of Hill 112, a broad, flat expanse of highland which dominated the ground between the Odon and Orne rivers. Over the next few days the panzers brought maximum pressure to bear against the British advance. Counterattacks from the three panzer divisions already committed to the battle (Panzer Lehr, 1st SS Panzer, and 2d SS Panzer) were reinforced by the II SS Panzer Corps, composed of the 9th and 10th Panzer divisions, newly arrived from their rest area in Poland. The repeated German attacks failed to penetrate the flanks of the salient, but they forced the 11th Armoured to withdraw from Hill 112.

The battle, a tactical draw, was over on 1 July. The Scots still held the corridor, but they had not been able to reach their Orne objectives. Operation Epsom, at the cost of some 2,500 casualties in the 15th Division, had forestalled Rommel's counteroffensive and bought time for the American buildup, but it had failed to loosen the German hold on Caen. Montgomery kept up the pressure on the forces holding the city by ordering massive naval and air bombardments and by launching a frontal assault on the city (Operation Charnwood). By then, Caen was mostly rubble, but still the Germans clung to its southern and eastern sections. SHAEF's worst fears of a developing tactical stalemate seemed near realization.

Prodded by an impatient Eisenhower, who was acutely aware of the impact the V-1 flying bomb attacks were having on London, Montgomery called for a two-pronged offensive to get under way in late July. His plan called for the British to attack first with an armored thrust east of Caen, code-named Goodwood, followed in a few days by a major drive by Bradley's First Army south of the St.-Lô–Périers–Lessay line, code-named Cobra.

In the planning and execution of Goodwood, Montgomery seems to have hedged his bets. He apparently hoped that his armored attack out of the British bridgehead east of the Orne might actually break through the German positions on the Bourguébus ridge, thus opening the way for a British drive toward Falaise. Failing that outcome, Goodwood would serve to pin down the bulk of the panzer divisions on the Normandy front, allowing the Americans the opportunity to break the tactical stalemate in their sector.

On his part, Bradley never had any doubts about the objectives of Cobra. It was designed to punch through the German defenses prior to unleashing his armor in a drive to roll up the German left flank.

At first glance, Goodwood and Cobra seem to be halves of the same tactical as well as strategic plan. Both called for an attack along a narrow front, preceded by a massive carpet bombing of the German front lines by Allied strategic bombing forces. Both operations aimed at breaking the stalemate that the *bocage* and the tenacious German defenders had imposed on the battlefield. Yet, however similar, the plans differed in at least two important ways—the weight of the attack and the use of armor.

Montgomery committed the bulk of his armored strength to Goodwood—the 11th Armoured Division would lead off, fol-

lowed by the 7th Armoured and the Guards. Their attached infantry brigades were to trail the tank regiments in the attack.
Bradley's order of attack was the opposite. He planned to mass
the four infantry divisions of Collins's VII Corps along some
seven thousand yards of the St.-Lô–Périers road. Behind them
were two armored divisions and the motorized 1st Division,
ready to exploit any openings the infantry might create in the
German lines. Cobra was designed to strike on a narrow front
with all the power that Bradley could muster.

Lieutenant General Sir Miles Dempsey, Second Army commander, kicked off Goodwood first. Right on schedule, at dawn
on 18 July, Allied bombers saturated with fragmentation bombs
the corridor down which the British armor was to attack. Before
the dust had cleared, and covered by a rolling artillery barrage,
the 11th Armoured struck out for the Bourguébus ridge. Less
than two hours later, the advance was slowed by fire from
Cagny and other villages along the embankment carrying the
railroad from Caen to Vimont. By 1100, a few troops of tanks
had reached the ridge, some six miles from their starting line,
but the momentum of the attack slowed in the face of stiffening
German resistance and because of a breakdown in air–ground
communications.

Dempsey and his corps commander, Lieutenant General Sir
Richard N. O'Connor, pressed the attack by passing first the
Guards, then the 7th Armoured up the corridor. Despite this
commitment of all the VIII Corps' armor, progress was dis-
couragingly slow through the afternoon. Infantry attacks along
both flanks of the corridor also met with limited success, with
two Canadian divisions mired in the rubble of Caen and the 3d
British Division heavily engaged with German forces holding
Troarn.

Flushed with the limited successes of the day's fighting, Montgomery announced to the world that "early this morning British
and Canadian troops of the Second Army attacked and broke
through into the area east of the Orne and south-east of Caen. . . .

General Montgomery is well satisfied with the progress made in the first day's fighting of this battle." That communiqué proved to be somewhat premature. There had been no breakthrough, nor, if Monty and his public defenders today are to be believed, was any intended. That communiqué damaged his credibility with his superiors and nearly cost him his job.

The Goodwood offensive continued through 19 and 20 July with diminishing gains. A torrential rainstorm in the afternoon of the twentieth forced Dempsey to withdraw his spent armored divisions, which had lost half their tank strength in three days of fighting. But counting the battle a success for pinning down the panzers, Montgomery now placed his hopes for a clean breakout on the American VII Corps, poised to strike south across the St.-Lô–Périers–Lessay road.

Two dramatic events now interposed themselves in the course of the Battle of Normandy—the fighter-bomber attack which critically wounded Field Marshal Erwin Rommel and the attempted assassination of Adolf Hitler. Both events had definite, if uncalculable, effects on the battle and the war.

Rommel's fate can be briefly dealt with. On 17 July, as he was driving back to his headquarters from an inspection tour of Seventh Army defenses east of the Orne, his staff car was attacked by British fighter-bombers. In the ensuing crash, Rommel was thrown from the car, sustaining a severe concussion. By the time his health would have permitted him to return to active duty, the Normandy front had collapsed, and he had been implicated in the plot against Hitler. Rommel, the most renowned of the Wehrmacht commanders, took his life to save both his honor and the lives of his family. His removal from command at the moment of crisis for the German forces in Normandy had an unsettling effect on the German conduct of the coming battle.

The plot against Hitler is a complicated story and can only be outlined here. Suffice it to say that a loosely connected group of Reichsheer (the pre-1933 army) officers and government officials, protected by an Abwehr (military intelligence) cover and led by a few disaffected generals and Colonel Count Claus von Stauffenberg, plotted to assassinate Hitler, then seize the government and sue for peace. Elaborate plans were laid to take power throughout occupied Europe, as well as in Germany, when the code word Valkyrie, signifying the death of Hitler, was received.

After many delays, the plot was set in motion in early June after Stauffenberg became chief of staff to the commander of the Home Army. Given access to Hitler at a staff meeting on 20 July, Stauffenberg managed to smuggle a bomb into his headquarters at Rastenburg. Unfortunately for the plotters, and for Germany, Hitler survived the blast, shielded by a heavy table.

In the weeks which followed, the plotters and those implicated with them were exposed and ruthlessly dealt with. Although Hitler's health was seriously impaired, his power over the German people and the military establishment was strengthened. Playing on the twin fears of a communist takeover and an abject "unconditional surrender" of the Reich, Hitler and Goebbels steeled the German people for the approaching Götterdämmerung. Meanwhile, his Seventh Army in Normandy faced a more immediate crisis on its western flank.

Generals Bradley and Collins, the chief architects of Cobra, hoped to launch their attack as early as 20 July, while the bulk of German armor fought to contain Dempsey's Goodwood offensive. More of the bad weather which had cramped Allied air power throughout much of June and July forced a four-day postponement. Despite the short bombing by the Eighth Air Force on 24 and 25 July, American infantry opened their attack across the St.-Lô–Périers road in the face of stiff opposition from the veteran Panzer Lehr Division. The attack was initially disappointing, with gains measured in yards and fields, but it was far from a failure. A majority of the Shermans advancing with the infantry were now equipped with steel prongs welded to their prows (an invention attributed to Sergeant Curtis G. Culin, Jr., 102d Cavalry Reconnaissance Squadron) which allowed them to cut through the hedgerows with ease. These "Rhino" tanks, and others equipped with dozer blades, gave the American armor the ability to operate off-road as if the *bocage* hardly existed.

Collins waited impatiently as his three assaulting infantry divisions advanced a little more than a mile on the first day, then, sensing the resistance on his front was crumbling, ordered his armored divisions to attack on the twenty-sixth. His estimate was correct. Brigadier General Maurice Rose, commanding Combat Command A of the 2d Armored, pushed his tanks and motorized infantry south through St.-Gilles and Canisy and did not halt them until 0300 the next morning, some six miles from their starting line. The breakout had begun.

For the next four days, American armor and supporting infantry, superbly aided by the Lightnings and Thunderbolts of Major General Elwood R. "Pete" Quesada's IX Tactical Air Command, streamed south, then angled southwest to cut behind the columns of retreating Germans. On the American right flank, Major General Troy H. Middleton's VIII Corps met determined resistance on the twenty-sixth, then lost contact as the Germans quickly withdrew to avoid being enveloped. Bradley hoped to trap the retreating Germans between the advancing columns of his two corps. Coutances was captured by elements of the 4th and 6th Armored divisions (VIII Corps) on the twenty-eighth. Brigadier General Isaac D. White's Combat Command B drove southwest from Canisy through Notre-Dame-de-Cenilly to Lengronne, then halted to avoid collision with VIII Corps armor probing south from Coutances. CCB blocked German columns at Notre-Dame, St.-Denis-le-Gast, and Lengronne, precipitating sharp fights; and while White's tankers inflicted heavy casualties, they never quite succeeded in sealing off the retreating Germans. Other than slowing the American advance, the fleeing Seventh Army could only stage ineffective counterattacks on the American left flank. Lieutenant General George S. Patton, to take command of the Third U.S. Army on 1 August, but now acting as a deputy army commander under Bradley, ordered

Major General John S. "P" Wood's 4th Armored Division to drive south with all speed. Wood's men reached Avranches late on July 30; the next day they captured the bridge over the Sélune at Pontaubault and prepared to swing west into Brittany.

At this moment in the breakout, the Overlord plan clashed with reality. According to the plan, Patton's Third Army, now activated around Middleton's VIII Corps, was to have fanned out into the Brittany peninsula with the objective of capturing the Breton ports—Brest, Lorient, Vannes—thought essential to maintain the Allied advance. No one, including Eisenhower and his staff, immediately grasped the extent of the Seventh German Army collapse. The possibility now presented itself for the rapidly advancing American armies to ignore the relatively weak German forces in Brittany and to drive east in an all-out attempt to trap the German armies against the Seine. Only "P" Wood, who had pushed his armored cavalry east to Angers before having to recall it, seems to have realized that the original Brittany operation had become anachronous. He later called the failure to use his and Gerow's armored divisions in an immediate drive for the Seine "one of the colossally stupid decisions of the war."

In any event, VIII Corps armor drove furiously through Brittany, first isolating then capturing Rennes, storming into Nantes, Vannes, and St.-Malo. Only Middleton's ill-timed order halting the 6th Armored for twenty-four hours prevented the early capture of Brest—that port would not fall into American hands until mid-September, after a bloody battle costing almost ten thousand American casualties. Other ports—most notably St.-Nazaire and Lorient—were simply sealed off until the war had ended. Because the Allied armies moved so rapidly across France, the Breton ports were never logistically important.

While the 4th and 6th Armored divisions raced across Brittany, Patton hurried the remainder of the Third Army across the Sélune bridge at Pontaubault, then on a wide sweep to the northeast toward Le Mans.

In a desperate move to pinch off the narrow corridor down

which Third Army units were now streaming, Hitler ordered a
massive counterattack through Mortain to the sea at Avranches.
As he conceived it from the remoteness of his bunker in eastern
Germany, the Mortain attack was the master strategic stroke
which would pinch off the American breakout at its most vulnerable point. There was logic, if not merit, in the Führer's plan.
If the attack had succeeded and if the Germans had been able to
hold the ground recaptured—both big ifs—much of the Third
Army would have been left in an exposed position and the
breakout possibly contained.

To give weight to his plan, Hitler ordered Field Marshal
Guenther von Klug, now OB West after von Rundstedt's forced
departure, to commit the XLVII Panzer Corps (the 116th, 2d,
and 2d SS divisions) to a simultaneous frontal attack. The 116th
was directed to advance north of the Sée, while the 2d SS
Panzers were to capture the medieval fortress town of Mortain
to protect the flank of the 2d Panzers, driving west between the
other two divisions. Although their tank strength was sadly depleted, these divisions were to clear the way for the 1st SS
Panzers, who were to drive to the sea at Avranches. Von Klug
fixed the jump-off time for 2200 on 6 August, knowing that none
of his divisions would have adequate preparation time.

To take the weight of this armored attack, Collins had to rely
on the 30th Infantry Division, which had only recently taken
over 1st Infantry positions around Mortain. There were belated
warnings from Ultra that the Germans were planning a counterattack in the Mortain area, but few on Bradley's staff believed
von Klug would commit his armor so far to the west; thus the
night attack took the Americans by surprise. The reinforced 2d
SS Panzers, moving in two columns, quickly drove the 30th Division from all its positions around Mortain save that on Hill 317
above the town. By noon, German panzers were just outside St.-
Hilaire, twelve miles from Avranches. However, the 2d Battalion of the 120th Infantry held Hill 317, from which observers
could call down artillery fire on the advancing panzer columns.

North of Mortain, the 116th German Division failed to attack on the sixth because its commander was implicated in the 20 July plot and had given up the war for lost. In the center, the 2d Panzers rapidly advanced against light opposition until stopped near Juvigny. Avranches seemed easily within reach of the panzer columns.

Reacting quickly to the threat, Bradley ordered Barton's 4th Division out of reserve and committed it along the Sée north of the German salient. On the southern flank, two combat commands of the 2d Armored and the 35th Infantry were rushed into blocking positions. They proved to be enough. American resistance on the ground stiffened; and, unprotected by the Luftwaffe, German armor hid during the day to escape detection by the IX Tactical Air Command's ever-present fighter-bombers.

Von Klug considered reopening the offensive on the eleventh, but realizing that armored spearheads were driving across his rear, he chose to withdraw his panzers eastward to avoid encirclement. Thanks to Ultra, good flying weather, the steadfastness of the 120th Infantry's 2d Battalion, and the steady hand of the American high command, the threat at Mortain had been quickly and decisively ended.

Bradley hoped to take advantage of von Klug's overextension of his armor at Mortain to trap the German forces in Normandy (now reshuffled into the Fifth Panzer Army and the Seventh Army) between the pincers of the First and Third American armies and the British and Canadian armies now pushing south of Caen. Whatever plans Hitler may have had to resume the attack toward Avranches were abruptly abandoned when Montgomery launched Operation Totalize to break the German hold on Caen and the Orne valley.

Jumping off in the dark on 8 August, minus the dubious benefit of carpet bombing, Lieutenant General H. D. G. Crerar's Canadians made good progress, overrunning the Bourguébus ridge where Goodwood had foundered in July. The advance soon

faltered as German defense along the Laison River and the Potigny ridge proved tougher than expected. Crerar used four days
to regroup, then sent his spearheads against the Potigny ridge
under cover of a smoke screen. This time the Canadian advance
carried all the way to Falaise, which the 2d Canadian Division
entered on 16 August. One arm of the pincers had at last closed
on the retreating German armies.

On 10 August, Major General Wade H. Haislip's XV Corps
moved north from Le Mans toward Alençon and the slowly advancing Canadians. However, Haislip soon found his divisions
overextended with both flanks open to counterattack. Besides,
Argentan, another forty kilometers to the north, was an inter-
Allied boundary that Bradley intended to respect, despite Patton's jeering question: "Shall we continue and drive the British
into the sea for another Dunkirk?" Jesting aside, Patton was furious with Bradley's decision and repeatedly tried to have it over-
turned. Whatever the reasons for not closing the pincers—and
they range from the danger from time-delay bombs dropped
along the roads, to the possibility of interfering with fighter-
bomber attacks, to the danger of the two Allied armies accidentally shelling one another, to the belief that the Germans had already slipped the pocket—the Falaise–Argentan Gap was never
closed, and through it the survivors of the two routed German
armies poured.

On 14 August, believing that the German armies had fled the
Falaise trap, Bradley ordered two of Haislip's divisions to begin
a movement eastward for a long envelopment—an attempt to
pin the retreating Germans against the bridgeless Seine. But, in
fact, von Klug had not yet withdrawn his battered troops from
their exposed positions. When Montgomery realized this on the
sixteenth, he ordered a full-scale effort to cut off their retreat by
driving a wedge between Chambois and Trun.

The unit picked to spearhead the attack on Chambois was the
1st Polish Armored Division, an untested unit formed from Polish refugees who were spoiling for a crack at the Germans. The

Poles received their marching orders in the evening of the seventeenth, and the lead units, the 2d Armored Regiment and the hitchhiking 8th Light Infantry, set off in the dark without waiting for their resupply. During their night march the Poles lost their way, passed through a German column undetected, and fought a dawn skirmish with the 2d Panzers, a unit that had routed the poorly equipped Polish armies in 1939. Near Chambois, Major General Stanislaw Maczek divided his force. Half continued on to the city, where they were joined by GI's of Company G, 359th Infantry; the remainder took up positions on Mont Ormel to the north. All units soon found themselves isolated and under heavy attack from German formations both inside and outside the pocket. Maczek's Poles held on to Hill 262 (dubbed the "Mace") at the southwest edge of Mont Ormel until they were relieved in the afternoon of the twenty-first. By then, more than three hundred of them were dead.

The relief of the Poles on the "Mace" marked the final closing of the Falaise Pocket. Despite the escape of German support units, including staffs, the Allied armies had won a stunning victory. They had "written down" the Seventh Army and the Fifth Panzer Army. Ten thousand German soldiers were dead; another fifty thousand were prisoners. Tank strength among the eight surviving panzer divisions was less than seventy-five. The stench from the 1,800 dead horses strewn along the lines of the retreat was overwhelming. The climax of the Battle of Normandy created scenes of destruction with few equals during the war. It was now D Day plus 77.

Tour of the Breakout Battlefields

We have created two suggested tours of the breakout areas—one for the American armies, a second for Montgomery's 21 Army Group. The two tour routes meet in the Falaise–Argentan area where the Allied armies came together in an effort to encir-

132

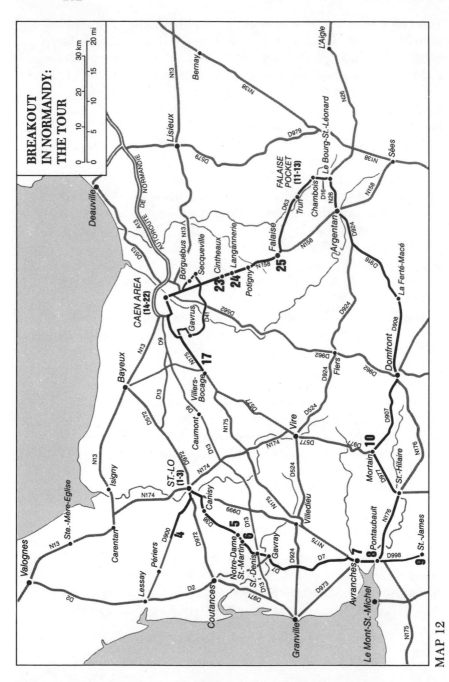

MAP 12

cle the German armies in Normandy. Together, they somewhat retrace the arms of the Allied pincers which sought to close the Falaise Gap.

The American sector tour begins in St.-Lô and follows the route of the American breakout south to Avranches and Pontaubault. From there it leads you to Mortain and thence through Argentan to Mont Ormel.

The tour of the British and Canadian battlefields is slightly more complicated because of the battles in and around Caen. The route begins in Caen and takes you first to Villers-Bocage, then retraces the advance of the 15th Infantry and 11th Armoured divisions (Operation Epsom) through Gavrus to Hill 112, where the attack spent itself. It then backtracks through Caen to the Bourguébus ridge, where Operation Goodwood foundered. Next it takes you south along N 158 through open countryside to Falaise, following the advance of the second Canadian Army in mid-August.

Both routes converge on the small village of Chambois in the Dives valley, the "Corridor of Death" (the escape route of many shattered German formations), and the Polish memorial atop Mont Ormel.

Not counting detours, the tour of the American breakout route (St.-Lô to Chambois) covers approximately 182 kilometers; the tour of the 21 Army Group battlefields runs between 110 and 120 kilometers. The distances are deceptive. We suggest that you plan to spend a day on each tour.

Tour of the American Battlefields

St.-Lô

St.-Lô is accessible by auto from almost any direction. From Bayeux it is a pleasant 35-km drive along D 572; from Caen the distance is a little over 70 km along D 9, D 13, and N 174. Whichever route you take, continue into the city

*until you reach the intersection of D 972 with N 174 and D
6 (the highways from Bayeux, Vire and Isigny respectively).
Since there are no public car parks, you will have to park on
the street, then walk to the intersection, where there is a memorial to Major Thomas D. Howie (1).* *

General Bradley considered the capture of this medieval town
essential for the protection of the left flank of Operation Cobra
because it was the hub of an important road net. The highway
running west to Périers also marked the end of the marshy river
bottoms which had confined the American advance to narrow
north-south corridors.

Bradley gave the task of capturing the already devastated
town (St.-Lô had either been bombed or shelled continuously
since D Day) to the V and XIX corps attacking east of the Vire
River. By mid-July, battalions of the 134th and 115th Infantry
regiments (35th and 29th divisions) had moved within two miles
of the town along the Isigny highway. At the same time, three
battalions of the 116th Infantry (29th Division) fought their way
westward along the Martinville ridge—the northernmost of
three low ridges leading into St.-Lô from the east. On 15 July,
the 2d Battalion of the 116th advanced to an isolated position on
the St.-Lô–Bayeux highway, where it was cut off. Major General
Charles H. Gerhardt, commanding the 29th Division, ordered
the 3d Battalion to relieve the isolated unit, then continue the
attack toward St.-Lô. Ordering them not to pause to return fire,
Major Thomas D. Howie, commanding the 3d Battalion, pushed
his men between enemy positions to the village of La Madeleine, astride the Bayeux highway, where they made contact
with the 2d Battalion. When Howie reported that the 2d Battalion was in no condition to resume the attack, he was asked if his
men could go it alone. "Will do," Howie answered back. A few
minutes later mortar rounds hit the 3d Battalion CP, killing the
major.

* Bold numbers are keyed to Maps 12, 13, 14, and 15.

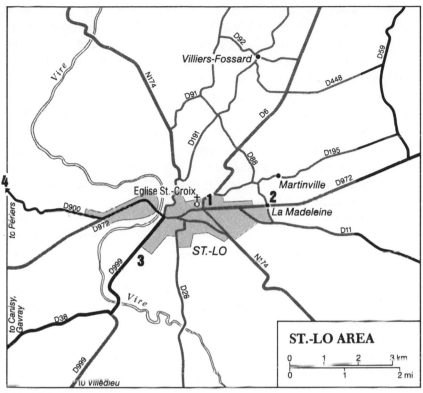

Villiers-Fossard

D92

D59

Vire

D174

D448

D91

D6

D191

D195

D88

Martinville

D972

Eglise St.-Croix

1

2

D900

La Madeleine

D972

D11

D999

3

ST.-LO

N174

to Périers

Vire

D28

to Canisy,
Gavray

D38

D999

to Villedieu

ST.-LO AREA

0	1	2	3 km
0		1	2 mi

MAP 13

Meanwhile, Gerhardt ordered the formation of an armored task force under command of Brigadier General Norman D. Cota. Cota assembled his six hundred men and their vehicles northeast of the town, and around 1500 hours on the eighteenth, Task Force C moved into St.-Lô. Four hours later, most resistance had collapsed, although the surprised Germans continued to pour down fire on the town from the surrounding high ground. Cota himself was wounded by shrapnel that evening.

The town that the Americans had captured with so much pain and blood had been pounded into rubble. Even so, at Gerhardt's order, Task Force C brought with it the flag-draped coffin of Major Howie. The coffin was placed on the steps of the bombed-out St.-Croix church to symbolize the price of victory.

Today, St.-Lô shows no sign of the devastation of 1944, although its reconstruction took twenty years. The battle is commemorated by the memorial to Thomas Howie, the "Major of St.-Lô," and by a municipal hospital built in part with American funds.

Task Force C entered St.-Lô from the northeast along D 6, then passed through the intersection where you are standing before turning west toward the center of town.

Some 1.75 kilometers east of your present position (on D 972) a secondary road will take you north to Martinville. This crossroad (2) marks the approximate positions held by the 2d and 3d battalions on 15–18 July. Major Howie was killed nearby.

The Hôpital Memorial France–Etats-Unis (3) is located on the south side of D 999 (Rue de Villedieu) about a quarter of a mile from its junction with D 972.

OPERATION COBRA

To visit the Cobra starting line (4) drive west from St.-Lô on D 900 for 7 km.

In the afternoon of 24 August, with Collins's VII Corps poised for the attack, the heavy bombers of the Eighth Air Force had taken to the air before deteriorating weather conditions led Air Chief Marshal Leigh-Mallory to cancel the strike. Leigh-Mallory's order failed to reach several squadrons, with disastrous results. Flying in from the north, perpendicular to the American lines, they began dropping their bombs on German positions south of the St.-Lô–Périers road. As later waves of bombers reached the target area, smoke and dust obscured the ground, and the bombs began to fall inside American lines. As the last of the heavies droned off in the distance, the 30th Division was left to sort out the pieces—156 men killed and wounded.

Bradley was furious at the short bombing. He maintained then and later that he had been led to believe at a meeting with Leigh-Mallory that the bombing runs were to have been made parallel to the highway. When informed that it was too late to change plans for the twenty-fifth, he acquiesced in the plans for a second perpendicular approach. The heavies bombed short again on the twenty-fifth, this time killing and wounding some 601 men in the 9th and 30th divisions. Another casualty was General Lesley McNair, principal prewar architect of the U.S. Army, who had gone forward to observe the bombing. McNair's funeral service (all that remained was his ring finger and West Point class ring) was held in secret, so that German intelligence would continue to buy the Fortitude deception—that McNair, instead of Patton, would soon assume command of a field army in France.

The area that was bombed on the twenty-fourth and twenty-fifth (not counting the numerous misses) lies south of D 900 and begins about five kilometers after that highway branches off to the northwest from D 972. It then parallels the highway for seven kilometers. Today there is no visible evidence from D 900 of the five thousand tons of high explosives dropped on the twenty-fourth and twenty-fifth, nor is there a memorial to the 136 American soldiers killed in the short bombings.

To follow the route of the breakout by the most direct roads, drive D 999 south from St.-Lô to Villedieu-les-Poêles

(34 km), then pick up N 175 to Avranches (22 km). This fol-
lows the route taken by Brigadier General Maurice Rose's
Combat Command A of the 2d Armored Division.

We also suggest an alternate route—that taken by Briga-
dier General Isaac D. White's Combat Command B. To
follow in the tracks of CCB, leave St.-Lô by D 999 as above,
then, some 3.5 km south of the town, veer west on D 38 (a
secondary road) toward Canisy (4.5 km). At Canisy you will
join the advance of CCB moving south along D 77 from St.-
Gilles. From Canisy follow D 38 southwest to Gavray, then
D 7 to Avranches (53 km).

Unlike CCA, which Collins committed to the battle on the twenty-sixth, CCB was held in reserve until the twenty-seventh, when it was ordered to move south and southwest to cut off retreating enemy units. General White responded by pushing his columns, led by the 82d Reconnaissance Battalion, through Canisy as far south as Notre-Dame-de-Cenilly before halting in the early hours of the twenty-eighth. Later that day, reconnaissance units fanned out to capture bridges over the Sienne River and the town of Lengronne.

There now followed a number of sharp actions between units of CCB (reinforced by the 4th Infantry Division) and German columns streaming south to escape the pocket CCB had created. Two of the more memorable firefights occurred near Notre-Dame-de-Cenilly (5) in the predawn hours of 29 July. One involved the attempted breakthrough of about thirty enemy tanks and vehicles some three miles southwest of the village, near St.-Martin-de-Cenilly (6). The German column struck a company of American tanks, supported by infantrymen, and were on the verge of breaking through when American rifle fire killed the driver of an 88-mm self-propelled gun, thereby blocking the road. The ensuing firefight lasted until dawn, when the enemy withdrew leaving 167 dead and wounded behind. Close by, another armored German column pushed back a company of infantrymen before being halted by fire from nearby artillery and tank destroyers. That effort cost the Germans seven Panzer IVs and 125 killed. More fighting erupted near St.-Denis-le-Gast, Lengronne, and Cambry during the evening.

In three days of fighting, CCB and its supporting units had killed fifteen hundred and captured another four thousand enemy soldiers, while suffering four hundred casualties.

AVRANCHES–PONTAUBAULT

The task of capturing Avranches and its key bridges over the Sée River fell finally to Major General John Wood's 4th Armored Division poised north of Cerences. Halted through the morning of 30 July until its engineers had bridged the Sienne River, one column of Combat Command B began to move south, only to be stopped during the night by stiff enemy resistance. CCB's other column, further to the west, made better progress, driving through light resistance to halt just north of Avranches. Unknown to the men of CCB, they just missed capturing the Seventh Army's advanced command post, including General Paul Hausser, Seventh Army commander, and members of his staff.

Finding both highway bridges over the Sée intact, CCB quickly secured the town, as well as a third bridge at Tirepied five miles to the east.

Once certain that Avranches was securely in American hands, Middleton ordered the 4th Armored to continue south to capture the bridges across the Sélune River at Pontaubault. Brigadier General Holmes E. Dager, commanding CCB and now given control of all forces in the area, including Colonel Bruce Clarke's CCA, ordered the immediate capture of Pontaubault and several nearby bridges and dams. By nightfall of the thirty-first, Clarke's troops had accomplished their tasks, including the capture of the intact Pontaubault bridge. On 1 August, with three bridges over the Sée and four over the Sélune in American hands, the way into Brittany was wide open.

There is a monument (7) dedicated to General George S. Patton, Jr., in Avranches at the junction of D 78 and N 175 on the south side of town. (If you accidentally end up on D 104, the loop that circles Avranches to the west, you will have to backtrack north on N 175 to find Patton's monument.)

Drive 7 km south to Pontaubault on N 175 to see the nineteenth-century arched bridge (8) captured intact on 31 July. The new highway, N 276, now bypasses the old bridge to the east.

The Brittany American Cemetery and Memorial
To visit this cemetery drive south from Pontaubault on D 998 to St.-James (11 km). The cemetery is located a mile east of the town. Follow the signs.

The Brittany cemetery (9) contains 4,410 graves in twenty-eight acres of gentle countryside. The memorial chapel is in the form of a small Romanesque church, typical of the area. Open summer 0900–1800 (1000 on weekends and holidays); open winter 0900–1700 (1000 on weekends and holidays).

MORTAIN

To reach Mortain from Pontaubault, take N 176 east to St.-Hilaire-du-Harcouet (20 km), then D 977 north to Mortain (14 km).

"Ralph," General J. Lawton Collins remarked to the commander of the 1st Infantry Division, "be sure to get Hill 317." "Joe," General Clarence Huebner shot back, "I already have it." And it was fortunate that he did. Only four hours before the Germans launched their counterattack through Mortain, men from the 30th Division had moved into the positions around the town being vacated by the Big Red One. The ground taken over by the 2d Battalion, 120th Infantry, included Mortain and Hill 317, the heights east of the town.

In its initial drive through Mortain in the early morning of 6 August, the reinforced 2d SS Panzer Division overran the 2d Battalion command post and the next day captured the battalion's senior officers, who were trying to rejoin their men on Hill 317. Although isolated and under heavy, continuous attack, the 2d Battalion clung stubbornly to its positions for six days. It posed a constant threat to German communications by calling down artillery fire on panzer columns driving eastward. On 10 August, C-47s managed to drop a two-day supply of food and ammunition to the beleaguered battalion. Help also came from the nearby 230th Field Artillery Battalion and other fire-support units that were able to fire smoke shell cases filled with medical supplies into the 120th's perimeter. Thus supported from without, and supplied with chickens by the French farmers, the battalion's seven hundred men fought on. By the time they were relieved on 12 August, three hundred were casualties. In recognition of their leadership, five of the junior officers on the hill received DSC's. Army historian Martin Blumenson called the 2d Battalion's fight on Hill 317 "one of the outstanding small unit achievements in the course of the campaign in Western Europe."

Just before entering Mortain, D 977 takes a sharp turn to the southwest, then joins D 907 which leads north into the rebuilt town. Drive north on D 907 a quarter of a mile, then turn right (east) on D 487, then quickly left on D 487ᵉ. This road will take you on a circle around Hill 317. We recommend that you park in the lot near the Petite Chapelle (10) and walk past it to the belvedere for a view over the Sélune valley.

A note on the Brittany Campaign. Because the flow of the main armies in August and later was away from Brittany, we have chosen not to extend our tour to the westward. That is not to say that there are no battlefields or relics worth visiting west of Avranches. On the contrary, there are several notable World War II sites scattered across the peninsula. For those travelers willing to make the detours necessary to visit them, we have briefly noted the most important below.

ST.-MALO

The Ile de Cézembre, just offshore from St.-Malo, was a heavily fortified German position in 1944. Duane Denfield calls it "a must visit for the World War II history enthusiast . . . possibly . . . the best preserved battlefield of World War II." Now a bird sanctuary, the Ile de Cézembre can be reached by regular boat service from St.-Malo.

ST.-NAZAIRE

The massive concrete submarine pens are still intact and can be visited.

BREST

Brest is the location of an American World War I naval monument. Its connection with World War II events is a commentary on prewar German-American relations. The monument was torn down by the Germans on 4 July 1941. The construction of the exact replica that you see today was completed in 1958.

SAUMUR AND MUSÉE DES BLINDÉS

Saumur has no connection with the Brittany campaign, but it lies in the lower Loire valley and therefore is more accessible from Avranches or St.-Nazaire than from any other spot on our tour. The ancient town is the location of the French Armored

School (once a cavalry school); the tank museum is found within the grounds of the school on the western side of the town. Signs (which are difficult to pick up from a moving car) will direct you to an adjacent parking area. Open 0900–1130 and 1400–1730. Admission charge.

THE FALAISE POCKET AND CHAMBOIS

To reach Chambois from Mortain, take D 907 from Mortain to Domfront (24 km), D 908 to La Ferté-Macé (22 km), D 916 to Ecouché (33 km), where you will pass a Sherman tank before picking up D 924 to Argentan (9 km). From Argentan take N 26 east to Le Bourg-St.-Léonard (10 km) and D 16 north to Chambois (5 km). Drive into Chambois and stop by the park surrounding the medieval keep (donjon).

Polish infantry of the 10th Dragoons fought their way into Chambois from the north around 1700 on 19 August, capturing forty German soldiers who were using the keep for an observation tower. Two hours later they were joined by GI's from the 359th Regiment, 90th Division. After a hurried toast of Polish vodka, the two commanders organized their men in defensive positions. Together, alone, although supported by artillery fire from the Bourg-St.-Léonard ridge, the two units held Chambois for three days against repeated German attacks.

A stone monument (11) commemorating the joining of Polish and American forces stands in the park. Back of it, against a wall, is an excellent map explaining the Battle of the Falaise Pocket.

To visit the 1st Polish Armored Division Monument on Mont Ormel, drive north from Chambois on D 16. The road soon begins to climb Mont Ormel, and you can see the array of flags to the west (left) of the highway which marks the memorial. Turn in and park in the small lot provided.

144

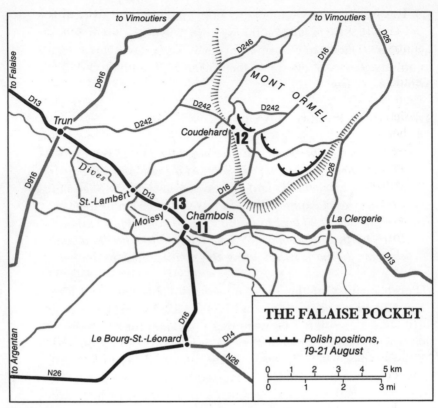

MAP 14

It was here and on the other side of D 16 that the Poles of the 1st and 2d Armored regiments (eighty Shermans) and three infantry battalions (fifteen hundred men) took up positions on 19 August. From here, Hill 262, soon dubbed the "Mace," the Poles made their gallant fight to close the Falaise Pocket. They were soon isolated by desperate German units seeking to escape the Allied pincers. But, holding their positions, they were able either to fire or to call down fire on the jam of men, vehicles, and horses seeking to cross the Dives between Chambois and Trun. From the nineteenth through the twenty-first of August, the roads below you were littered with dead and dying men, burning vehicles and hundreds of slaughtered horses—the death of an army.

For those three days the Poles made life a hell for the retreating Germans and were in return repeatedly counterattacked by units from within and without the pocket. By the afternoon of the twentieth, German artillery had the Polish positions under fire and had hit five of their Shermans. Under cover of this harassing fire, panzer grenadiers repeatedly tried to overrun the Polish positions. As night fell, the Germans withdrew, but they were back at dawn the next day. Their attacks continued until the Poles made contact with the tanks of the Canadian Grenadier Guards sent to reinforce them. By then, the Polish dead numbered 325.

The monument (12) on top Mont Ormel commemorating the Polish units which fought there consists of a modern metal sculpture resembling a mace set against a stone wall. A Sherman tank and an armored car stand nearby. While the latter vehicle bears the insignia of the Free French Forces, the Sherman is stenciled with the names GEN MACZEK and MACZUGA.

CORRIDOR OF DEATH

Return to Chambois, then leave town by D 13 toward Trun. In about 2 km you will reach the crossroads village of

Moissy (13). Turn right (northeast) onto the secondary road and proceed along it.

You are now traveling the Corridor of Death (Le Couloir de la Mort) along which a large part of the remaining Seventh German Army and Panzer Group West was destroyed. As you drive toward Mont Ormel, keep an eye on the flags flying over the Polish monument. That should give you a way to gauge the vulnerability of the German columns. This road and others paralleling it between Chambois and Trun were lined with wrecked and burning vehicles during the final days of the battle. Warning—you may feel lost on this farm road, but eventually you will end up in the village of Coudehard, where you can work your way east to D 16. The drive is well worth the effort, although all signs of the battle have disappeared.

From Chambois it is possible to drive north to Caen, thereby retracing the route of the 21 Army Group's breakout in reverse, or to continue east following the Allied armies in their advance across France to Paris and beyond.

Tour of the British and Canadian Battlefields

CAEN

Caen was destroyed by heavy air and naval bombardment on the sixth and seventh of June, and devastated again in July by one of the most concentrated air attacks of the war.

Although warned by leaflets of the coming raid, the Caennais who remained in the city still must have been dismayed by the sight and sound of the bomber stream—six hundred heavies of the U.S. Eighth Air Force—as it relentlessly approached the city in the afternoon of D Day. The rain of bombs destroyed many quarters of the ancient Norman city and started fires that raged for eleven days. Many of Caen's inhabitants were trapped and killed by the explosions; survivors sought refuge in the Abbaye

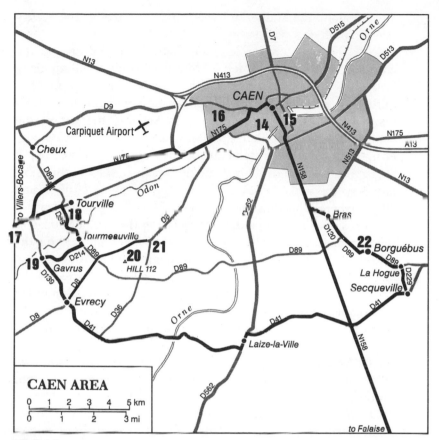

CAEN AREA

0 1 2 3 4 5 km
0   1   2   3 mi

MAP 15

aux Hommes, the Malherbe Lycée, and the caves of the Fleury quarry south of town.

Over the next few weeks while fighting spread around the city, only scattered shells fell within its perimeter, lulling many into a false sense of security. But the climax of destruction came during the evening of 7 July, when, desperate to break the German-imposed stalemate, Montgomery secured the use of the heavy bombers of the RAF Bomber Command in direct support of his infantry assault. Reluctantly, for they did not consider it an appropriate use of their strategic bombers, the air chiefs ordered up the strike. Thus, in the early evening of 7 July, some 460 bombers droned across the Channel to dump 2,300 tons of bombs (many of the time-delay variety) on the northern edge of the city. Set to detonate just before the attack jumped off the next morning, the time-delay bombs completed the devastation of the city and may have actually impeded the advance of the 3d Canadian Division. Unfortunately, most German defenses lay outside the target area, so the Canadians still had to batter their way into the city. Caen was not entirely in Allied hands until 20 July.

The Abbaye aux Hommes and its St.-Etienne church, founded by William the Conqueror in the eleventh century, were not seriously damaged during the long siege of Caen.

On the wall of the Prefecture garden, at the end of the Boulevard Bertrand, is a plaque (14) to the first Canadian soldier killed in the city.

A monument (15) to the cooperation between the resistance and the Regina Rifle Regiment stands at the Pont de Vaucelles.

In the Place Monseigneur-des-Hameaux, west of the Church of St.-Etienne is a plaque (16) commemorating the liberation of the city on 9 July.

VILLERS-BOCAGE

To reach Villers-Bocage from Caen drive west on N 175 some 26 kilometers. Two kilometers east of Villers-Bocage you will cross a high point—point 213 (17)—*before descending into the town.*

In the morning of 13 June, A Squadron (Cromwell tanks, Fireflies, and assorted tracked vehicles) of the 4th County of London Yeomanry (Sharpshooters), 7th Armoured Division, was parked along these two kilometers of road, crews dismounted, just having rolled through Villers-Bocage without opposition. It was attacked here by a lone Tiger tank commanded by SS Lieutenant Michael Wittmann, one of a squadron of five belonging to the 501st SS Heavy Tank Battalion, just arrived from northern France. Wittmann earlier had fought on the Eastern Front, where he personally accounted for 117 Russian tanks. By all accounts, he was the greatest tank ace of the war.

Wittmann now slipped into Villers-Bocage from the east and surprised four Cromwells of the Headquarters Group. He quickly "brewed up " three of the British tanks while the fourth backed out of sight into the front garden of a nearby house. He then proceeded west to D 71, where he found B Squadron's vehicles parked along the highway just outside the village. At this juncture, Wittmann's Tiger took a hit from a Firefly. Seeing that he was outnumbered, he reversed course back through the village, whereupon he knocked out the Cromwell he had missed earlier.

After replenishing his ammunition supply, Wittmann next attacked A Squadron, which was still parked along N 175 just east of Villers-Bocage. In a few minutes he destroyed A Squadron, knocking out more than fifty of its vehicles. However, when he later drove back through Villers-Bocage with two other Tigers and a Panzer IV, he was ambushed by tanks from B Squadron. British point-blank fire quickly accounted for two Tigers and the Panzer IV, but Wittmann and his crew escaped in the melee.

Some two months later Wittmann was back in action again, this time against Canadian armor. On 8 August, during Operation Totalize, his Tiger was destroyed when he attempted single-handedly to hold off an attack by eight or nine Shermans.

Wittmann's body lay buried in an unmarked grave along the east side of N 158 at Gaumesnil (between Caen and Falaise) until its discovery by Jean Paul Pallud in the summer of 1983. Wittmann and two of his crewmen now lie in a communal grave in the German military cemetery at La Cambe (Block 47, Row 3, Grave 120).

OPERATION EPSOM AND THE "SCOTTISH CORRIDOR"

To retrace the advance of the 15th Scottish Division during Operation Epsom, retrace your route along N 175 for 13 km, then turn right (south) on D 89 at Tourville. In a quarter of a mile you will reach a stele (18) surmounted by a rampant lion and bearing the inscription "Scotland the Brave," commemorating the 15th Division. Park in the small space nearby.

Epsom represents the second of Monty's efforts to unhinge the German defenses around Caen. First conceived as coordinated attacks both east and west of the city, the logistical problems brought on by the storm of 19–21 June forced him to redesign his offensive as a single thrust west of the Orne.

The Scots of the 15th Division hardly had time to sort themselves out on the beach before they were advancing across N 13 to begin their attack "two brigades up"—some seven hundred men, supported by artillery and tanks, attacking across a thousand-yard front. In two days of fighting on the twenty-sixth and twenty-seventh, the Scots carried their advance through Cheux to Tourmeauville, across the ground where you are now standing.

On the twenty-eighth, Major General MacMillan decided to shift the axis of the attack west to the village of Gavrus. There the 2d Battalion, Argyll and Sutherland Highlanders, collided with the II SS Panzer Corps, fresh from the Eastern Front. With little effective tank support, the Scottish infantry used their six-pound anti-tank guns and Piats (a spring-loaded anti-tank weapon) to engage the German armor at point-blank range. The Highlanders held, and the "Scottish Corridor" remained in Allied hands, although the 11th Armoured Division was withdrawn from its exposed position on Hill 112. The 15th Division had lost 2,500 men in the five days of Epsom.

To visit Gavrus (19), continue along D 89 to Tourmeau- ville, then turn right (southwest) on D 214 to Gavrus (4 km).

In the summer of 1984, there was a small private exhibition containing artifacts found in the vicinity, housed in a farm building on the south side of town. Also note the steepness of the banks of the Odon—making it a natural anti-tank ditch—and the shell marks on many of the town's stone buildings.

To visit Hill 112, leave Gavrus by D 139 to Evrecy (2.5 km), before turning left (east) on D 8 toward Caen. Stop by the monument (20) on the south side of D 8 some 6 km from Gavrus.

This monument commemorates the sacrifices of the 43d Wessex Division, one of the three VIII Corps divisions committed to Epsom. The 43d held the east flank of the corridor during the initial attack, then was given the task of recapturing Hill 112 on 10 July during the opening phase of Operation Charnwood.

On the tenth, the division's Dorsetshire Regiment attacked down D 8 toward Hill 112, capturing Eterville, Château de Fontaine, and Maltot, before it was stopped by a line of dug-in Tigers belonging to Colonel Kurt Meyer's 12th SS Panzer Division. The Dorsets gained Hill 112 and lost it, then gained it again. The 43d Division and attached armor lost two thousand men in the first two days of the offensive. But it held Hill 112.

Drive one kilometer further along D 8 and park by the
modest monument (21) to the 5th and 6th battalions of the
Dorsetshire Regiment.

From anywhere along this part of D 8 it is obvious that Hill
112 was so bitterly fought over because it dominates the western
approach to Caen. From this monument, Maltot is a kilometer
to the southeast, Fontaine the same distance to the north, and
Eterville two and half kilometers ahead.

OPERATION GOODWOOD AND THE BOURGUÉBUS RIDGE

To reach the Bourguébus ridge, which is southeast of
Caen, from Hill 112 you can follow either of two routes. The
first takes you into Caen on D 8 and N 175. In the city, fol-
low the N 13 signs eastward until you reach the turn (south)
onto N 158 toward Falaise. Some 4 km along N 158 turn off
on D 120 to Bras. The alternate route avoids Caen altogether
by backtracking southwest on D 8 to Evrecy, then follows D
41 in an arc south of the city to Secqueville. From there,
drive north on D 229 to La Hogue, then west on D 89 to
Bourguébus (22).

Concentrated high-velocity fire from German anti-tank guns
and tanks positioned in the villages of Four, Soliers, Bras, and
Hubert-Folie stopped the British attack to the north of you, well
short of the Bourguébus ridge, where you are located. On the
west (to your left as you face Caen) the 3d Royal Tank Regiment's Shermans crossed the Caen–Vimont railroad embankment and had almost driven as far as Hubert-Folie before they
were hit by flanking fire. Both A and B squadrons were soon out
of the battle, many of their tanks ablaze, belching the smoke
rings peculiar to burning tanks with ammunition periodically
cooking-off in their turrets.

Further to the east, the Fife and Forfar Yeomanry Regiment

came up against a similar concentration of fire from the fortified villages of Four and Bourguébus. Their attack died before Soliers. Later, an attempt to reinforce the Fifes by the 23d Hussars was defeated by flanking fire from Panthers and anti-tank guns in Four. Although the battle would go on for another two days, British armor failed to gain control of the Bourguébus ridge and the open country that would enable them to crack the German defenses around Caen.

OPERATIONS TOTALIZE AND TRACTABLE

To follow the advance of the Second Canadian Army toward Falaise (25), return to N 158 and drive to Falaise (about 30 km).

On this drive you will pass a Canadian cemetery (23) a half-kilometer north of Cintheaux and a Polish cemetery (24) just north of Langannerie. Two kilometers south of Potigny, N 158 crosses the Laison River, which marks the farthest advance of Canadian armor during Totalize.

Operation Tractable, which continued the Canadian advance south, jumped off on 14 August, much too slowly for an impatient General Bradley, who wanted to spring a trap in the Falaise area. Despite a shaky start caused by yet another short bombing and the difficulty in fording the tiny Laison, the Canadians entered Falaise on 16 August. Possession of the ruined town was contested for another day by fifty of Colonel Meyer's Hitler Jugend fanatics who refused to surrender the Ecole Supérieure. Actually, the Canadians and the men of the 12th SS Panzer Division had given each other no quarter since shortly after D Day, when a number of Canadian and British prisoners had been shot near Audrieu.

Today Falaise, by tradition the birthplace of William the Conqueror, is completely restored from its devastated state in August 1944. In the summer of 1984, the Municipal Library sponsored an exhibit dealing with the liberation of the city and the Battle of the Falaise Pocket. The photographs of the bombed-out city were especially impressive. Unfortunately, this exhibit may not be on display in future years.

CHAMBOIS AND THE FALAISE POCKET

Chambois can be reached from Falaise by driving D 63 (which becomes D 13 after 9 km) to Trun (18 km) and Chambois (7 km). Park by the keep in Chambois (11).

Here in Chambois you meet the tour route which follows the American breakout. You now have the choice of retracing that route back to St.-Lô, retracing the route you have just driven back to Caen, or following the route to Paris that we describe in the next chapter.

155

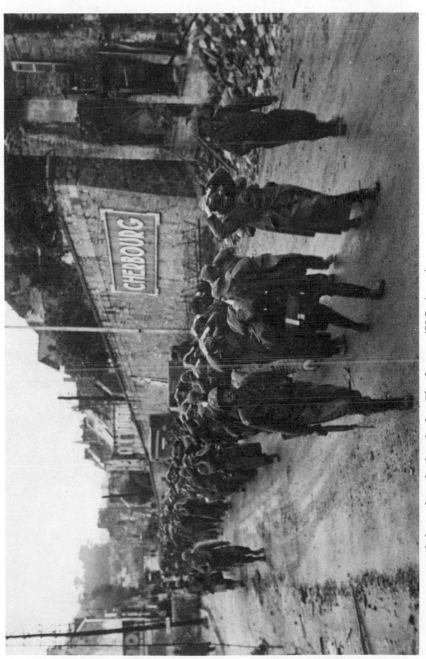

German troops in defeat after the battle for Cherbourg. (*U.S. Army*)

The flag-draped coffin of Major Thomas Howie rests before the Eglise St.-Croix in St.-Lô. (*U.S. Army*)

157

Crew of 3d Armored M-4 Shermans await orders to advance west of Mortain on 7 August 1944. (*U.S. Army*)

4

Pursuit Across France

An Overview

While Polish and American troops fought desperately to destroy the remnants of the German armies fleeing the Falaise Pocket, elements of Patton's Third Army, advancing between Alençon and Le Mans, were headed for the Seine. There, Patton hoped to pin the retreating enemy against the virtually bridgeless river, thus completing the destruction of the German forces routed from Normandy, and to take the liberation of Paris on the run. "I have used one principle in these operations," he wrote his son on 21 August, "and this is to—

> Fill the unforgiving minute
> With sixty seconds worth of distance run.

That is the whole art of war and when you get to be a general, remember it!" As Patton set down this advice, Major General Wade H. Haislip's XV Corps was approaching the Seine at Mantes, while Major General Walton H. Walker's XX Corps, having already liberated both Angers and Chartres and blockaded Nantes, was closing on the river east of Fontainebleau.

After an adjustment of the inter-Allied boundary on 19 August, XV Corps' 79th Division established a fortified bridgehead across the river at Mantes. During the afternoon of the twentieth, the rest of XV Corps, soon to be reinforced by the 30th Division (XIX Corps), was probing along the west bank of the Seine toward Vernon.

Patton now ordered two of his corps, XX and XII (Middleton's VIII Corps was still engaged in Brittany), to drive through the Paris–Orléans Gap toward the Seine above Paris. The Third Army was on the move. Manton Eddy's XII Corps, having already cleared the Loire valley of enemy troops, pushed from Orléans (captured on 16 August) to Sens, some 120 kilometers, in one jump. Colonel Bruce Clark's Combat Command A of the 4th Armored Division, the spearhead of the XII Corps drive, carried the advance to Troyes on the twenty-fifth. In a stunning attack, with its Shermans charging abreast, guns firing continuously, CCA stormed into the city, although it took another day of door-to-door fighting to dig out the last defenders. By then, American reconnaissance units were already across the Seine, restlessly probing toward the Marne.

The advance of Walker's XX Corps was equally rapid. On 15 August, before his last units had arrived from Omaha Beach, Combat Command B of Major General Lindsay McD. Silvester's 7th Armored Division was on the outskirts of the cathedral city of Chartres. After meeting determined resistance from the city's hastily assembled defenders, the 7th Armored, reinforced by the 5th Division, took the city on the eighteenth. The 7th next pushed east to Melun on the Seine, where its Combat Command Reserve was stopped on the twenty-second. Although German sappers managed to blow the Melun bridge the following morning, some seven miles downstream CCA's armored infantry crossed in boats and was soon joined by the other two combat commands.

With these crossings by the XX and XII corps, any hope that the German High Command had of establishing a defensive line on the Seine vanished. Patton continued to drive his two corps eastward, in part with captured German gasoline. The XII Corps crossed the Marne at Châlons-sur-Marne on the twenty-

160

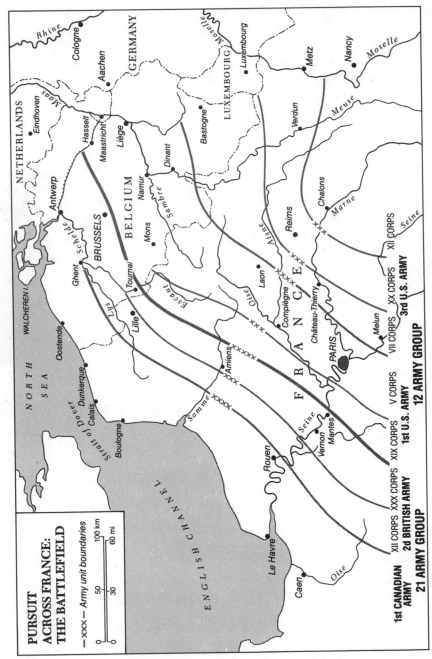

PURSUIT
ACROSS FRANCE:
THE BATTLEFIELD

—xxx— Army unit boundaries

0   50   100 km
0   30   60 mi

1st CANADIAN ARMY XII CORPS
2d BRITISH ARMY XXX CORPS
21 ARMY GROUP

1st U.S. ARMY XIX CORPS
12 ARMY GROUP V CORPS
VII CORPS

3rd U.S. ARMY XX CORPS
XII CORPS

MAP 16

NETHERLANDS
Rhine
Cologne
Aachen
GERMANY
Eindhoven
Maas
Hasselt
Antwerp
Maastricht
Liège
BRUSSELS
BELGIUM
Ghent
Scheldt
Namur
Sambre
Dinant
Bastogne
LUXEMBOURG
Luxembourg
Moselle
Metz
Nancy
Moselle
Verdun
Meuse
Chalons
Marne
Reims
Aisne
Mons
Escaut
Lys
Tournai
Lille
Laon
Oise
Compiègne
Château-Thierry
Melun
Seine
Melun
PARIS
FRANCE
NORTH SEA
WALCHEREN I.
Oostende
Strait of Dover
Dunkerque
Calais
Boulogne
Somme
Amiens
Seine
Vernon
Mantes
Rouen
Le Havre
Caen
Oise
ENGLISH CHANNEL

ninth. Twentieth Corps, driving across American World War I battlefields near Château-Thierry, first surrounded, then captured Reims the following day. Continuing their headlong advance on the thirty-first, tanks of the 7th Armored crossed the Argonne Forest and entered Verdun. The next day reconnaissance units were across the Meuse and probing toward the Moselle. But there the critical shortage of gasoline stopped the onrushing Third Army in its tracks.

On this date, 1 September, we must leave the Third Army with its nearly empty gas tanks to go back in time to describe both the Allied landings in southern France and the liberation of Paris.

The Americans, especially Eisenhower, had always insisted on the necessity of a second landing in France to support the main effort in Normandy. Their reasons were many and sound, ranging from the logistical need for another major French port, to the need to protect the exposed right flank of the Allied armies to the north, to the ease with which both American and Free French forces in the Mediterranean Theater and American divisions staging through the British Isles could be brought into the main battle. Operation Anvil—as the plan was originally named—was, in fact, a gigantic double envelopment that would put maximum pressure on the German armies in France.

The British, namely Churchill and Brooke, saw Anvil in a somewhat negative light, one decidedly self-serving. They realized that Anvil meant weakening the Allied effort in Italy—a theater still dominated by British arms and commanders—to support a risky amphibious operation dominated by the Americans. It would also end any hope of realizing Churchill's cherished dream of an Allied drive from northern Italy to the Danube. Whatever the reasons—pride or grand strategy— Churchill fought the plan until the last hour.

As it was, the shortage of landing craft in the ETO meant that Dragoon (as Churchill now insisted Anvil be renamed) could not be staged with Overlord; rather it was rescheduled for 15 August. The assault area finally chosen was the French Riviera between Cannes and Cap Negre.

Command of the new Seventh U.S. Army was given to Lieutenant General Alexander M. Patch, Jr., like J. Lawton Collins a veteran of the Guadalcanal campaign. Under him, Lieutenant General Lucian K. Truscott, Jr., commanded the VI Corps (3d, 36th, and 45th divisions), chosen for the assault landing. Additional assault troops would be provided by the 1st Airborne Task Force, the 1st Special Service Force (the Devil's Brigade), and various French units. The landings began at 0800 and were uniformly successful. French forces under General Jean de Lattre de Tassigny quickly captured Toulon and Marseille with its vital port. General Johannes Blaskowitz's Army Group G was soon in a pell-mell retreat up the Rhône valley narrowly escaping being cut off at the Montélimar narrows. By the middle of September French and American divisions were in Dijon and Besançon and were approaching the Third Army's southern boundary. Dragoon's success had amply justified Eisenhower's adamant insistence on the operation.

The liberation of Paris would likewise tax the Supreme Commander's patience. From a purely logistical standpoint, Eisenhower and members of his SHAEF staff wished to delay the liberation until the German armies in the West had been decisively defeated. Staff estimates predicted that just supplying the city with food and fuel would consume the same tonnage necessary to keep eight infantry divisions in the field. Already the rapid advance of the Allied armies was straining port facilities and the convoys of trucks now being organized into the Red Ball Express. In addition, many could and did argue that the surest way to liberate the city unharmed was to bypass it, allowing its defenders to surrender later. These arguments undoubtedly sounded reasonable at SHAEF's London headquarters; they simply neglected to take into account the French.

Neither the several resistance organizations within the city nor General Charles de Gaulle would brook any delay in the liberation of the city. The stakes were no less than control of the post-liberation government of France, concerning which no firm decision had yet been made by the Allies. As early as 17 August, somewhat prematurely anticipating the movement of the Allied armies, communist elements within the Paris resistance movement had independently called for the takeover of all government offices by their supporters. That uprising never took place, but two days later the Paris police occupied a number of public buildings and raised the tricolor for the first time since 1940. Gaullist supporters seized other public buildings and offices; soon impromptu barricades began to appear in the streets. Throughout 19 August, sporadic fighting swept through various quarters of the city as the German garrison attempted to restore order.

All this sudden activity on the part of the Paris resistance cadres presented Major General Dietrich von Choltitz, placed in command of the Paris garrison only two weeks before, with a painful dilemma. On one hand, he had been told by Hitler during a personal briefing to defend Paris at any cost, destroying the city if necessary. Clearly the Führer wanted a Stalingrad in the West. Von Choltitz's inclination was to offer only token resistance to the advancing armies, thereby saving the city from destruction while preserving his honor. Although Paris had not been bombed by the Allies (outlying areas, including rail yards around the city had been repeatedly struck), the city's bridges had been rigged for demolition. Von Choltitz rightly believed that Paris could best be defended from positions south of the city, and that blowing the Seine bridges would hinder the defenders more than the attackers. Working through Swedish Consul Raoul Nordling, he arranged for a cease-fire on 20 August, but the fragmented resistance movements were unable to honor the agreement. Von Choltitz became so alarmed by the breakdown of order in the city that he later agreed to pass Nordling through his lines so that he could arrange for the prompt entry of the Allied forces.

164

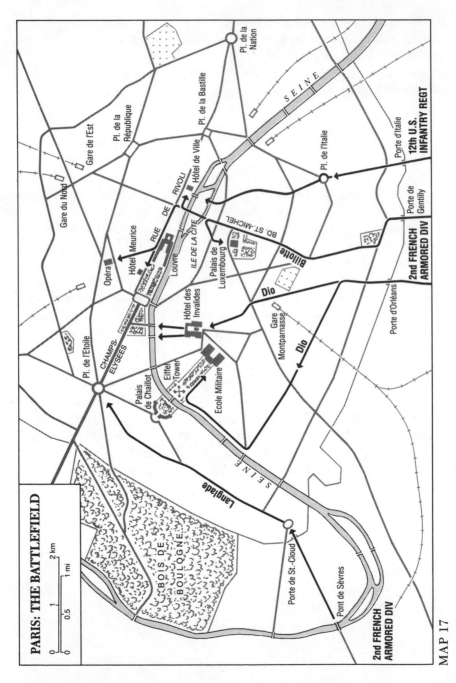

PARIS: THE BATTLEFIELD

MAP 17

The moment was critical for Charles de Gaulle. In an effort to consolidate his political position shortly before D Day he had proclaimed his National Committee of Liberation to be the provisional government of liberated France. Furthermore, he had managed to have his chief military commander, General Pierre Koenig, appointed commander of the French Forces of the Interior (FFI), as the Overlord planners had designated the military arm of the French resistance. In all this, the French people had had no say. Their nominal government remained that of Marshal Philippe Pétain, located at Vichy. Collaborationist or not, the legitimacy of the Vichy government was accepted by many Frenchmen, as evidenced by the large cheering crowds that had greeted Pétain on his visit to Paris in March 1944.

Thus it was an uncertain De Gaulle who came to France on 20 August—the second time since D Day—this time to stay. He had Ike's promise that his Free French forces would play an important and conspicuous role in the liberation of Paris. That promise really came down to allowing the 2d French Armored Division, soon to be famous as the "Deuxième DB," to lead the Allied armies into the city. The men of this American-trained and -equipped armored force, as well as its commander, Major General Jacques Philippe Leclerc (the nom de guerre of Viscount Philippe-François Marie de Hautecloque), were staunchly Gaullist. First organized from colonial units of the French army in Africa, this Free French force had fought its way across North Africa to participate in the victory over Rommel's Afrika Corps in early 1943. Subsequently moved to England, reorganized, and equipped as an armored division, the reborn 2ème Division Blindée landed on Utah Beach on 1 August and soon found itself part of the V Corps engaged south of the Falaise Pocket. In mid-August the division was bivouaced near Argentan awaiting orders to move toward Paris.

Aware of the critical situation in the capital, De Gaulle met with Eisenhower in the morning of the twenty-first to urge the immediate liberation of the city by the Deuxième DB. Apparently unsatisfied with the Supreme Commander's procrastinations, De Gaulle later sent Ike a formal letter reiterating his earlier request and hinting that he would order Leclerc to Paris if Ike would not. De Gaulle had already gone so far as to endorse Leclerc's decision to order a reconnaissance unit toward the city. When Major General Leonard T. Gerow, V Corps commander, learned of Leclerc's action, he did not mince words: "I desire to make it clear to you that the 2d Armored Division (French) is under my command for all purposes and no part of it will be employed by you except in the execution of missions assigned by this headquarters." He then recalled the reconnaissance unit.

For all his reservations concerning the Gaullists and their motives, Eisenhower preferred them to the communists as the liberators of Paris. Late in the afternoon of 22 August, Eisenhower and Bradley decided to pass the Deuxième DB through Gerow's V Corps and give De Gaulle his triumph. As insurance, they also ordered the 4th Infantry Division, poised south of the city, to close on Paris.

The men of the Deuxième DB spent the night of 22 August fueling and arming their vehicles, and the next morning set out for Paris, 120 miles away. Leclerc sent one combat command under Colonel Pierre de Langlade along a northern route through Rambouillet and Versailles. Altering his plans at the last moment (and not bothering to inform his American superiors), Leclerc chose to make his principal effort to the south. The combat commands under Colonels Billotte and Dio were ordered to approach Paris through Arpajon, along the route from Orléans.

Moving out at dawn on the twenty-fourth, Colonel Langlade eventually reached the Pont de Sèvres and established a small bridgehead across the Seine by dark.

Billotte's tanks had rougher going, being constantly slowed by harassing fire from enemy strong points. By midafternoon of the twenty-fourth, he was still seven miles from the center of the city. Bradley and Gerow were unhappy with the Deuxième

DB's slow progress, blaming it on the crowds of French civilians lining the route and the reluctance of Leclerc's men to endanger French lives and property by pushing forward aggressively. An exasperated Bradley, unwilling to wait for the French "to dance their way to Paris," ordered Gerow to "tell the 4th to slam on in and take the liberation." Gerow ordered Major General Raymond O. Barton to have his division on the road by 0200 on the twenty-fifth. Thus spurred, Leclerc managed to get a small force from Billotte's column to the Hôtel de Ville before midnight on the twenty-fourth. Paris was officially liberated the next day.

Langlade's column entered the city via the Pont de Sèvres and the Place St.-Cloud. By 1300, it had reached the Etoile. The Americans were not far behind. With the 102d Cavalry Group screening the way, the 12th Infantry Regiment of the 4th Division punched its way into the city via the Porte d'Italie. By noon, the GI's had occupied the Ile de la Cité. They were closely followed by the other two combat commands of the Deuxième DB. Thus Paris was taken in a rush on 25 August by units of two Allied divisions, one French, one American.

French tanks flushed von Choltitz and his staff from the Hôtel Meurice on the Rue de Rivoli. Later he agreed to a formal cease-fire at Leclerc's temporary headquarters in the Gare Montparnasse. With a calculated disregard for the military chain of command under which he was operating, Leclerc received the surrender in the name of the Provisional Government of France. The acknowledged head of that government, Charles de Gaulle, was at that moment making his way into the city from Rambouillet, where he had been occupying the Presidential Palace in anticipation of the liberation. His enthusiastic reception by the throngs of Parisians celebrating in the streets prompted him to plan a formal entry the following day, complete with a parade by the Deuxième DB down the Champs Elysées. Generals Gerow and Barton, aware of the danger from German snipers, protested to no avail. Barton even suggested that Gerow cut off Leclerc's gasoline ration if he would not comply with his orders. Fortunately, some 2,600 German soldiers entrenched in the Bois de Boulogne surrendered just prior to the parade. They might have shelled the parade route instead.

There was another parade through Paris four days later. To satisfy both De Gaulle's desire for a show of American force in his behalf and his own desire to emphasize the American role in the liberation, Eisenhower ordered the 28th Infantry Division to parade down the Champs Elysées as it moved through the city on its way north in pursuit of the retreating Germans. Bradley, De Gaulle, and other Allied officers reviewed Cota's veterans from an upside-down Bailey bridge.

Montgomery declined to play any part in the liberation of Paris despite Eisenhower's desire for an Allied presence. Avoiding that political tangle, Montgomery instead pushed 21 Army Group across the Seine on 29 August. Although he again missed trapping the retreating Germans, there was little they could do to impede the 21 Army Group's advancing armor. With the Third Canadian Army sweeping up the Channel coast headed for the V-1 launching sites in Holland, Montgomery unleashed Lieutenant General Brian G. Horrocks's XXX Corps for a sweep north of Paris. On 29 August, XXX Corps drove thirty kilometers beyond the Seine. Another two days, which brought clearing weather and weakening opposition, found the British in Amiens, where they captured Lieutenant General Heinrich Eberbach, newest commander of the German Seventh Army. By 3 September the Guards Armoured was probing the Belgian border toward Brussels, while the 11th Armoured struck for Antwerp. Both cities were in British hands the next day, with Antwerp's port facilities virtually intact.

Unfortunately, XXX Corps neglected to capture the bridges over the Albert Canal north of the port—an inexplicable oversight which cost the Allies dearly by allowing elements (some 86,000 troops in all) of the German Fifteenth Army to escape across the Schelde estuary to regroup in Holland. German control of South Beveland and Walcheren Island north of the es-

tuary meant that Antwerp would remain closed to Allied ship-
ping during the critical months of September and October.
Those divisions would also constitute a threat to Montgomery's
left flank, as well as being able to cover the V-2 launching sites
near The Hague (the first V-2 ballistic rockets hit London on 8
September).

While British tankers rolled across former battlefields, recall-
ing the bitter fighting of 1914–18 and 1940, the First U.S. Army
moved north of Paris to cover their right flank. On the left, the V
Corps cleared the Compiègne area, then drove to Cambrai,
where its vehicles ran short of gas on 2 September. Still further
to the west XIX Corps pushed to the outskirts of Tournai. Using
the Third Army bridgehead at Melun, Collins's VII Corps
pushed rapidly northeast across the World War I American battlefields at Soissons and Château-Thierry. Rose's 3d Armored
reached Mons on 2 September and, with some help from the 1st
and 9th Infantry divisions, was able to net some 25,000 prisoners
in the "Mons Pocket." With hardly a pause, VII Corps struck
out for Liège and the German border south of Aachen. Many
in the Allied command were predicting the collapse of the
Reich in a matter of weeks. They were not watching their gas
gauges.

By early September the full logistical consequences of the
rapid drive across France were becoming apparent. The Allied
armies, by jumping the Seine with hardly a pause, weeks ahead
of SHAEF's schedule, were simply outrunning their logistical
support. Even with some rail traffic restored and the Red Ball
Express truck convoys operating around the clock, not enough
tons of supplies (especially POL—petroleum, oil, and lubri-
cants) could be brought forward to sustain such rapid movement
on all fronts. Toward the end of August, Eisenhower, about to
assume tactical command of the Allied armies, found himself
wrestling with the question of priorities, caught in the unenvi-
able position of having to say no to either Montgomery or Patton.

As far back as 23 August, Montgomery had sought to sell both Eisenhower and Bradley a scheme that would have given him the men and material for what he termed "a full-blooded thrust to Berlin." What Monty had in mind was the massing of forty divisions under his command, with absolute logistical priority, for an attack through the Ruhr to Berlin. That meant giving him command of the First U.S. Army and halting the other two American armies (Patton's Third and Patch's Seventh). Monty, of course, believed his plan was the surest way of ending the war quickly, although weighing against it was the fact that, on the twenty-third, the British were not yet across the Seine. By then, the Third Army was far to the east of Paris, driving for the borders of the Reich. Nevertheless, Monty came away from his meeting with Ike convinced that he had carried the day, that Hodges's First Army would be placed under his command for a drive through the Low Countries to the Ruhr. But Ike prudently refused his request that all gasoline shipments to the Third Army be diverted to 21 Army Group.

Some awareness of the limitations that logistics would place on Montgomery's plan must have occurred to Eisenhower when he flew to 12 Army Group tactical headquarters (Eagle Tac) in Chartres on Saturday, 2 September, to confer with Bradley, Patton, and Hodges. During this meeting, he agreed to modify his August decision and now agreed to support a concurrent Third Army advance to the Saar. Between 5 and 8 September, Patton's divisions received 1,636,975 gallons of fuel, enough to start them again for the West Wall. While still emphasizing Montgomery's northern push, Eisenhower had returned to his favored broad-front advance.

Montgomery shortly protested Eisenhower's latest change of mind in a bluntly worded communiqué which restated his desire for a single "full-blooded thrust" to the Ruhr. Ike countered by pointing out that both advances could be supported if Le Havre and Antwerp could be quickly opened. To allay any misunderstanding because of communication difficulties (SHAEF head-

quarters was still in the Cotentin), Ike flew to Monty's headquarters for a conference on 10 September. Because of a
sprained knee, Ike was unable to move about with ease, so the
meeting took place in the cabin of his light plane. Things got off
to a bad start when the field marshal (Monty's promotion had
come on 1 September, as Ike assumed tactical command) insisted that the Supreme Commander's chief administrative officer must leave, while his stayed. Then, in the middle of Monty's
lecture on strategy, Ike found it necessary to warn: "Steady,
Monty! You can't speak to me like that. I'm your boss." Nevertheless, Monty won another victory—he would get the use of
the newly formed First Allied Airborne Army for his plan
to drive an armored column north through Holland to cross
the Rhine at Arnhem. The operation—to be known as Market-
Garden—was scheduled for 17 September. Beyond the Rhine,
Monty still dreamed of a thrust through the Ruhr to Berlin, now
with sixteen or eighteen divisions instead of forty.

While the Allied High Command squabbled over priorities,
two American corps, Collins's VII and Gerow's V, were preparing to breach the West Wall. In the V Corps zone, the 5th Armored Division liberated Luxembourg City on Sunday, 10
September. On Monday, a patrol from the 85th Cavalry Reconnaissance Squadron crossed the Our River into Germany. To the
north, later that day, two other V Corps units—a reinforced
company of the 109th Infantry (28th Division) and a patrol from
the 22d Infantry (4th Division)—also crossed into Germany,
but were soon withdrawn. Hodges ordered a full-scale attack by
both corps on the fourteenth, when sufficient ammunition could
be brought up. However, Collins received permission for his VII
Corps to probe the fortifications two days early. Even so, the VII
Corps attack came too late. The 1st and 9th Infantry and the 3d
Armored divisions were able to penetrate both lines of pillboxes
south of Aachen, but their attack died as the Germans rushed to
plug the gap. There was to be no quick rupture of the West
Wall by the Americans, nor were the British to be more suc-

cessful in outflanking it in the north. The heady pursuit across France had ended with the summer.

Tour of the Pursuit Across France

The following tour first takes you from Normandy to Paris by one of two routes, depending on your point of departure. One possible route follows the Autoroute de Normandie from Caen, with a suggested detour to visit La Roche-Guyon. Because of the driving conditions, this is the easiest route; although, because of the tolls, it will also be the most expensive. A second route, leaving Normandy from the Chambois area, follows N 12 through Dreux to Paris. We also include a detour to Chartres along this route.

From Paris, the route follows the Autoroute du Nord toward Cambrai, with a suggested detour to Compiègne, then bypasses Brussels to deposit you at the intersection of E 39 and N 15, some 50 kilometers south of Eindhoven, in position to drive the Market-Garden corridor north into Holland.

If one chooses, Paris can be bypassed and, by driving Autoroute all the way, the trip from Normandy to Holland made in a long day.

NORMANDY TO PARIS

To leave Normandy from the Bayeux–Caen area drive A 13 east to Rouen, then southeast along the Seine to Paris (240 km).

Along the way, you will pass Elbeuf, Vernon, Mantes, and Meulan, all spots where either British or American armies reached the Seine.

173

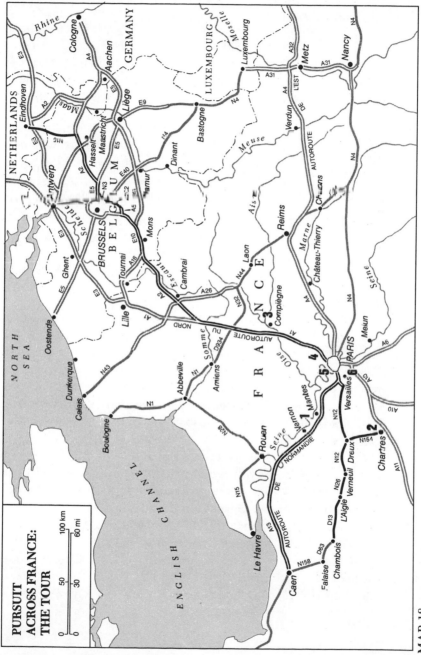

PURSUIT
ACROSS FRANCE:
THE TOUR

MAP 18

La Roche-Guyon Detour

Leave the Autoroute at the Vernon exit, then, immediately after crossing the Seine, turn right on D 5. Drive through Giverny (site of the Claude Monet Museum) to Gasny, where you bear right on D 313 to La Roche-Guyon (22 km). Stop near the château.

Mantes was captured by a task force of the 79th Infantry Division on 19 August without opposition. The opportunity now presented itself to bag the German forces still west of the Seine. Throwing the inter-Allied boundary to the winds, Patton ordered Haislip to have the 5th Armored attack along the west bank. At the same time Haislip told Major General Ira T. Wyche to get the 79th Infantry across the river that night and establish a fortified bridgehead on the east bank.

Covered by a driving rain and darkness, GI's of the 313th Regiment crossed the river in single file by groping along a footpath leading across a dam. At dawn they were joined by the 314th Regiment, which crossed in rafts and assault boats. By afternoon, XV Corps engineers had thrown a bridge across the Seine, allowing the rest of the division and its vehicles to cross. Wyche's men quickly moved downriver to La Roche-Guyon, where they captured Army Group B headquarters in the Château de La Rochefoucauld. Field Marshal Walther Model's staff managed to escape to Soissons, where they were able to regroup.

Meanwhile, on the west bank, elements of Major General Lunsford E. Oliver's 5th Armored captured Vernon on 20 August. However, it took five days of hard fighting against a scratch *Kampfgruppe* for the tankers to advance the next twenty miles to the outskirts of Louviers. That town was eventually taken by the 30th Infantry Division moving up from the south. At that point, the Americans began a gradual withdrawal eastward as the Second British Army closed the Seine. Before the month was out, the British would jump the river west of Vernon.

La Rochefoucauld Château (1)*

The château has been in the La Rochefoucauld family since the seventeenth century, when it was acquired through marriage by the son of Duke François de la Rochefoucauld, the famous author of the *Maximes*. Field Marshal Rommel used the château as his personal command post from December 1943 until he was injured in July. His office is said to have been located on the ground floor. Today, the château is closed to visitors.

To return to A 13, leave La Roche-Guyon by D 913 and follow it east until it intersects N 183. That road will take you south through Mantes, across the Seine to the Mantes-Est interchange on A 13 (19 km). Paris is some 45 km away.

Alternate route: *If you leave Normandy from the Chambois area, take D 13 to L'Aigle (43 km), where you can pick up N 26 to Verneuil (23 km). From Verneuil you can detour 56 km to Chartres and there pick up A 11-A 10 to Paris (83 km). Or you can continue on N 12 via Dreux to Versailles (88 km). As N 12 approaches Versailles, turn north at the Bois-d'Arcy exit onto A 12, then east after 6 km onto A 13. At that point you are approximately 12 km from the Paris périphérique.*

Whichever road you take to Paris, we advise you to plan your route carefully beforehand, including that into and through the city itself. The inner city is accessible from all sides from the *périphérique* which circles it. Driving there is a challenge.

L'Aigle and the Musée Parlant, Juin 44

The town of L'Aigle opened this invasion museum in 1953. Open April through October 1000–1200 and 1400–1830; closed Mondays in winter.

* Bold numbers are keyed to Map 18.

Chartres (2)

This famous cathedral city was liberated by units of the Third Army after overcoming stubborn German resistance. The first attack came in the early evening of 15 August when Combat Command B of the 7th Armored, XX Corps, advancing from Nogent-le-Rotrou, attempted to enter the city, then withdrew after meeting unexpected resistance. CCB resumed its attack the next day, encircled the city, but was unable to reduce its inner defenses. Tanks being at a disadvantage in the confines of city streets, General Walker ordered up his 11th Infantry Regiment (5th Division) to help in the fight. The 11th Infantry eliminated the last pockets of resistance on the eighteenth. The cathedral itself narrowly escaped damage from American artillery fire because some war correspondents climbed a tower to wave a white flag. That the cathedral survived intact may have been in part due to the efforts of Sergeant Clarence E. White (11th Infantry) who won the DSC for continuing to direct artillery fire against German positions in the city, although seriously wounded.

There is a monument to Jean Moulin, the resistance leader who was a native of Chartres, in the Place Châtelet, a few blocks southwest of the cathedral.

PARIS

Paris contains numerous museums, monuments, and places of interest relating to World War II and the liberation of the city. We have listed the museums below according to our judgment of their World War II importance. More information about them is provided in Appendix A. We have also included the name of the closest metro station.

Musée de l'Armée (1)*

The Army Museum is located in the Hôtel des Invalides. Open April through September 1000 to 1800 (1700 in winter);

* Bold numbers are keyed to Map 19.

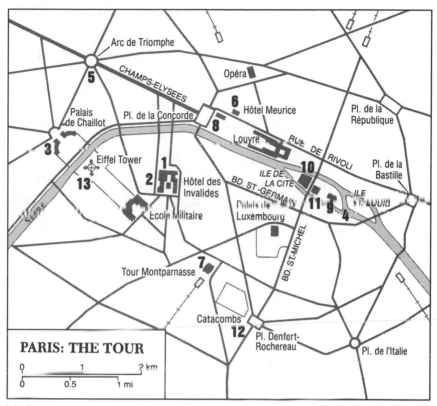

Arc de Triomphe

5

CHAMPS-ELYSEES

Opéra

6 Hôtel Meurice

Pl. de la
République

Palais
de Chaillot

Pl. de la Concorde

8

Louvre

RUE DE RIVOLI

Pl. de la
Bastille

3

Eiffel Tower

1

13

2

Hôtel des
Invalides

10

ILE DE
LA CITE

BD. ST -GERMAIN

ILE
ST. LOUIS

4

Ecole Militaire

Palais de
Luxembourg

11

9

Seine

BD. ST-MICHEL

7

Tour Montparnasse

Catacombs

12

Pl. Denfert-
Rochereau

Pl. de l'Italie

PARIS: THE TOUR

0 — 1 — 2 km
0 — 0.5 — 1 mi

MAP 19

closed 1 January, 1 May, 1 November, 25 December. Metro stop: Invalides.

Musée de l'Ordre de la Libération (2)

The Museum of the Order of Liberation is on the Boulevard Latour-Maubourg next to the Hôtel des Invalides. Open 1400 to 1700; closed on Sundays, the month of August, and on holidays. Metro stop: Invalides.

Musée de la Marine (3)

The Naval Museum is located in the Palais de Chaillot. Open 1000 to 1800; closed Tuesdays and holidays. Metro stop: Trocadéro.

Mémorial de la Déportation (4)

This underground memorial is located on the Ile de la Cité east of Notre Dame Cathedral. Metro stop: Cité.

Arc de Triomphe (5)

Commissioned by Napoleon in 1806 and completed in 1836, this famous Parisian monument commemorates both the Emperor's victories and his victorious generals. It is also the site of the tomb of France's unknown soldier.

In the early afternoon of 25 August, Colonel Pierre de Langlade's column spun down the Avenue Foch to the Place de l'Etoile, where they were greeted by the now standard throngs of Parisians celebrating in the streets. Accompanying this column was a small coterie of Americans who had tagged along with the French to witness the liberation, including war correspondent Ernest Hemingway, OSS Colonel David Bruce, Army historian Colonel S. L. A. Marshall, and his assistant, Captain John Westover. After they had parked their jeeps, members of the group went sightseeing. Marshall joined the Parisians in the street for a better view of the Arc de Triomphe and of a nearby banner proclaiming "Hart, Schaffner & Marx Welcomes You" (a French gunner later took care of the sign). Bruce, later United States Ambassador to England, climbed to the top of the Arc, from where he could see burning vehicles in the Place de la Concorde and the Tuileries Gardens. Gunfire still rattled through the streets, and a stray 88-mm shell nicked the Arc. That desecration and the glimpse of a Tonkinese laundryman at a nearby window prompted a final burst of fire from the French half-tracks. Marshall's jeep took two hits, one in a tire. When the firing stopped, Hemingway's somewhat shaken driver, Sergeant Red Pelskey, saved a collaborationist mademoiselle from having her head shorn, shouting at her assailants with more verve than tact: "Leave her alone, goddamn you, you're all collaborationists!"

Back in the saddle, tire repaired, the little group of liberators detached itself from the French and set out to conquer the rest of Paris unaided. Marshall and Westover found their way to the Hôtel Claridge, where a flustered clerk tried to deny them rooms by maintaining that the hotel was reserved, but probably only wanted time to remove the bathroom signs welcoming German officers. Meanwhile, Hemingway and Bruce sped down the Champs-Elysées to liberate the Travelers Club Bar. That evening, the members of the group, now swollen to nine, showed up for dinner at the Hôtel Ritz, where Jack Ritz presented them with souvenir Dunhill pipes. After vociferously refusing to pay the Vichy government's tax, they capped the evening by dropping a hundred-dollar tip and by signing each other's menus under the caption: "We think we took Paris."

After the liberation, De Gaulle received the accolades of the Parisians at the Arc de Triomphe and along the Champs-Elysées.

A small museum in the Arc, reached by either elevator or stairs, contains exhibits which trace its history. Access to the platform and museum 1000 to 1745 from April to September

(1645 in winter); closed Tuesdays, 1 January, 1 May, 1 and 11 November, 25 December. Admission charge. Metro stop: Etoile.

Hôtel Meurice (6)

This large and luxurious hotel on the Rue de Rivoli was the German headquarters for "Greater Paris." After the hotel was surrounded by French-manned Shermans, some of which were firing on German vehicles parked under the arches along the Rue de Rivoli, French troops under Lieutenant Henri Karcher rushed the building under cover of smoke grenades. "Do you speak German?"a French officer shouted at General von Choltitz as he entered the commander's office. "Probably better than you do," the general replied. Von Choltitz was first taken to the Prefecture of Police, where he signed the articles of capitulation, then driven across town to Leclerc's headquarters in the Gare Montparnasse to put his signature on a general cease-fire order.

Today, the Hôtel Meurice rates luxury status in the Michelin Red Guide. Metro stop: Concorde.

Gare Montparnasse (7)

The old station was rebuilt in 1968–70 and is now the site of the imposing Tour Montparnasse, a skyscraper which dominates the Montparnasse section of the city. Room 32, where the cease-fire was signed, no longer exists. Instead, the event is commemorated by a plaque (mentioning only the surrender) on the wall of the C & A department store, a quarter of a mile away from the original site.

Place de la Concorde (8)

On the wall below the Jeu de Paume Museum, there are a few memorial plaques to soldiers of the 2d French Armored Division and to civilians who were killed in the liberation of

Paris. The wall faces the Rue de Rivoli and is close to the metro station entrance. Metro stop: Concorde.

Cathédrale de Notre-Dame (9)

While visiting this great medieval cathedral look for the simple brass plaque fastened to a column on the right side of the nave as you approach the transept. It reads: TO THE GLORY OF GOD AND TO THE MEMORY OF ONE MILLION MEN OF THE BRITISH EMPIRE WHO FELL IN THE GREAT WAR, 1914–1918, AND OF WHOM THE GREATER PART REST IN FRANCE. British statesmen and soldiers in 1944 could never forget that simple truth, and it influenced their decisions and actions all through the campaign. Metro stop: Cité.

Palais de Justice (10)

As you enter the courtyard of the Law Courts on your way to visit the Sainte Chapelle, that marvel of stained glass tucked away inside the compound, notice the shell marks over the archway and on various parts of the building's facade.

Paris police seized the Prefecture de Police (11) on 19 August and held it, despite attacks from German armored vehicles, until von Choltitz agreed on a truce. It was here that the tricolor was raised for the first time since 1940. Metro stop: Cité.

The Catacombs (12)

This famous Paris ossuary was used as a resistance headquarters during the occupation. Open most Saturdays (first and third only from 16 October through June) after 1400. Admission charge. Metro stop: Denfert-Rochereau.

Tour Eiffel (13)

This Paris landmark, built in 1889 and threatened with demolition by the Germans, survived the war. For a short time after the liberation, the Tower Restaurant was requisitioned for use as an enlisted men's club.

Paris Environs

Chartres (2)*

Chartres can be reached from Paris by leaving the city from the périphérique on A 6. Follow the signs (A 10–A 11) to Chartres (83 km).

Compiègne (3)
Leave Paris by the Porte de la Chapelle and follow A 1 north to its intersection with N 31 (73 km). Drive N 31 through Compiègne to the Clairière de l'Armistice (20 km).

After World War I, the railroad car (actually a dining car being used as Marshal Foch's command post) in which the Armistice had been signed was installed in a park outside Compiègne near the spot where the ceremony occurred. At the park entrance, the French erected a memorial stele (Alsace-Lorraine Monument) depicting the Hohenzollern eagle being pierced by a sword. Near where Foch's car had stood, they built a low stone monument inscribed in bold relief with these words:

HERE ON THE ELEVENTH OF NOVEMBER 1918 SUCCUMBED THE CRIMINAL PRIDE OF THE GERMAN EMPIRE—VANQUISHED BY THE FREE PEOPLES WHICH IT TRIED TO ENSLAVE.

Its gloating tenor was obvious and intended.

For that reason, Hitler visited Compiègne on 21 June 1940, after humbling the French army, to symbolically reverse the decision of 1918. He had new tracks laid so that Foch's dining car could be moved from its protective building to the location where the signing had taken place. Hitler and entourage (Goering, Ribbentrop, Raeder, and others) entered the car to hear the German terms of surrender read to the French, then left. Two

* The sites are keyed by numbers to Map 18.

days later, they arrived at Le Bourget airport for a tour of the conquered capital.

It was just before his visit to Compiègne that Hitler was photographed dancing in triumph over the French debacle, but historians now suspect that the film footage was later carefully edited for Allied propaganda purposes.

After the French surrender, the Germans dismantled the Alsace-Lorraine memorial and shipped it to Germany in crates. The railway car was sent to Berlin, where it was eventually destroyed in an RAF raid.

Today, the Clairière de l'Armistice has been restored to its pre–World War II state. The Alsace-Lorraine memorial was found in Germany and returned. A contemporary dining car (first passed off as the original), equipped as in 1918, is on display. Admission charge.

General Gerow's V Corps (5th Armored, 4th, and 28th Infantry divisions) fought a sharp action against elements of the LVIII Panzer Corps in the Forêt de Compiègne during the last days of August 1944.

Aeroport du Bourget and the Musée de l'Air (4)

Le Bourget Airport can be reached by exiting the périphérique by the Porte de la Chapelle, then following A 1 north to the Bourget 5 exit (8.5 km). Once you have entered the airport, bear right. The museum is located in the buildings to your left (west).

Open November through April 1000–1700 (in summer to 1800); closed 1 January, 25 December, and Mondays. Admission charge.

Suresnes, American Military Cemetery (5)

Since there is no close metro stop, the Suresnes Cemetery is best reached by taking one of the commuter trains that leave the Gare St.-Lazare every twenty minutes for the

Suresnes station and beyond. The cemetery is about a ten-minute walk up Mont Valerien.

Besides the American Military Cemetery, this western suburb of Paris is also the site of a "Memorial to Fighting France." During the occupation some 4,500 resistance fighters were shot down on the slopes of Mont Valerien.

This World War I cemetery, occupying 7.5 acres, originally contained the graves of 1,541 Americans. Today it accommodates the graves of twenty-four unknown American soldiers killed in World War II. Additions to the original chapel include World War II commemorative materials.

Versailles (6)

It is possible to catch a train from the Gare des Invalides to the Versailles Rive-Gauche station. If you choose to drive, leave the périphérique by the Porte d'Auteuil exit, A 13 to Versailles. Exit the autoroute at the Versailles-Nord interchange, then drive south and southwest to the château (13 km).

No visitor to Paris should miss touring the château and its grounds. Versailles was the residence of the French court from the time of Louis XIV until the Revolution. The palace's Hall of Mirrors is best remembered for the signing, on 28 June 1919, of the treaty of peace between the Allied Powers and the Imperial German Empire. Admission to parts of the palace and the two Trianon palaces is by guided tour only. The gardens and parts of the palaces can be visited without a guide. Call 950.58.32 for details. Admission charge.

From September 1944 to May 1945, the town of Versailles was the location of SHAEF Headquarters. Eisenhower had quarters in the Trianon Palace Hotel.

PARIS TO THE DUTCH BORDER

Leave Paris by the Autoroute du Nord (A 1). This route will take you by Le Bourget Airport and Compiègne (see Paris Environs section). Veer east toward Cambrai (A 2). In Belgium the route becomes E 10. To skirt Brussels, follow A 5 (A 202, M 3) by Waterloo until it intersects E 5. After 12 km, leave E 5 on A 2. Continue on A 2 for 63 km, then exit (No. 29) north on N 15. Eindhoven is some 50 km to the north. The total distance from Paris to the N 15 turnoff is 388 km.

186

Generals Hodges, Bradley, and Patton (left to right) confer at 12th Army Group headquarters near St. James, France. (*U.S. Army*)

187

General Leclerc, commander of the 2d French Armored Division, near Rambouillet on the road to Paris. (*U.S. Army*)

The 28th U.S. Infantry Division marches down the Champs-Elysées shortly after the fall of Paris. (*U.S. Army*)

MP directs Red Ball Express traffic in early September 1944. (*U.S. Army*)

5

Operation Market-Garden

An Overview

Following the breakout at Avranches on 31 July, Allied forces pursued a disorganized enemy across the Seine. In the space of four weeks, Patton's Third Army had raced 250 miles to Verdun. Advance units were on the banks of the Moselle near Metz on 5 September. Montgomery's armies in the north had wasted no time either. The Guards Armoured Division of the Second British Army swept into Brussels on 3 September, and the next day the 11th Armoured Division captured Antwerp and its port intact. These successes inspired confidence and fostered hope in an early end to the war in Europe.

If entrance to Germany itself was soon to be gained, however, unrelenting pressure had to be maintained on the retreating German armies. Any respite would afford time to harried commanders to reorganize their scattered troops and to consolidate defenses. But in early September, just at the moment when Allied prospects seemed brightest, the advancing columns slowed and in many places ground to a halt; they had reached the end of their logistical tether.

The campaign across France and Belgium had been sustained very largely by supplies brought over the beaches in Normandy or through Cherbourg and carried by truck to the front—by

September, three to four hundred miles distant. The victories of Allied arms included no ports closer to the front. The Channel ports would not be captured until September was out. And although Antwerp was seized early in the month, negligent British commanders failed to clear the seaward approaches.

In pre-invasion planning, it had been projected that Allied forces would not reach the Seine until 4 September (D plus 90). By that date, bases would have been established to supply the advance to the German borders. The very rapidity of that advance prevented a buildup in depth of the means of supply. Try as they did, the truckers of the Red Ball Express could not bring forward sufficient ammunition, food, and, particularly, gasoline. On 30 August, Patton's tank units received only 32,000 gallons of gasoline and were told they would get no more until 3 September; they required 400,000 gallons daily. In a meeting with Eisenhower at Chartres on 2 September, Patton exclaimed, "My men can eat their belts, but my tanks have gotta have gas!"

Despite the difficulties of maintaining four armies on the march, Eisenhower refused to give up his broad-front strategy in favor of the single thrust which Montgomery had been advocating since mid-August. But the Allies were stuck; and so at Brussels on 10 September, Eisenhower listened to the British field marshal's proposal to get them moving again. Montgomery, who had a well-deserved reputation for caution, surprised nearly everyone by presenting a daring plan. He proposed that three and a half airborne divisions be dropped behind German lines in Holland to seize and hold the road and bridges over the waterways to the north. Along this corridor XXX British Corps armor and infantry would dash through the cities of Eindhoven, Nijmegen, and Arnhem and over the Neder Rijn to the Zuider Zee, a distance of ninety-nine miles.

If successful, the operation, code-named Market-Garden, would cut off the Germans in western Holland, outflank the West Wall and put the British army in a position to attack the Ruhr from the north. The plan won Eisenhower's approval. Its success depended much on the absence of a strong, organized enemy and the presence of good weather for the troop-carrying aircraft and for the bombers and fighters in tactical support. And, as always in war, time imposed its imperatives. The ground column had to advance quickly to relieve the lightly armed paratroopers and to prevent the reinforcement of German defenses. Montgomery estimated that XXX Corps, under Lieutenant General Brian Horrocks, would cover the sixty-four miles from the bridgehead on the Schelde–Maas Canal to Arnhem in two days. The airborne commander, Lieutenant General Frederick Browning, thought that the forces at Arnhem could hold for four days.

However, the field of battle would afford even small bands of determined defenders opportunity to delay the ground column. Nine waterways traversed the area: three major rivers, ranging from two hundred to four hundred yards wide, the Maas, the Waal and the Neder Rijn; three smaller rivers, the Upper and Lower Dommel and the Aa; and three major canals, the Wilhelmina, the Willems, and the Maas–Waal. These waterways and the soft polderland in the area would confine the motorized column to the road most of the way. Should even one of the crossings be denied the Allies, the operation might be seriously jeopardized.

In the second and third weeks of September, German commanders managed to arrest the flight of battlefield troops and occupation forces toward the German border and to introduce some cohesion to German defenses along the Belgian-Dutch border. German forces in the area were also strengthened in mid-September by the arrival of two divisions from the Fifteenth Army. In a minor Dunkirk, the Fifteenth Army had evaded the encircling First Canadian Army south of the Schelde by ferrying across the mouth of the estuary at night and then slipping through a narrow isthmus to the mainland just twenty miles north of Antwerp. More significantly, Field Marshal Walther Model, commander of Army Group B, whose responsibilities in-

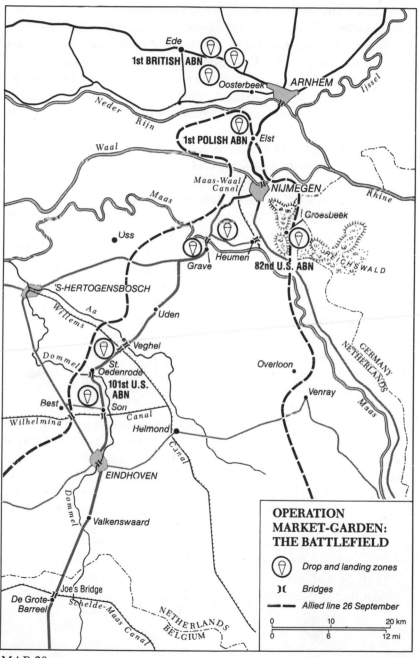

Ede
1st BRITISH ABN
Oosterbeek
ARNHEM
Ijssel
Neder
Rijn
1st POLISH ABN
Elst
Waal
Maas-Waal
Canal
NIJMEGEN
Rhine
Groesbeek
Maas
Uss
REICHS WALD
Heumen
Grave
82nd U.S. ABN
'S-HERTOGENSBOSCH
Aa
Willems
Uden
Dommel
Veghel
St.
Oedenrode
Overloon
GERMANY
NETHERLANDS
101st U.S.
ABN
Best
Son
Venray
Wilhelmina
Canal
Maas
Helmond
Canal
EINDHOVEN
Dommel
Valkenswaard

**OPERATION
MARKET-GARDEN:
THE BATTLEFIELD**

Drop and landing zones

)(Bridges

Allied line 26 September

| 0 | 10 | 20 km |
| 0 | 6 | 12 mi |

Joe's Bridge
De Grote-
Barreel
Schelde-Maas Canal
NETHERLANDS
BELGIUM

MAP 20

cluded the Netherlands, ordered two armored divisions to Arnhem for refitting and reassignment. Although under strength, these two units, the 9th SS Panzer "Hohenstaufen" Division and the 10th SS Panzer "Frundsberg" Division, far outmatched any airborne division. In their eagerness to renew the offensive, Allied commanders dismissed intelligence reports of stiffening German resistance along the front and of the presence of German armor in the target area.

On 17 September, there began the largest airborne operation of the war. In the middle of that Sunday morning the sky above southeastern England filled with some two thousand aircraft—troop-carrying C-47s and, behind their tugs, Horsa, Waco, and Hamilcar gliders. Even this great number, however, was insufficient to transport the whole airborne force in one day. Twenty thousand men, along with matériel, were dropped on D Day. Over the next four days, the remaining fifteen thousand troops as well as additional armament and supplies were scheduled to be carried to the landing and drop zones.

The lift on D Day was remarkably successful. The hundreds of sorties flown by American and British bombers and fighters during the preceding night and morning had crippled many German flak batteries and airfields. And the escort of Tempests, Spitfires, Mosquitoes, P-47s, P-38s and P-51s, a thousand strong, dissuaded enemy fighters from attack. Losses in the air were very low—just 2.8 percent among transport aircraft. The drops and landings themselves were made, almost without exception, on the correct zones. It was an auspicious beginning.

The airborne forces moved swiftly to their objectives. The 101st U.S. Airborne Division seized all the bridges in its sector, save one, the bridge over the Wilhelmina Canal at Son. The 82d U.S. Airborne captured the high ground southeast of Nijmegen and secured the crossings over the Maas at Grave and over the Maas–Waal Canal at Heumen. At Arnhem elements of the 1st British Airborne "Red Devils" under Colonel John Frost won control of the northern end of the bridge over the Neder Rijn.

For all the successes of D Day, however, there were also portentous developments which, in the end, proved fatal to the Allied cause. First, German resistance was stronger and swifter than expected. The armored column was not able to dash up the corridor. It made only six miles the first day, and by the evening of D plus 3 had not yet crossed the Waal at Nijmegen. Second, the inability of the 82d to capture the Nijmegen bridge on D Day permitted the Germans to reinforce their defenses and forced a bloody and time-consuming battle. Third, the British paratroopers at the end of the corridor found that the reports of German panzers in the area were true. The 9th and 10th SS Panzer divisions would play the key role in the destruction of 1st British Airborne and in the halting of XXX Corps, first at Nijmegen and then finally on the "island" road south of Arnhem.

In addition to these difficulties, the weather took a turn for the worse on D plus 2. For four days, fog and rain over England and the Continent delayed or prevented resupply and reinforcement of the airborne forces. The 82d's fourth regiment of infantry, the 325th Glider Infantry, did not arrive until D plus 6; it had been scheduled to land on D plus 2. The 101st received only half the artillery and anti-tank guns scheduled for drop on D plus 2, and not until D plus 6 would the 101st have anything larger than the 75-mm pack howitzer. Poor weather also delayed arrival of the 1st Polish Parachute Brigade south of Arnhem for two days. Thus, the airborne forces on the ground were left thin in infantry and artillery during the critical early days of Market-Garden. Consequently, XXX Corps had to devote a greater part of its strength to opening and keeping open the corridor than had been planned. It could give no help to 1st British Airborne. Despite all, the men on the ground did all that could have been asked, and more.

The 101st "Screaming Eagles" under Lieutenant General Maxwell Taylor fought for control of a fifteen-mile stretch of road between Eindhoven and Veghel. In the course of the fighting it would be known to the men of the division as "Hell's

Highway." While the bulk of Taylor's command advanced on the nine highway and rail bridges along the main road, Colonel John Michaelis detached a company from his 502d Regiment to seize bridges over the Wilhelmina Canal at Best, four miles to the west. This company encountered elements of the 59th German Infantry Division—one of the survivors of the Schelde evacuation. The fight which developed was the most bitter experienced by the Screaming Eagles on D plus 1 and D plus 2. Ultimately Michaelis committed two battalions at Best. Although the Germans blew up the bridges, the left flank of the 101st had been secured—for the moment.

Following linkup with the ground column in Eindhoven at 1900, 18 September, the 101st adopted a defensive stance aimed at keeping open the corridor it had created. Beset on both flanks by German forces of increasing strength, the paratroopers had their hands full. General Taylor later likened the situation to that of the isolated post of cavalry in the Old West which had to defend long stretches of railway against marauding Indians. In part, this situation was due to the inability of the VIII and XII British corps to make much headway in the polderland on either flank of the corridor.

Despite aggressive patrols designed to break up German troop concentrations, the enemy twice severed the lifeline to XXX Corps. On the first occasion, the Germans broke through between Uden and Veghel on 22 September (D plus 5) and halted traffic for twenty-four hours. Horrocks sent the 32d Guards Brigade, half the Guards Armoured Division, south from Nijmegen to assist in reopening the road. Twenty-four hours after this was accomplished, the Germans cut the road again north of St. Oedenrode. Although units of the 101st Airborne and the 50th British Infantry Division succeeded in driving off the enemy by the morning of 26 September, mine clearing delayed reopening the road until well into the day.

Further north the 82d "All American" Division under Brigadier General James Gavin concentrated its efforts on clearing and holding the Groesbeek heights. This hill mass southeast of Nijmegen rises some three hundred feet above the surrounding countryside and dominates the bridges and roads in the area. Unless the 82d controlled the heights, the corridor could not be counted secure. Because the ground column with its tanks and artillery would not reach the 82d for several days, Gavin had opted to leave behind a regiment of glider infantry—to arrive on D plus 2—in favor of a parachute artillery battalion.

The objectives of the 82d were many: the bridge at Grave over the Maas, the bridges over the Maas–Waal Canal south and west of Nijmegen, the great highway bridge over the Waal in Nijmegen, and, in general, the maintenance of a ten-mile corridor from Grave to Nijmegen. As it turned out, there were too few men available to accomplish all these tasks. The 504th Parachute Infantry was in control of the Grave bridge within three hours after landing and, at nightfall, had a crossing over the Maas–Waal Canal at Heumen. The 505th and 508th also knew success in establishing themselves on the Groesbeek heights. It was not until late afternoon, however, that units of the 508th moved on Nijmegen to capture the bridge over the Waal. The 9th SS Panzer Reconnaissance Battalion beat them there by a few hours.

The 82d launched four attacks with no result against the German defenses at the bridge until the fifth, and successful, attack in the afternoon of 20 September (D plus 3). Backed by tanks of the Guards Armoured, Lieutenant Colonel Ben Vandervoort's 2d Battalion of the 505th cleared the way. Simultaneous with this assault on the south end of the bridge, another assault was mounted against the north end.

In one of the most daring exploits of the war, the 82d made an amphibious crossing of the Waal to strike the Germans on the north bank. By evening British tanks were across the river. The amphibious attack had succeeded. General Dempsey, commander of the Second British Army, upon meeting Gavin after the Waal crossing said, "I am proud to meet the commander of

the greatest division in the world today." Gavin would later return the compliment. He called the performance of the Red
Devils on Arnhem bridge "the outstanding independent parachute battalion action of the war."

Unknown to paratroopers of the 82d and the tank crews of the
Guards Armoured, the Germans had driven Colonel Frost and
his men off the Arnhem bridge the same afternoon on which
they had captured the bridges at Nijmegen.

On D day, three battalions of Brigadier Gerald Lathbury's 1st
Parachute Brigade set off for Arnhem from their drop zones six
miles to the west. The 1st and 3d battalions ran into armored
screens which the Germans threw across the two major roads
running from Arnhem to the west. Only Lieutenant Colonel
John Frost's 2d Battalion bypassed the German strength on a
secondary road alongside the Neder Rijn. At the outskirts of the
city one company peeled off to seize a rail bridge, only to have it
blown up as Lieutenant Peter Barry and his platoon sought to
cross. Another company under Major Digby Tatham-Warter got
hung up in a firefight in outlying buildings. This left just one
company and the men of the battalion headquarters to seize the
bridge. Frost's men encountered little resistance in occupying
eighteen buildings overlooking the northern end of the bridge.
They had missed by a bare hour Captain Paul Graebner's 9th SS
Panzer Reconnaissance Battalion, which had crossed the bridge
on its way south to Nijmegen to investigate reports of parachute
drops in the area.

On Sunday night (D Day), the British twice attempted to
storm the southern end of the bridge, only to be beaten back.
The Germans also mounted an infantry assault, but they too
were forced to retreat. Throughout the night other Red Devils
in twos and threes filtered through the German lines and most of
Tatham-Warter's company rejoined Frost to boost his numbers
to six hundred or so.

By Monday morning the British paratroopers commanding
the northern end of the bridge were completely surrounded. For
the next three days the fiercest kind of combat occurred—house

to house, room to room. There were more than a few veterans of Stalingrad among the German troops, and in after-action reports it was to Stalingrad that they likened the fighting around the Arnhem bridge.

1st British Airborne commanders sought, to no avail, to relieve Frost's beleaguered band. The 1st and 3d battalions fought constantly for the better part of two days to force a way down the major highways but were halted little more than a mile from the bridge. As two more battalions, the South Staffordshires and the 11th, joined the fight, the 1st and 3d battalions slipped south to the river road used earlier by Frost. This time the Germans were ready at the brickworks across the river; they cut the British to pieces with anti-aircraft guns firing horizontally. Faced with the extinction of more than a third of his command, Major General Roy Urquhart ordered his troops to withdraw from Arnhem. About two hundred of the 3,500 men who had marched on Arnhem managed to make it back.

At the bridge, the 2d Battalion was now on its own. On Tuesday (D plus 2) General Heinz Harmel, commander of the 10th SS Panzers, asked for Frost's surrender and was turned down. By this time, the 2d occupied only ten of their original eighteen buildings. The Germans proceeded to reduce these by point-blank bombardment from tanks and artillery. The few who could—one to two hundred—fought on through Wednesday; by dusk on D plus 3 it was all over but the mopping up.

To the west, around Oosterbeek, the remnants of the 1st Airborne formed a finger-shaped perimeter two miles long and one and a half miles wide—the "Cauldron." Here, against an enemy of steadily increasing strength, they held out in anticipation of the arrival of XXX Corps. For six days the besieged defenders sought to keep open a corridor to the north of the Neder Rijn. Not even the long-delayed arrival, south of the river, of units of the 1st Polish Parachute Brigade and of infantry of the 43d Wessex Division averted disaster. Only a handful of reinforcements got across. In the evening of 25 September (D plus 8) Horrocks and Browning decided to withdraw the survivors of the 1st British Airborne from the north bank. Under cover of night and a driving rain, about 2,300 of the original 10,000 who had fought north of the Neder Rijn came back.

This withdrawal marked the end of the airborne phase of the operation. In those nine days total Allied casualties exceeded those suffered on D day in Normandy. British casualties were the highest—over 13,000. The 1st British Airborne was largely destroyed. Counting the Poles and glider pilots, casualties totaled 7,578. Horrocks's XXX Corps lost 1,480 and the VIII and XII British corps another 3,874.

American losses, including glider pilots and 9th Troop Carrier Command, were 3,974. The 82d had casualties of 1,432, and the 101st had 2,118.

German casualties remain uncertain. In a radio message intercepted by the Allies on 27 September, the Germans gave their losses at Arnhem alone as 3,300 in dead and wounded. On the basis of interviews with German commanders, Cornelius Ryan in *A Bridge Too Far* estimated that the Germans suffered an additional 7,500–10,000 casualties along the corridor.

The fighting in the salient created by Market-Garden was not over for the 82d and 101st Airborne. Owing to manpower shortages in the Second British Army, the 82d and 101st moved north of the Waal to help maintain the tip of the salient. The 82d fought on until early November, and the 101st remained until the last week of November. In this fighting the two American airborne divisions had losses as great as those taken in the airborne phase. They were much bloodied divisions when they retired to Reims for a well-deserved rest. In three weeks they would be fighting in the Ardennes.

Tour of Operation Market-Garden

The Market-Garden tour follows, in the main, the route taken by XXX Corps in its drive northward to Arnhem. The roads and bridges over which you will travel make up the "Corridor"

201

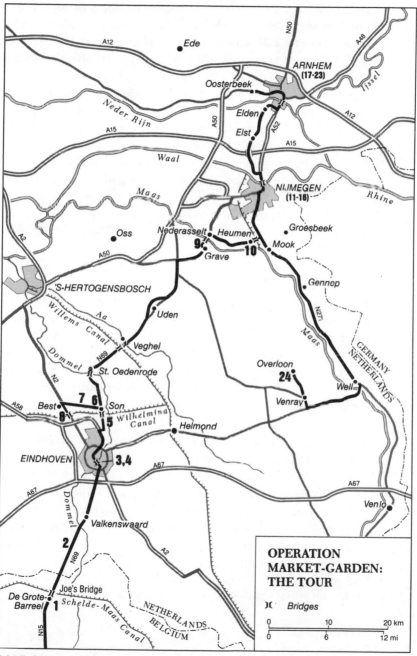

OPERATION MARKET-GARDEN: THE TOUR

)(*Bridges*

0		10		20 km
0		6		12 mi

MAP 21

seized by the airborne. The tour begins at "Joe's Bridge" a few kilometers south of the Belgian-Dutch frontier on N 15. This road runs north and south between Hasselt and the frontier some 70 kilometers east of Antwerp. At the frontier, N 15 becomes N 69.

The first major city on the tour is Eindhoven, where several sites are located. At Son, a short detour to the west gives access to the battleground around Best. Upon rejoining the "Corridor" at Son, the tour proceeds up N 69 to Grave. Just north of Grave, you leave N 69 to go east through Heumen to N 271. This road takes you to Nijmegen, another large city and site of the Waal bridge.

Care must be taken after crossing the bridge to get on the road to Elst, as the main road to Arnhem—A 52—was built after the war. The village of Elst marks the northern terminus of the drive by XXX Corps. The projected route of XXX Corps north of Elst is that described in the text.

Be sure you rejoin A 52 south of Arnhem lest you cross the Neder Rijn on the new highway bridge rather than the bridge held by Frost's 2d Battalion. There is much to be seen in Arnhem and in the adjacent town of Oosterbeek—allow half a day, at least, if you can. The tour concludes with a visit to a major museum east of Eindhoven which may conveniently be reached in driving south to other battlefields.

Drive north on N 15 in Belgium toward the Netherlands. Cross the bridge (1)* over the Schelde–Maas Canal just past De-Grote-Barreel. On the north side of the bridge to the west is a slip road where you should park. Walk to the canal bank. You are now standing on the springboard for the offensive. You can see to the east the factory buildings on the south side of the canal from which General Horrocks watched the opening of operations by XXX Corps.

* Bold numbers are keyed to Maps 21, 22, and 23.

   Lieutenant Colonel Joe Vandeleur's Irish Guards of the British Guards Armoured Division had established a bridgehead here in the days immediately preceding Market-Garden. In Vandeleur's honor the bridge was called "Joe's Bridge." The current bridge is of postwar construction. After the invasion, the Germans had rebuilt of timber the bridge blown up by the retreating Belgians in 1940.

   Stretching behind on the road over which you just passed, twenty thousand vehicles waited on the day of the attack. At 1435 on 17 September 1944, three hours after the first paratroopers had floated to earth further north, British XXX Corps began the drive up N 15.

Continue north on N 15 toward Eindhoven. Cross the Belgian-Dutch frontier where N 15 becomes N 69. Eight km from the frontier is a British military cemetery (2) on the west side. Park in the slip road to the south.

   The cemetery contains 222 graves. Almost all died in the fighting around Valkenswaard.

As you drive north on N 69 through Valkenswaard, notice the dense vegetation along the road and waterways which severely restricted observation by the British and provided cover for the Germans during the drive northward.

   The XXX Corps got no further than Valkenswaard on D Day. Eindhoven, the first day's objective, lies nine kilometers to the north. On 18 September (D plus 1), the advancing British armor encountered opposition on the outskirts of Eindhoven. Unable to leave the road to maneuver, the tanks stopped in the face of fire from 88-mm guns. After a two-hour delay, a reconnaissance group got behind the defenders and knocked out the guns. Only the large welcoming crowds of Dutch civilians now delayed the advance through the city.

EINDHOVEN

Enter Eindhoven on N 69—Aalsterweg, then Stratumse-dijk. At the swimming pool, zwembaden, turn northwest on P. Czn. Hooftlaan, which shortly becomes Keisersgracht Wal. Once you cross the Dommel River, the town hall, stadhuis, appears to the east. Park in the public lot across the street. Cross the street to the monument (3).

The Dutch artist Paul Gregoire sculpted this "Statue of Liberty." The three figures represent soldier, civilian, and resistance worker. Around the base is a frieze depicting occupation, oppression, and liberation with the words "Remember their dead, their great sacrifice, so that you may live here."

Standing next to the liberation monument is a torch holder which receives the "Freedom Flame" carried from Bayeux every year on 18 September. The holder bears the legend "Unis par l'Amitie" and the coats of arms of Eindhoven and Bayeux. Linkup between the Irish Guards and Colonel Sink's 506th Parachute Infantry, part of Taylor's 101st Airborne, occurred in Eindhoven at 1900, 18 September.

Drive north on Keisersgracht Wal to Emmasingle. Bear north following the signs to the railway station and VVV. Turn east at Mathilde-laan to the large traffic circle—18 September Plein. Go around the circle; bear off to pass under the railroad viaduct. Turn east on Fellennoord at the Holiday Inn, then north on John F. Kennedy Laan toward Nijmegen. Watch for signs to "Airborne Monument." Turn east on Airborne Laan, and then north on Koppele. Park by the school. Walk back to the monument on the east side of the road (4).

At the edge of the garden is a wooden sign commemorating the liberation of Eindhoven on 18 September 1944. The stone

monument in the center bears a map of this section of the Market-Garden corridor.

SON

*Return to John F. Kennedy Laan (N 69) and turn north
toward Son. At the bridge over the Wilhelmina Canal (5),
stop and park on the frontage road just south of the bridge.
Walk to the canal bank.*

The present lift bridge was built in 1983 on the site of the old
one. On Market-Garden D Day 1944, with paratroopers of the
506th within fifty yards, the Germans blew up the bridge—the
only bridge on the corridor within its responsibilities which
the 101st failed to get. Advance units of the Guards Armoured
Division reached the canal by 1900, D plus 1, and they waited
the night through for the engineers to erect a Bailey bridge. At
0645 on 19 September, the Guards began to move northward
once again, hours behind schedule and forty-six miles from Arnhem.

*Drive into Son. At the traffic lights in the town center,
turn west toward Best. In 150 yards, turn north at the lights
onto Europalaan. Park 150 yards further on the west at the
memorial (6).*

This memorial is dedicated to the 101st Airborne Division.
The 506th Parachute Infantry landed two kilometers away and
immediately moved toward the Son bridge. German guns in the
woods and the town impeded their advance for more than two
hours.

BEST

*Turn around and return to the traffic lights. Turn west to-
ward Best. At the sign "Paveljoen Joe Mann," turn south*

through the white concrete arch onto Joe Mann Weg. Turn
west at the small crossroads and park in front of the memo-
rial (7).

The people of Best erected this memorial in honor of Private
First Class Joe E. Mann. On 18 September, the day after the
bridge at Son was blown, 502d paratroopers sought to capture a
bridge over the Wilhelmina Canal at Best, three kilometers to
the west. Mann, heavily bandaged about the arms from wounds
suffered earlier, fell upon a German grenade to prevent injury to
six of his fellows. Private Mann was awarded the Medal of
Honor posthumously.

The memorial represents Mann by a pelican, a symbol of self-
sacrifice in Dutch legend. The figures in bas-relief around the
base depict his valor.

Return to the main road; turn west toward Best.

The wood on both sides of the road is the Zonsche Forest, the
scene of bitter fighting between two battalions of the 502d and
elements of the 59th German Infantry Division.

Continue on to Best, where you should turn south on N 2
toward Eindhoven. Two km brings you to a bridge over the
Wilhelmina Canal (8). Park on the secondary road north of
the canal.

This is not the bridge which stood here in September 1944.
The bridge that a small detachment of Screaming Eagles—H
Company, 502d Regiment—had come to capture was blown up
by the Germans on 18 September. Along the banks of the canal,
several hundred yards east of the bridge, Lieutenant Edward
Wierbowski and his men fought off successive attacks for two
days. Attempts at reinforcement were unsuccessful, and Wierbowski was forced to surrender. He and his men escaped before
the day was out.

Son, Grave, and Heumen

Reverse course and return to Son by way of Best. At the traffic lights in the center of Son, turn north on N 69 toward Nijmegen. Proceed over the bridges seized by the 101st at Sint Oedenrode and Veghel.

The Guards Armoured really got going on this stretch. Urged on by cheering, flag-waving Dutch along the road, the column swept through Uden and reached Grave by 0830, 19 September, where contact was made with the 82d Airborne.

Continue driving north past Grave. After 1 km, turn east near the village of Nederasselt in the direction of Heumen. Stop at the bridge over the Maas River (9). Park on the slip road at the southern end.

This is the Grave bridge, the southernmost objective of the 82d Airborne. By midafternoon, just three hours after the drop, the 2d Battalion of the 504th Parachute Infantry held the bridge.

Proceed over the bridge and through Heumen to the bridge over the Maas–Waal Canal (10). Pull off the road and park near the bridgekeeper's house. Notice that you are now on a small island. Behind the building to the west of the bridgekeeper's house is a footbridge connecting the island to the mainland.

Small-arms fire from the island held up capture of the Heumen bridge until the evening of D Day. Capture of this bridge became vitally important when it was discovered that the main bridge into Nijmegen from the west, seized earlier in the day, had been weakened by demolitions. Only the Heumen bridge could support armor. Soon after nightfall, 504th paratroopers stormed across the footbridge and overwhelmed the German defenders.

Drive over the bridge to the intersection with N 271.

South of here, from the direction of Mook, units of the II German Parachute Corps launched a determined attack on 20 September. General Gavin rushed down from Nijmegen to command the 505th Parachute Infantry and the Coldstream Guards in the successful effort to beat back this threat to the corridor.

Nijmegen

Turn north on N 271 and drive into Nijmegen. In the city N 271 becomes Sint Anna Straat. At the large traffic circle—Keiser Karel Plein—turn east on the large boulevard named Oranje Singel. Watch for signs to VVV and Arnhem. Turn north at the traffic lights onto Van Schevic Havenstraat. On the east side is the main post office (11) distinguished by the tower. Park.

In this building a platoon of the 508th was besieged for two days. On entering the city on D Day late in the evening, the 1st Battalion learned from the Dutch resistance that the detonating mechanism for blowing up the Nijmegen highway bridge was in the post office. Engineers cut wires and destroyed the suspected apparatus. As the platoon made to withdraw, it found itself surrounded. With the aid of Dutch fighters, the platoon held out until relieved on 19 September (D plus 2) by Grenadier Guards.

Turn east at the next intersection on Van Broeckhuysenstraat. At the traffic circle—Hertog Plein—take Derde Walstraat to Sint Joris Straat. Turn west and into the large parking lot on the north side. The Valkhof (12) lies due north and Hunner Park (13) immediately to the east.

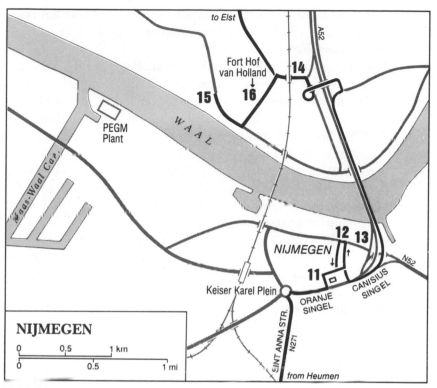

MAP 22

It was in and around the Valkhof and Hunner Park that resistance to the Allied advance was fiercest. The high ground afforded good observation for the self-propelled guns among the trees. German infantry occupied the buildings on the streets approaching the highway bridge. The 505th paratroopers supported by Grenadier tanks finally succeeded in getting to the bridge by advancing through and on top of those buildings and up these fire-raked streets.

At the south end of the park is a monument commemorating the liberation of the city. It is dedicated in particular to Jan van Hoof, a young member of the Dutch resistance, whom the Dutch credit, on inconclusive evidence, with cutting the wires to demolition charges which the Germans tried, and failed, to detonate as British tanks crossed the bridge. Nearby is a circular area surrounded by a small brick wall. It contains a time capsule with information on Operation Market-Garden. Sealed in September 1974, it will be opened in September 2044. To the north stands the Belvedere Tower. Originally part of the old city wall, it is now a restaurant. From the site one gets a fine panorama of the battleground: the approaches to the bridge, the bridge itself, and the Waal River.

Return to your car. Leave the parking lot and make an immediate turn south on Hertogstraat. Drive through the Hertog Plein to the main boulevard, Canisius Singel. Turn east and continue across the bridge. Take the first turn, following the signs to Elst. Stop at the railroad overpass (14).

Sergeant Peter Robinson brought his own and one other Grenadier Guards' tank here after a dash across the bridge at 1830 on 20 September. He was joined later in the day by two other tanks. Under orders to stay put, the tankers waited through the night to continue the drive to Arnhem. Meanwhile Colonel Reuben Tucker, commander of the 504th Parachute Infantry, whose men had forced the crossing of the Waal, fumed at

British tardiness in following up on the seizure of the bridge. Not until 1100 the next morning did Irish Guards tanks begin to move northward.

Drive under the bridge and bear south toward the river. Stop on the road embankment overlooking the river at that point where the power cables cross the river (15).

The Waal is about four hundred yards wide at this point and the current swift. The large building to the south of the river is the PGEM electrical plant. The first bridge to the east is a railway bridge where, after its capture, the Allies found thirty-four machine guns, two 20-mm anti aircraft guns, and one 88-mm dual purpose gun.

Just to the east of the electrical plant, Major Julian Cook's 3d Battalion of the 504th made ready to launch their boats on 20 September. Only twenty-six boats, constructed of plywood and canvas, each nineteen feet long, were available. Behind the paratroopers, thirty British tanks, lined up track to track, and one hundred British and American artillery pieces sent round after round northward. Overhead, Typhoons struck positions along the north bank. At 1500, the 260 men of Companies H and I who made up the first wave ran for the river. Half the boats made the north bank, and only eleven made the return trip.

Once ashore, the American forces dashed across the open field to the embankment. In less than thirty minutes the first German defense line was overwhelmed. The paratroopers then struck east for the Nijmegen bridges.

Reverse course—carefully! Between the previous site and the railway overpass is a lane to the west named Zaligestraat. Turn into the lane and stop at the small wooden bridge which leads into the Fort Hof van Holland (16). *The house beside the bridge is privately owned; you should ask for permission to cross.*

The Dutch built this fort late in the nineteenth century. At the time of Operation Market-Garden, the Germans had mounted 20-mm cannons on and around the walls. Company H, which had made the crossing with Cook, stormed the fort. The paratroopers swam the moat and scaled the walls. In a short time, the surviving defenders, trapped in the central building with the slot-shaped windows, surrendered.

ARNHEM

Return to the crossroads west of the railway overpass and take the road north to Elst.

This is the so-called island highway over which XXX Corps sought to relieve the 1st Airborne in Arnhem. All other routes to Arnhem were too thin-surfaced to support armor. The present main highway north—A 52—was built after the war. In 1944, the road you are now on was even narrower and had ditches on either side.

North of Elst, the Germans established a screen of tanks, artillery, and infantry which effectively barred any further advance by the Irish Guards.

Drive through Elden and then make a turn to the east on Batavierenweg. Proceed to A 52 (Nijmeegseweg). Turn north and cross the John Frost bridge. Turn right at the traffic circle and park. Walk back up the approach ramp to the bridge (17) on the west side of the road.

This is "The Bridge Too Far." The original bridge was built in 1935 and then blown up by the Dutch in the face of the invading Germans in 1940. It was rebuilt by the Germans in 1942. The Germans blew up the bridge in February 1945. The present bridge was constructed on the original plans and opened in 1950.

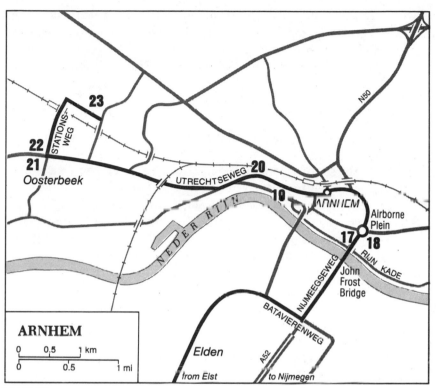

MAP 23

You first pass a plaque commemorating the renaming of the bridge as "John Frost Brug." A little further on by the steps descending from the bridge to the street below is a shelter containing a memorial to the men of Frost's command. The memorial stands on the site of a German pillbox which was put out of action by a flamethrower.

Continue walking to a point over the water's edge.

At the southern end of the bridge were SS Panzer Grenadiers who repulsed two attacks by the Red Devils on the night of D Day. A German armored column, returning from a reconnaissance to the south, attempted to force passage on D plus 1. The bulk of the column got hung up in a hail of gunfire halfway across. The Germans retreated, leaving flaming wrecks behind. Along the southern bank, to the west of the bridge, anti-aircraft guns fired constantly at the British positions on the bridge.

Face north.

The street which runs under the bridge is Rijn Kade. Colonel Frost's men held buildings in the blocks adjacent to the bridge along Rijn Kade as well as buildings to east and west of the grassy embankment sloping away from the approach ramp. The buildings which you now see are almost all of postwar construction. The area around the northern approaches to the bridge was largely devastated in the battle.

The Red Devils held out here for three days. By D plus 2, they were short of everything: men, medical supplies, ammunition, food, and water. Frost's contingent, far fewer than the planned two battalions, suffered appalling casualties. The wounded lay nearly on top of one another in the cellars of the occupied buildings. Bandages taken off the dead were used to bind fresh wounds. Thirst added to the woes of able and disabled alike. Rations ran out, and men scrounged fruit from the cellars of the surrounding homes. It is a testament to the fighting qualities of the 1st British Airborne that they held for as long as they did. As late as the evening of D plus 3, a few still fought on.

Walk down off the bridge and through the tunnel to the center of the traffic circle. This is Airborne Plein (18).

The broken pillar from the Palace of Justice—destroyed during the war—was placed here to memorialize the 1st British Airborne Division.

Return to your car Drive north away from Airborne Plein on Eusebiusbuiten Singel. This road makes an arc around the city center. Follow the signs to the railroad station and VVV office. Go past the station and straight on to Utrechtseweg.

This is the road down which the 3d Parachute Battalion sought to reach the bridge.

At the top of the hill, park on the north side by the PGEM building—No. 68 Utrechtseweg. Walk across the street to the Dutch War Memorial (19).

Below you is the road used by Major Frost and the 2d Battalion to reach the bridge in the evening of 17 September. To the east is the new road bridge and a quarter mile beyond the John Frost bridge. On the other side of the river lies a large brickworks where the Germans had emplaced anti-aircraft guns. These were fired horizontally on British paratroopers seeking to use the lower road after 17 September. Behind you, on the hill beyond the railroad marshaling yards, are houses from which the Germans fired machine guns onto Utrechtseweg.

Walk to No. 72 Utrechtseweg, "Airborne House." On the wall is a commemorative plaque.

Some thirty Red Devils defended this building for two days as part of the effort to reinforce their comrades on the bridge. This is as close to the bridge as the 1st Airborne got along this route.

Return to your car and continue west along Utrechtseweg to St. Elisabeth's Hospital (20) on the north side. Park.

In the main hall of the hospital is a plaque, and another can be seen in one of the wards—ask at the reception desk. St. Elisabeth's and two other Arnhem hospitals treated both British and German wounded during the battle. The houses around the hospital were the scene of bitter fighting between the 1st and 3d Parachute battalions and German units on 18–19 September.

Drive west on Utrechtseweg to Oosterbeek. Follow signs to the Airborne Museum in the old Hartenstein Hotel (21).

The Hartenstein served as headquarters for General Urquhart, commander of the 1st Airborne. In 1977, the Airborne Museum was established in the hotel. Open 1100–1700 weekdays and 1200–1700 on Sunday. Admission charge.

Cross Utrechtseweg in front of the museum to the Airborne Monument (22).

This monument was erected to commemorate the valor and sacrifice of the 1st Airborne.

Return to your car. Turn east toward Arnhem. Follow signs to the British military cemetery—north on Stationsweg over the railway tracks, then east on Van Limburg Stirumweg. Park in the lot adjacent to the Arnhem/Oosterbeek Cemetery (23).

Most of the British airborne dead are buried here. The cemetery contains 1,747 graves, including those of three recipients of the Victoria Cross and three of the nine 1st Airborne battalion commanders.

In heading south to visit other battlefields, you can conveniently stop by a major museum in the southeastern Netherlands. The museum is located in an area, the Peel Marshes, which witnessed combat from 30 September to 3 December 1944. In the battle, Allied forces sought to eliminate a German salient which extended west of the Maas from Wessem in the south to Vortum in the north. In a five-day period, the 7th U.S. Armored Division lost twenty-nine medium tanks and six light tanks in moving two miles from Oploo to Overloon.

Drive south out of Arnhem on A 52 to Nijmegen. In Nijmegen, turn southeast on N 271. Drive south just past Well, where you should turn west across the Maas toward Venray. In 10 km, turn north to Venray and proceed to Overloon, where signs direct you to the museum (24).

The Oorlogsmuseum is open 0900–1900 daily; closed 24–26 and 31 December and New Year's Day. Admission charge.

British commanders confer during Market-Garden. Left to right: General Allan Adair, commander of the Guards Armoured Division, Montgomery; General Brian Horrocks, commander of XXX Corps, and General George Roberts, commander of 11th Armoured Division. (*The Trustees of the Imperial War Museum, London*)

Crowds of Dutch civilians welcome 101st Airborne troops in Eindhoven. (*U.S. Army*)

General Sir Miles Dempsey confers with Brigadier General James Gavin toward the close of Operation Market-Garden. (*U.S. Army*)

A 1st British Airborne patrol moves through the rubble of Arnhem.
(*The Trustees of the Imperial War Museum, London*)

6

The Battle of the Bulge

An Overview

On 16 September 1944, with Allied forces battering at the borders of the Reich, Hitler announced to unbelieving Field Marshals Keitel and Jodl his plan for a bold counterstroke. A great army was to be organized in secret to strike through the Ardennes and across the Meuse to Antwerp—some one hundred miles from the jump-off line along the West Wall. By separating the British armies from the bulk of the Americans and delivering a wounding blow to both, he hoped to create political division between the Allies and to bring them to question the utility of the alliance; perhaps the British might even be brought to withdraw from the Continent. Even if these ambitions were unrealized, Germany would have acquired a strategic port and relieved the mounting pressure on the Ruhr.

Undissuaded by the objections of all in the High Command who learned of the plan—they thought its aims fanciful in light of available resources—Hitler ordered preparations to begin. Several target dates for the attack in late November and early December passed before the mighty host could be organized and moved into place. At last, on the night of 13 December, the German infantry settled into their forward lines, and tanks and artillery crawled forward over roads strewn with straw to

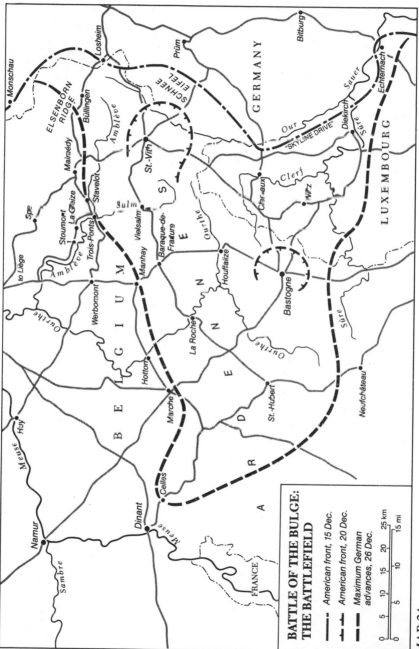

BATTLE OF THE BULGE:
THE BATTLEFIELD

American front, 15 Dec.

American front, 20 Dec.

Maximum German
advances, 26 Dec.

MAP 24

deaden the sound. Overhead, planes flew low to mask any sounds which might be picked up by American listening posts.

Out of these same dark forests, General von Kleist's panzers had pushed to the sea in 1940 on the heels of the retreating French and British armies. Whatever inspiration Hitler may have drawn from the victories initiated here four years before, the force poised at the gateway to Belgium in 1944 was not the juggernaut of 1940. There were far fewer tanks, and the Luftwaffe had lost command of the air. The number of divisions which could be devoted to the attack fell short by at least five of those envisioned in the early planning. The more experienced divisions, moreover, had all been mauled in Normandy and in the retreat across France. The Germans were also short of motor transport, spare parts, ammunition, fuel, and engineering equipment. These shortcomings would tell in the end, but they were far from apparent at the beginning. On 17 December, General Bradley could only ask, "Just where has this sonuvabitch gotten all his strength?"

Hitler had managed to assemble thirteen infantry divisions and seven armored divisions comprising some 200,000 men and 970 tanks and self-propelled guns along a meandering sixty-mile front from Monschau in the north to Echternach in the south. In addition, five infantry divisions and one armored and one mechanized brigade with 450 tanks were in close reserve. This force was organized into three armies.

The Sixth Panzer Army under General Josef "Sepp" Dietrich had five infantry and four SS armored divisions on the right wing. Hitler accorded it the principal role: to cross the Meuse on both sides of Liège and then to turn northwest along the Albert Canal to Antwerp. At the start, the Sixth Panzer Army would attack through the Ardennes between Monschau and Losheim to capture the road junctions at Monschau and Butgenbach and further west at Malmédy and Stavelot. Three infantry divisions were then to take up a blocking position on the northern flank of the advancing armor.

General Hasso von Manteuffel's Fifth Panzer Army occupied the center of the German line. Four of its infantry divisions were to encircle the Schnee Eifel in the north and press on to St.-Vith. In the southern part of its sector the infantry was to seize Our River crossings at Clervaux (Clerf) and other points. These objectives won, the three armored divisions would take the lead in the capture of Bastogne and Houffalize and in the drive beyond to Namur and Dinant on the Meuse.

The Seventh Army, commanded by General Erich Brandenberger, made up the southern wing. These four infantry divisions were to force crossings over the Our and Sauer from Vianden to Echternach. They were to push south as far as Arlon and west to the Meuse in establishing a flank block against counterattack from Patton's Third Army.

The Germans made every effort to conceal the buildup and to deceive the Allies as to their intentions. Not even corps and divisional commanders learned of the offensive until late in November. They, like the Allies, were led to believe that all the activity was aimed at countering an anticipated American offensive east of Aachen. Thus Dietrich, commander of the Sixth Panzer Army, was permitted to stage a noisy buildup to the north for the benefit of Allied intelligence. Only at the last minute was he directed to slip his panzers south to take up the point of the drive through the Ardennes.

The surprise, virtually complete, which the Germans achieved was due in part to the great forests just to the east of the target area—permitting large concentrations of troops and armor away from the spying eyes of reconnaissance planes. In greater part, however, it was due to Allied attitudes about the enemy's intentions and capabilities. Allied commanders believed that German resources were stretched thin and that the rational von Rundstedt, German commander on the Western Front, would husband those resources for defense along the Rhine. None reckoned on the thought processes of the real commander—Hitler.

On the front where the German blow would fall, only a handful of American divisions stood guard. For over two months the Ardennes had been a quiet sector, with only an occasional patrol and exchange of artillery to break the routine. Bradley had deliberately thinned the line to free additional troops for offensives in the north against the Roer dams and in the south against the Saar. To the Ardennes, divisions newly arrived from the States were assigned, and it was here that divisions bloodied in combat retired.

From Monschau south to Losheim, the 99th Division of Major General Gerow's V Corps manned the line. Another V Corps division, the 2d, was in the area but engaged in an attack on the West Wall. Responsibility for the rest of the front lay with Major General Troy Middleton's VIII Corps. Middleton had little more than four divisions with an assigned strength of 68,822. In the north, around Losheim, the 14th Cavalry Group with a few squadrons of tanks held the boundary between VIII and V Corps. The 106th Infantry Division, green as any in the European Theater, had just taken over positions in the Schnee Eifel. Two veteran divisions held the line to the south with Combat Command A of the 9th Armored Division between them. The 28th Infantry of Major General Norman Cota was south of the 106th along a highway dubbed the "Skyline Drive," which paralleled the Our River two miles to the east. Major General Ray Barton's 4th Infantry Division made up the corps right and the First Army's join with the Third Army.

Long before first light on 16 December, some 1,900 German guns opened up on American positions in the Ardennes. Following a bombardment of an hour and a half, German infantry began to emerge out of the dark and fog. The Battle of the Bulge had begun. In the ensuing weeks the mettle of the American soldier would be sorely tried and proved. Initially the defenders engaged a force far larger than their own—three times as large along the whole Ardennes front and up to six times as large at points of concentration. For the first week, and periodically thereafter, overcast skies and fog prevented Allied fighters and bombers from coming to the aid of those on the ground. Throughout the battle the shortness of the day—just eight hours—reduced the opportunities for the Allies to assert their superiority in the air.

It was a battle for infantry, artillery, and tanks. Much of it was fought in half-light and dark. Much of it was also fought in bitter cold and snow. Frostbite and respiratory diseases were common. Those who suffered battle wounds, if unattended, froze to death in half an hour. The snow also served to cast all in high relief—a shooter's gallery of targets. The Germans had come prepared for this; the infantry wore white snow capes. Americans responded by requisitioning Belgian bedsheets for themselves and white-wash for their vehicles.

The woes of the American defenders were further compounded by a special unit of German commandos. In the days just before the great offensive, Hitler directed Lieutenant Colonel Otto Skorzeny, the man who had rescued Mussolini from the Italians, to organize a group of English-speaking troops to infiltrate the American lines in an operation code-named Greif. As finally organized, the 150th Panzer Brigade numbered about 2,000, of whom 150 spoke English. Outfitted in American uniforms and supplied with captured American vehicles, these men sought to capture bridges over the Meuse and to create confusion in the Allied rear. In the first of these tasks, they were unsuccessful. Several jeep teams which had set out on 16 December did reach the Meuse bridges, but they were captured before they could take any action. Other small teams did carry out minor sabotage. The main party of Skorzeny's command, however, was unable to get far forward and entered battle as a unit only once in an abortive attack on Malmédy on 21 December.

The appearance of the masquerading Germans behind American lines did succeed in sowing suspicion among the defenders. In order to distinguish friend from foe, GI's closely queried unknown men as to the identity of Betty Grable's husband, the names of baseball teams, and other Americana. German thoroughness unmasked several commandos. They had been supplied with U.S. identity cards upon which a misprint had been corrected. Even Eisenhower experienced difficulty as a result of Operation Greif. One captured German asserted that the main purpose was to assassinate the Supreme Commander, and for nearly a week Eisenhower was kept at his Paris headquarters under close guard by his zealous security men.

In the north, the infantry of the Sixth Panzer Army fell upon the 99th Infantry Division from Monschau to Losheim. Despite heavy losses, the 99th gave ground grudgingly, while panzer commanders waited impatiently for the way to be cleared. Increased German pressure on 17 December forced Gerow to withdraw the 2d Infantry Division from the West Wall to avoid its encirclement and to backstop the now crumbling 99th. The veteran 2d managed to break off its own attack, cover the retreat of the 99th, and withdraw to positions on Elsenborn ridge.

Unable to break through the eastern front of the 2d and the 99th, the Germans on 19 December shifted their efforts to the southern sector of the Elsenborn defense. North and west of Bullingen they struck the 26th Infantry Regimental Combat Team of the 1st Infantry Division, which had come south in the early morning of the seventeenth. The resolute troops of the "Big Red One" fended off the enemy blows with the aid of artillery on Elsenborn ridge. These batteries fired over ten thousand rounds during an eight-hour period on the twenty-first. By then V Corps commanders had rallied American forces on the naturally strong position afforded by the ridge. There the 2d, 99th, 1st, and 9th Infantry divisions succeeded in jamming the northern shoulder of the growing German salient. In so doing, they denied the Sixth Panzer Army three of the five roads slated to carry the attack to Liège and brought one of the remaining two roads under artillery fire.

On the southern shoulder the German Seventh Army also encountered firm resistance put up by the 4th Infantry Division. At Echternach, Company E, 12th Infantry, held out for five days in a hat factory, where, surrounded, it was finally forced to surrender. In the Parc Hotel in Berdorf, Lieutenant John Leake and sixty men of Company F, 12th Infantry, maintained their position for five days. These and other strong points prevented the enemy from quickly overrunning the American artillery emplaced in the hills to the west of the Our and Sauer rivers. The big guns delayed the German engineers as they sought to bridge the rivers and bring across armor and assault guns. The artillery and the early arrival of Third Army tanks—Combat Command A (CCA), 10th Armored Division, under Brigadier General Edwin Pilburn—did much to mitigate the numerical advantage enjoyed by the German infantry in the first days of the offensive.

To the north, Brandenberger's Seventh German Army had greater success in breaching that section of the American front held by the 109th Infantry of the 28th Division. There, artillery and armor reinforced the push of the German infantry around Vianden. The 109th, forced apart from its sister regiments, fell back to the southwest. It joined the 4th Division, CCA of the 9th Armored, and CCA of the 10th Armored in blocking the southern shoulder. As in the north at Elsenborn ridge, the significance of the riposte to the German left wing lay in constricting the field of operations open to the enemy.

Between the shoulders, German forces pushed forward, although neither as far nor as fast as Hitler had expected. On the northern flank of the Fifth Panzer Army, panzer grenadiers encircled two regiments of the 106th Division in the Schnee Eifel. Promised relief on the ground and resupply by air failed to arrive. Low on ammo, some eight thousand men surrendered late in the afternoon of the nineteenth—the largest single reverse suffered by American arms in the European Theater.

Further south Manteuffel's forces attacked with such violence and in such overwhelming numbers that the 28th Division was split apart. In small units, Colonel Hurley Fuller's 110th Infantry fought to delay the advancing panzers of the 2d Panzer Division and Panzer Lehr. At Clervaux and Wiltz and other road junctions and villages leading to the west, the 110th expended itself as a regiment but exacted a high price from the enemy. In terrain more advantageous to the defense, the 112th Infantry of Colonel Gustin Nelson maintained greater unity and suffered fewer casualties. Under orders to withdraw, the 112th slipped north and west, where it joined in the gathering defense of St.-Vith.

The only deep German penetration achieved early in the offensive occurred at the northern end of the Schnee Eifel. The 1st SS Panzer Division swept away the 14th Cavalry Group in the Losheim Gap. Through this tear in the front, Kampfgruppe Peiper bolted on a drive which, by the evening of 17 December, carried it to Stavelot. Along the way, Peiper and his men left an infamous trail of slaughtered Americans and Belgians: nineteen American POW's at Honsfeld, eight POW's at Ligneuville, eighty-six POW's at the Baugnez crossroads (the Malmédy massacre), and still others later as the *Kampfgruppe* sought an opening to the Meuse—an approximate total of 350 American POW's and 100 unarmed Belgian civilians.

In the first few days the American commanders were uncertain as to the strength and the objectives of the enemy. The destruction of telephone lines in the opening bombardment and German infiltration of the thin defense cut off communications up and down the line and from forward units to command posts in the rear. It was difficult to determine conditions at the front and just where the front was at any particular moment. Both Bradley, 12th Army Group commander, and Hodges, commander of the First Army, initially believed the attack to be local and limited. Eisenhower suspected something larger and ordered on 16 December the first reinforcements in aid of the VIII Corps: the Third Army's 10th Armored Division from south of Luxembourg City to Echternach and Bastogne and the Ninth Army's 7th Armored Division from north of Aachen to St.-Vith.

The next day Eisenhower brought the 82nd and 101st Airborne out of strategic reserve at Reims and rushed them north.

For the next two weeks, the Ardennes would act as a magnet on Allied forces. The divisions which first felt its force were those in the field and thus closest to the battle. It was to them that Eisenhower turned for help needed immediately. On 19 December, he ordered offensive operations north and south of the Ardennes to cease. In order to free Patton's Third Army for action in Belgium, General Devers's 6th Army Group assumed responsibility for most of the Third Army's sector. Simpson's Ninth Army shifted its boundary southward to Aachen to release additional divisions from the First Army. In the days following, the U.S. 11th Armored and 17th Airborne divisions were hurried out of training in the United Kingdom and transported across the Channel. Eisenhower also appealed for the immediate shipment from stateside ports of infantry regiments out of those divisions slated for early embarkation. By the time American forces had contained the German offensive and were ready to retaliate in early January 1945, the U.S. had committed eight armored, sixteen infantry, and two airborne divisions to the battle, with a total of some 335,000 men.

Although the Battle of the Bulge was almost entirely an American battle, the British too became involved. The expanding German salient promised to soon cut off Bradley's headquarters in Luxembourg City from Hodges's headquarters near Liège. Eisenhower decided on 20 December to ease the communications problem and to secure the presence of commanders of equal stature on both flanks by appointing Montgomery to direct operations north of the salient. This reorganization put the U.S. First and Ninth armies under Montgomery's 21 Army Group. Despite some initial hard feelings among American commanders, the division in command worked smoothly.

Montgomery had already moved the XXX British Corps south from Holland on 19 December to take up defense of the Meuse bridges. By the twenty-third, patrols in force were undertaken east of the river. On such a patrol, the 29th British Armored Brigade had a hand in blunting the tip of the salient forged by the 2d Panzer Division just to the east of the Meuse. More significantly, the RAF shared equally throughout the battle in providing tactical support for the ground forces and in pummeling the railheads and supply routes in the German rear.

Once American resistance along the original front had been overcome, German commanders sought to seize the towns of Bastogne and St.-Vith, which sat astride major roads to the Meuse. They got St.-Vith, what was left of it, on 22 December. For five days, the defenders at St.-Vith held a whole German corps at bay. Organized piecemeal by Brigadier General Robert Hasbrouck, they suffered six thousand casualties in their effort to deny the enemy. The greater German numbers finally forced withdrawal. In a running fight, the fourteen thousand survivors of the 7th Armored, Combat Command B of the 9th Armored, the 112th Infantry of the 28th Division, and the 424th Infantry of the 106th Division retreated through a narrow corridor over the Salm River at Salmchâteau and Vielsalm which had been kept open by the 82d Airborne.

To the south, the splintering of the 28th Division along the Skyline Drive had opened the way to Bastogne. The 101st Airborne was on the road, but whether the Screaming Eagles would win the race with the Germans was an open question. First, CCR of the 9th Armored, and then CCB, 10th Armored, fought savage engagements with the advancing enemy columns at roadblocks on the principal roads into the city. Their efforts denied any easy passage to the Germans and permitted the convoy carrying the 101st to slip into Bastogne before dawn on 19 December.

Brigadier General Anthony McAuliffe, temporarily in command in the absence of Maxwell Taylor (on leave in Washington), immediately began preparations for defense. In this he collaborated with Colonel William Roberts, commander of CCB, 10th Armored. The forces at their disposal were the four

regiments of the 101st, the two bloodied combat commands—
CCR (Combat Command Reserve), 9th Armored, and CCB,
10th Armored—and stragglers from various units overrun in the
east who were organized into Team Snafu. On the twentieth, a
small band of tankers from CCB, 4th Armored, arrived from the
south—the last reinforcements, as it turned out, before the Germans closed the ring around Bastogne. In all, the American
force amounted to a reinforced division.

The foe enjoyed a marked superiority in men and armor, although General Heinrich von Luettwitz, commander of the
XLVII Panzer Corps, initially committed only one infantry division to investing Bastogne. On 18–20 December, the 2d
Panzer Division dealt hard, glancing blows against the perimeter and then passed to the north on its way west. Panzer Lehr
stayed on the scene until 21 December, when it circumvented
the city to the south and headed toward the Meuse. In transit
these panzer divisions cut off the Bastogne garrison. The last
opening to VIII Corps—the highway to Neufchâteau—was severed on 21 December. With only limited supplies of ammunition and desperately short of medical personnel and supplies,
the paratroopers and tankers were on their own. These circum-
stances did not induce surrender but only hardened the resolve
of the defenders. "Nuts," said McAuliffe in reply to the German
surrender ultimatum of 22 December.

The 26th Volksgrenadier Division reinforced by several ar
mored teams succeeded in reducing the Bastogne perimeter to a
scant sixteen miles but failed to capture this important road hub.
On 23 December, the skies cleared for the first time since the
offensive began, and Allied fighter-bombers plastered German
concentrations around the city. C-47s also appeared and
dropped much-needed supplies. The 4th Armored lifted the
siege on the twenty-sixth by punching through from the southwest at Assenois. Lieutenant Colonel Creighton Abrams, commander of the 37th Tank Battalion and recipient of the DSC for
his part in the action, shook the hand of a relieved McAuliffe a

little after 5 P.M. Days later the 101st Airborne and CCB, 10th Armored, left the city as the "Battered Bastards of Bastogne"; they had taken in excess of two thousand casualties.

The storied defenders of St.-Vith and Bastogne impeded the German offensive, they did not halt it. Under the lash of Hitler's repeated cry "On to the Meuse," German commanders sought and found gaps in the American line.

Kampfgruppe Peiper, spearhead of the 1st SS Panzer Division, drove between the Elsenborn ridge and St.-Vith and reached Stavelot by the evening of 17 December. This penetration exposed to capture the First Army's map depot at Stavelot, fuel dumps containing three million gallons of gas north of Stavelot and Malmédy, and Hodges's headquarters at Spa. It also threatened a breakthrough to the Meuse, forty miles away. Peiper needed only passage across the Salm to gain the major highway to Huy.

What he got was grief in the valley of the Amblève. North of Stavelot, a company of the 526th Armored Infantry Battalion prevented capture of the fuel dump by erecting a roadblock of flaming jerry cans. At Trois Ponts, the 51st Engineers blew up the bridge over the Salm. Keeping to the Amblève River road, Peiper pressed on to La Gleize, where there was a western exit out of the valley over a secondary road and bridges at Cheneux and Habiémont. The 291st Engineers blew up the bridge at Habiémont. Thwarted in this attempt to break out, the *Kampfgruppe* continued on to Stoumont. By this time, 19 December, American forces were moving to block Peiper's panzers.

The 82d Airborne, assembled at Werbomont, moved up from the southwest. The 30th Infantry Division from the north sent the 117th Regiment to retake Stavelot and the 119th to Stoumont to block further advance westward. A task force from CCB, 3d Armored Division, closed on Stoumont from Spa. Kampfgruppe Peiper was hemmed in and out of gas. Before dawn on 24 December, with the shells of a great 155-mm gun raining down on his lines in La Gleize, Peiper led on foot the eight hundred men who remained out of his original two thousand to the safety of German lines. He left behind all his vehicles, including thirty-nine tanks.

The spearhead broken and the northern shoulder firmly stuck, General von Rundstedt transferred the burden of the main effort from Dietrich's Sixth Panzer Army to the Fifth Panzer Army. Manteuffel's panzers had already burst through the opening between St.-Vith and Bastogne. By 21 December, the 2d and 116th Panzer divisions were poised on the Ourthe, south and west of Houffalize, for a drive to the Meuse. The 2d SS Panzers, at last come forward, were fast closing on Manhay. Most of Panzer Lehr was around Bastogne and threatening St.-Hubert, fifteen miles to the west.

Against this threat, American forces were gathering. On 19 December at a meeting of the High Command in Verdun, Patton had promised a counterattack from the south on the twenty-second. On the appointed day, he delivered. The 4th Armored and 26th Infantry divisions began a drive to relieve encircled Bastogne, and the 80th Infantry Division moved to shore up the block on the German southern shoulder. By Christmas the greater part of two corps—the III and XII—had engaged the Germans. The Third Army had withdrawn in the face of the enemy, made a ninety-degree turn in direction, and moved to the attack—some units as much as 150 miles—with a speed unprecedented in military history. "Drive like hell," Patton had told his commanders.

In the north of the Ardennes, the First Army began to assemble a force for counterattack behind a screen provided by the XVIII Airborne Corps. General Matthew Ridgway's divisions were thinly stretched on a line from Stavelot to Hotton. The western flank was open. German pressure grew intense on both the screen and its open flank. Before General "Lightning Joe" Collins could organize the VII Corps for counterattack, he had a defensive battle on his hands.

On 22 December, the 2d SS Panzer Division began an all-out

push up the Houffalize–Liège highway. Elements of the 3d U.S. Armored and 82d Airborne succeeded in checking this drive, but not before Baraque de Fraiture and Manhay had fallen. So grave was the situation that Ridgway felt constrained to commit CCA of the 7th Armored—recently extricated from St.-Vith— and Collins to commit the 75th Infantry Division—recently arrived on the Continent.

A few miles to the west, the 116th Panzers attacked at Hotton and Marche. The 84th Infantry Division, just settled into the line, bore the major burden for meeting the enemy there, with the 3d Armored lending a hand. The 51st Engineers, also on the scene, distinguished themselves again by denying the foe the bridge over the Ourthe at Hotton.

Nowhere was the German threat greater, however, than south and west of Marche. The 2d Panzer Division glanced off the right flank of the 84th and advanced on the Meuse. It got as far as Celles by 24 December, just four miles from the river city of Dinant. There the tanks, out of fuel, ground to a halt. Before the 2d Panzer supply trains could get forward or Panzer Lehr, coming up from St.-Hubert, could reinforce, Collins threw his last division against the German spearhead.

By 27 December, the 2d "Hell on Wheels" Armored Division had chewed up the 2d Panzers at Celles, the 84th Division had repelled the 116th Panzers before Marche, and the 517th Parachute Infantry had retaken Manhay. Throughout this period, from 23 December forward, clear skies had permitted Allied air power, in close support of the troops on the ground, to make a significant contribution. Allied fighter-bombers did much to thwart the efforts of Panzer Lehr and the 9th SS Panzer Division to aid the 2d Panzers in their hour of trial in the Celles pocket.

Much savage fighting remained, but the Germans had lost the initiative. General von Manteuffel made one last desperate attempt to take Bastogne on 30 December. His forces met head-on a Third Army offensive. After a four-day fight, the Fifth Panzer Army had to settle for stalemate.

On 3 January 1945, the VII Corps launched its counteroffen-

sive from the north and Patton renewed his attack out of Bastogne. Advance patrols of the First and Third armies met at
Houffalize on 16 January. The rejoining of the American armies
failed to trap significant German forces west of the Ourthe. The
turn of the year had brought bad weather, which kept Allied
planes at their bases and impeded movement on the ground.
The Germans also demonstrated once again their ingenuity in
exploiting the terrain in defense. Consequently, they were able
to effect their escape with most of what they had brought with
them—save for what had been destroyed in combat or abandoned for want of fuel.

American forces fought their way back through Wiltz and
Clervaux to Echternach and the Skyline Drive, back through
St.-Vith and Rocherath to the Schnee Eifel. By 28 January, the
positions occupied at the beginning of the German offensive
were retaken, marking the end of the greatest pitched battle in
the history of American arms.

The losses on both sides were staggering. In matériel, each
had lost as many as eight hundred tanks and the Germans a
thousand aircraft. American casualties numbered upwards of
80,000, including 19,000 dead and 15,000 captured. The British
had 1,400 casualties including some two hundred dead. The
Germans suffered some 100,000 total casualties.

The Battle of the Bulge had cost the German dearly. He could
not make good his human or matériel losses. He had failed completely to gain his ultimate objective of Antwerp or even his in-
termediate objective of the Meuse. He had succeeded at best in
imposing a delay of six weeks on Allied offensives in the West
but at the expense of the collapse of the German armies in the
face of the oncoming Russians.

Tour of the Battle of the Bulge

This tour begins at an American military cemetery near Liège
and ends at another American cemetery near Luxembourg City;
it covers a distance of some 320 kilometers. The tour visits

many of the principal sites associated with the Battle of the Bulge and, incidentally, traverses some of the most beautiful countryside in all of Europe. The high, heavily wooded ridges, the narrow valleys, and the many rivers are reminiscent of the Appalachians. It was this likeness which inspired the GI's in 1944 to call one road—N 7—the "Skyline Drive."

The first part of the tour follows, in reverse, the trail of Kampfgruppe Peiper in the Amblève River valley. This route also marks the northern edge of the German salient. At Bullingen, you will leave Peiper's trail to visit Elsenborn ridge just a few kilometers to the north. The tour then goes south on N 27 and N 7 along the center of the American front in the first days of the offensive. St.-Vith and Clervaux are the principal sites in this sector. Clervaux would be a good place to stop for the night, as the setting is delightful and hotels and restaurants are plentiful.

From Clervaux, the tour cuts back to the west along roads used by German armor in their advance to Bastogne. On the eastern edge of Bastogne are the Mardasson Memorial and the Bastogne Historical Center. These sites are, respectively, the major memorial to those who died in the Battle of the Bulge and the major museum of the battle. There is much else to be seen here, and you should allow the greater part of a day to cover the ground. You will then travel southeast on N 34, N 15, and N 7 to Luxembourg City, with stops on the way at Wiltz and Ettelbruck.

Liege to Werbomont

From Liège take N 35 south for 16 km to Neuville-en-Condroz (1).* Watch for signs to the American military cemetery, which lies north of the road.

* Bold numbers are keyed to Maps 25, 26, and 27.

239

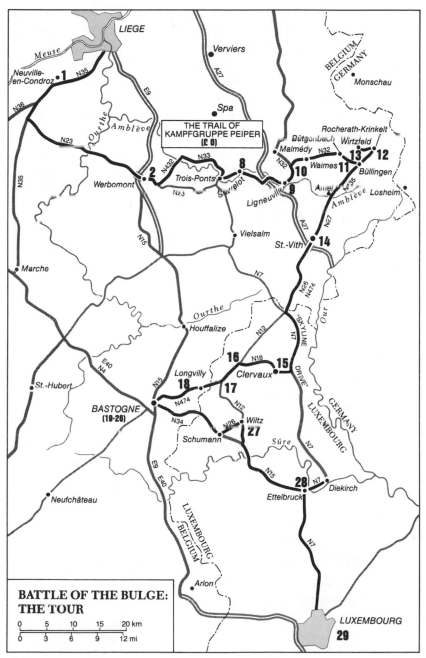

**BATTLE OF THE BULGE:
THE TOUR**

0   5   10   15   20 km
0   3   6   9   12 mi

MAP 25

This cemetery contains the graves of 5,326 dead, many of whom fell in the Battle of the Bulge. In the interior of the memorial are large maps describing American military operations in Europe. The map on the south wall over the entrance door is devoted to the Ardennes and Rhineland campaigns.

Another American military cemetery lies 30 kilometers east of Liège near the village of Henri-Chapelle. It can be reached by taking N 3 east from Liège to Henri-Chapelle.

Continue south on N 35 for 10 km. At the intersection with N 23 turn southeast for 30 km to Werbomont (2).

This town was headquarters for the 82d Airborne during the battle. Initially slated for Bastogne, the 82d was diverted to Werbomont to meet the threat posed by Kampfgruppe Peiper. General Gavin dispatched Colonel Reuben Tucker's 504th Parachute Infantry to the northeast to deny Peiper an exit out of the Amblève valley.

KAMPFGRUPPE PEIPER IN THE AMBLÈVE VALLEY

Go east out of Werbomont on N 23 toward Trois Ponts. At the foot of the long hill, pull off and park at the intersection with N 432 near Habiémont. Walk east along N 23 to Lienne Creek (3).

The 291st Engineers blew up the bridge over Lienne Creek which stood on this spot and thereby blocked further progress by German tanks, which had moved south from La Gleize on the road through Rahiers. On their return to La Gleize, the panzers were ambushed by 504th paratroopers.

Drive north on N 432 toward Targnon. Cross the Amblève to the intersection with N 33 and turn west toward Remouchamps. Go through Stoumont Station and stop after 1 km (4).

241

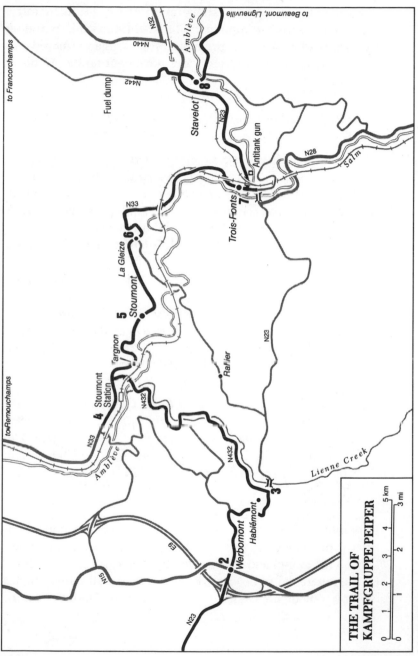

THE TRAIL OF
KAMPFGRUPPE PEIPER

0   1   2   3   4   5 km
0   1   2   3 mi

MAP 26

At about this point the 1st Battalion of the 119th Infantry, 30th Division, and a company of the 740th Tank Battalion erected a roadblock which prevented the German armored column from making further westward movement on the Amblève River road.

Reverse course and go east on N 33 to Stoumont (5).

Stoumont was the scene of intense fighting for three days, 19–21 December. The Germans captured the town in an attack initiated at first light on 19 December. The 3d Battalion, 119th Infantry, which bore the brunt of the fighting, lost 267 men. A task force from CCB, 3d Armored Division, moved down the Stoumont–Spa road to join the 119th Infantry in an effort to retake the town on 21 December.

The fighting centered around St. Edouard's Sanitorium, which lies north of the road (closed to the public). The sanitorium was all but destroyed; the present buildings are of postwar construction. While the battle raged above, three clerics sought to calm two hundred terrified children and old people who had taken refuge in the cellar.

Proceed east from Stoumont to La Gleize (6). Turn south on the road toward Rahier. Watch for signs to La Gleize Museum. Park in the square in front of the post office. The museum is located in the café Echo des Campagnes. The King Tiger tank parked on the side of the square was a casualty of the La Gleize battle.

Kampfgruppe Peiper, spearhead of the SS forces upon which Hitler had pinned his greatest hopes, came to an end in La Gleize. Out of fuel and surrounded by American forces, Peiper and the remainder of his command abandoned all their vehicles and stole out of La Gleize on 24 December. Under cover of darkness, they slipped through the lines of the 505th Parachute Infantry south of Trois Ponts.

> *Return to N 33. Turn east and proceed to Trois Ponts (7). Upon entering Trois Ponts, you will first cross the Amblève. Continue straight on. Turn west on N 23 toward Werbomont. Cross the Salm River bridge and park. Walk to the riverbank. Notice that the Salm, like the Amblève, is neither broad nor deep. The steep banks, however, bar passage to tanks.*

The bridges at Trois Ponts give access to the main highway—N 20—running west to the Meuse through Werbomont. Company C, 51st Combat Engineers, under Major Robert Yates occupied the town about midnight, 17 December, with orders to deny Peiper the bridges.

> *Reverse course. Drive back across the Salm and the Amblève and turn east on N 23 toward Stavelot. Go under the railway viaduct and park on the south side of the road next to the café.*

It was here that Yates posted a 57-mm anti-tank gun from the 526th Armored Infantry which had been abandoned in transit to Stavelot. As the engineers hastily completed demolition work on the bridges, the gun crew faced German tanks coming down the Stavelot road. This crew managed to hold up temporarily the German attack with a hit on the leading Panther. The short delay proved long enough. The members of the gun crew, McCollum, Hollenbeck, Buchanan, and Higgins, paid with their lives, but Peiper, once he had cleared the viaduct, had the bridges blown in his face. He had no choice but to turn north to La Gleize.

Renewed fighting occurred at Trois Ponts on 21 December when the 1st SS Panzers sought to reinforce Kampfgruppe

Peiper. The 2d Battalion, 505th Parachute Infantry, from positions west of the Salm successfully beat back this effort.

Proceed east on N 23 to Stavelot (8). Take N 422 north toward Francorchamps. Stop 1.5 km out of Stavelot.

Along this road lay a huge fuel dump containing thousands of gallons of gasoline in five-gallon jerry cans stacked for five miles. Major Paul Solis, commanding a reinforced company of the 526th Armored Infantry Battalion, was unable to prevent Peiper from taking Stavelot. With the Germans nipping at their heels, the American defenders withdrew up the hill. Lest the Germans capture the fuel which they so much needed, Solis created a roadblock of burning gasoline cans. Some 124,000 gallons were consumed before the fire was extinguished upon the arrival of reinforcements from the north.

Return to Stavelot and take the road south toward Ligneuville via Beaumont. Cross the Amblève at Stavelot and park.

The bridge over which you just passed was built in 1955. The old bridge which stood on the same spot could support the great weight of a King Tiger—sixty-five tons. Peiper had forty-two in his *Kampfgruppe.* Although wired for demolition by 291st Engineers, the bridge failed to blow upon the approach of German tanks in the early morning of 18 December. Leaving behind part of his force to hold Stavelot, Peiper struck out for Trois Ponts. The German occupiers were unable to fend off the counterattack of the 30th Division. The Germans withdrew across the Amblève. The 117th Infantry then blew up the bridge, which served to cut off Peiper's supply line from the east.

Continue on toward Ligneuville. Notice that between Stavelot and Beaumont old houses and farm buildings bear

shell marks on the east side. As the German tanks passed
these buildings, they fired for effect. In Ligneuville (9), park
in front of the Hôtel du Moulin on the west side of the road.
Just to the north of the hotel is a memorial to eight Ameri-
cans shot down behind the hotel.

Peiper's column intercepted here the tail of a supply train of
Combat Command B, 9th Armored, on its way to St. Vith. A
lone Sherman undergoing repair in front of the hotel briefly delayed the German tanks. The Sherman was soon dispatched, and
the American truckers who had been eating lunch in the hotel
were captured. Infuriated by the delay, the Germans shot their
prisoners.

Take N 23 north out of Ligneuville to the intersection
with N 32 (10). Park behind the Café du Monument in front
of the small museum.

This is the Baugnez crossroads and site of the Malmédy Massacre. The Café du Monument is the former Café Bodarwé,
which was rebuilt after the war. The massacre occurred in the
field south of the café. Across the road is the memorial erected
by the Belgian government to commemorate the dead. On the
stone wall are mounted individual plaques with the names of
eighty-four men.

On Sunday, 17 December, Battery B, 285th Field Artillery
Observation Battalion, left Malmédy on its way to St.-Vith to
join the 7th Armored. It had just cleared the crossroads heading
south on N 23 when halted by fire from a German tank column
traveling north on a parallel secondary road to the east. Lieutenant Virgil Lary and his men leapt from their trucks and dove
into the ditch on the west side of the road. The Germans
stormed across the field and soon forced the surrender of the
lightly armed Americans. Approximately 120 men were lined up
in eight rows in the field. While the main body of the German

column moved on to Ligneuville, two Mark IV tanks pulled out and opened up with their machine guns on the POW's. Eighty-six died.

When all but a few German guards had departed, the survivors—most wounded, including Lieutenant Lary—escaped north through the woods. By late afternoon, in twos and threes, these men stumbled into the roadblocks manned by the 291st Engineers south of Malmédy. News of the massacre reached First Army headquarters by 1630 and was soon circulated among American forces. Outrage at the event spurred even more intense efforts to stem the German tide.

ELSENBORN RIDGE

Drive north on N 32 through Waimes and Butgenbach. At the crossroads 3 km east of Butgenbach is a monument to the 1st Infantry Division (11).

The hills to the north of N 32 from Waimes to Bullingen constituted the southern face of the Elsenborn defense. The 16th Regiment, 1st Division, was dug in around Waimes and the 26th around Butgenbach. Both regiments saw considerable action in repelling attacks on 19–22 December.

Continue on N 32 east to Bullingen. Turn north on N 435 toward Rocherath and Krinkelt.

Kampfgruppe Peiper captured Bullingen in the morning of 17 December. Instead of turning north behind the 99th and 2d divisions, Peiper, with other fish to fry, headed west. In turning north, then, on N 435, you leave Peiper's trail.

Stop in Rocherath and Krinkelt (12).

These two villages lay some four miles behind the center of the 99th Division's front at the beginning of the German offensive. As that front crumbled under the sheer weight of the advancing Sixth Panzer Army, Rocherath and Krinkelt took on new significance. Here, Major General Walter Robertson, commander of the 2d Division, anchored a temporary line of defense behind which the engineers of V Corps could prepare Elsenborn ridge as a block to the German right wing and through which the shattered regiments of the 99th could pass to the comparative safety of the ridge.

Turn east down the narrow lane opposite the church. Drive across the valley and up the hill.

On this ridge the 1st Battalion, 9th Infantry, under Lieutenant Colonel William McKinley, grandnephew of the former president, met a determined assault late in the evening of 17 December. The battalion repulsed this and every other thrown at it. When McKinley finally withdrew from his forward position after a six-hour fight the next day, there were just 240 men left of the original battalion.

Return to the villages.

In and around the villages, the 2d Division battled units of four German divisions, including the 12th SS Panzer. American infantrymen stalked German tanks with bazookas in the fog-shrouded streets and met the oncoming infantry with knife and rifle butt. The Shermans, no match for the Tigers and Panthers in frontal attack, waited in the lee of a building or hedgerow for a shot from side or rear. Back and forth went the fight, hedgerow to hedgerow, building to building—some men captured, rescued, and captured again. The 38th Infantry alone suffered 625 casualties.

Drive south on N 435. Watch for signs to Wirtzfeld and Elsenborn. Turn west on the road to Wirtzfeld and proceed up the hill to the top. Stop (13).

The road over which you have just driven was that used by the 99th and 2d divisions to reach Elsenborn ridge—your present location. In 1944, the road was little more than a muddy track. Throughout the fighting of 17–19 December, the artillery on the ridge fired almost non-stop to put up a curtain of steel in front of Rocherath and Krinkelt. Nevertheless, enough German tanks and infantry penetrated the curtain to make things hot. When the last of the 99th had filtered through 2d Division lines and all was ready on the ridge, the men of the 2d withdrew from the twin villages in the evening of 19 December.

St.-Vith

Return to Rocherath and Krinkelt; turn south on N 435 to Bullingen. Continue on N 435 to Amel, where N 435 joins N 27. Take N 27 south toward St.-Vith. About 7.5 km south of Amel, you cross the front lines of CCB, 7th Armored, on 19 December—part of the St.-Vith defense. Proceed to St.-Vith (14). At the main crossroads in St.-Vith, N 27/N 26, look for signs to the American memorial. Turn west on the local road for a short distance. The memorial is on the north side of the road.

In 1959, the 106th Infantry Division erected this memorial to those of the division who died in the Battle of the Bulge.

Reverse course. On your return to the crossroads, notice the large stone building on the south, St. Joseph's Kloster.

On this site stood the building in which Major General Alan Jones, commander of the 106th, had established his headquarters in early December 1944. It also served as headquarters for Brigadier General Bruce Clarke when Jones turned over the defense of St.-Vith to him on 17 December.

At the crossroads, take N 26 east about 4 km.

On this hill, Lieutenant Thomas Riggs, an ex-football star at the University of Illinois, and about five hundred men of the 81st and 168th Combat Engineers repulsed the first probing thrusts of the Germans on 17 December.

Look back toward St.-Vith.

St.-Vith lay about twelve miles behind the front of 16 December. Although German planning placed the town on an axis of advance, the block erected at Elsenborn ridge changed matters. The few northern roads available to the Germans were so congested that whole divisions were unable to get forward. Control of the road net at St.-Vith became critical.

Return to St.-Vith. Take N 26/N 474 south to the intersection with N 7. Turn south on N 7 toward Diekirch.

You are now traveling along the front occupied by "Dutch" Cota's 28th Division. The men of the division dubbed this road connecting St.-Vith and Diekirch the "Skyline Drive." During the day they occupied outposts on the Our River a few miles to the east. At night they withdrew to lines higher on the ridge closer to the road.

CLERVAUX

At N 18 turn west toward Marnach and Clervaux.

Eight kilometers east of the N 7/N 18 intersection is a bridge over the Our. On 16 December, the Germans put the greater part of two infantry divisions across and, on the following day, the tanks of the 2d Panzer Division. This force hit the 110th Regiment. A reinforced Company B, 1st Battalion, defended the intersection but was eventually forced back on Marnach. Company B held on here throughout the sixteenth—its last communication received at regimental headquarters about dusk. The fight left Marnach a smoking ruin.

> *Continue on to Clervaux (15). You come into town on the south side. The town is dominated by a ridge running east to west. At the eastern end of the ridge is a château below which is a public parking lot on the south side. Use the stairs at the eastern end of the parking lot—away from the church—to enter the château.*

Mounted on the south foundation wall of the château is a memorial plaque to all who died in the Second World War.

> *From the courtyard of the château, look south. The Marnach road—N 18, down which you just drove—can be seen winding its way up the bluff.*

In late morning of 17 December, the 110th Infantry headquarters company of clerks, cooks, and MP's watched as German tanks slowly negotiated the sharp turns. The château's defenders were already under small-arms fire from German infantry who had gained the town's edge earlier in the day. The arrival of the tanks made the fall of Clervaux just a matter of time. Colonel Hurley Fuller, commander of the 110th, had appealed to division for reinforcements. There were none. Cota, with his eye on the security of Bastogne, had told Fuller to stay put: "Nobody comes back."

In the château is the Battle of the Bulge Museum, open 1000-1700 daily. Admission charge.

> *Descend from the château through the parking lot. Walk south one block to the Place de la Libération. In this square is a statue of an American infantryman in full battle*

*dress dedicated to "Our Liberators." Walk back toward the
château to the pedestrian mall. Follow the mall to the
Grand rue north of the château. Continue straight on along
rue de la Gare. On the south side of the road is the Claravallis Hôtel and, a little beyond, the northern bridge into
Clervaux.*

Fuller had his command post in the Claravallis Hôtel. With
German tanks on the street outside and enemy infantry on the
floors below, Fuller and twelve others went out a third-floor
window onto a narrow ladder to the cliff behind the hotel. They
clambered up steps cut into the cliff wall to the top. Compass in
one hand and the hand of a blinded soldier in the other, Fuller
set off to the west. He never made it; he and his fellows were
captured. Few men of the 110th escaped the onslaught. The regiment took some 2,750 casualties in those first few days in Clervaux and the surrounding hills and villages.

CLERVAUX TO BASTOGNE

Take N 18 out of Clervaux toward Wiltz and Bastogne.

This is the road taken by the 2d Panzer Division on the morning of 18 December.

*Eight km out of Clervaux stop at the intersection with
N 12/N 474 (16).*

Here the German column struck an American roadblock. In
an uneven fight, Task Force Rose was pushed aside, and the
panzers ground their way onto the St.-Vith–Bastogne road.

*Turn southwest on N 12/N 474 toward Bastogne. In 6 km
the road divides. N 12, up which Panzer Lehr toiled,*

branches off to the south into the Wiltz valley, and N 474
continues on to the southwest. Stop **(17)**.

At this point Lieutenant Colonel Ralph Harper established
the second of the CCR, 9th Armored, roadblocks. In a night attack, the Mark IVs and Panthers of the 2d Panzers overran Task
Force Harper. Pursued by tanks and infantry, the remnants of
the two American task forces—they had lost forty tanks—retreated to Longvilly.

Continue on N 474 toward Bastogne.

At the turnoff to Bourcy—N 477 north—the bulk of the 2d
Panzer Division broke off the pursuit to skirt Bastogne to the
north.

Just under 1 km west of Longvilly, stop at the religious
shrine on the south side of the road **(18)**.

Between Longvilly and Mageret occurred the third and fiercest firefight in the German advance on Bastogne. The action
centered on this shrine, the Grotto of St. Michael. The night of
18 December found the headquarters company of CCR, 9th Armored, the surviving men and vehicles of the two task forces,
and a handful of infantry from the 110th Regiment clustered
around Longvilly. These units sought to lend support to the 58th
and 73d Field Artillery battalions in positions close to Longvilly.
By midnight, the artillerymen were laying on targets a scant two
hundred yards to the front.

Earlier in the evening an armored team under Lieutenant
Colonel Henry Cherry had started up the Bastogne road. The
advance units of Team Cherry, CCB, 10th Armored, stopped at
St. Michael's Grotto. Several hours after the American armor
had cleared to the east, Panzer Lehr, closing from the south,
seized Margaret.

During the night, in a dense fog which would persist into the next day, American and German commanders sought to dispose their forces for the battle of the next day. About 0800, CCR began a withdrawal toward Bastogne. As the head of the column neared the German roadblock at Margaret, the Germans unleashed their attack from every direction. They shattered the line of men and vehicles along the road. Tanks, self-propelled guns, armored cars, trucks, and jeeps—two hundred in all—were destroyed or captured. It was not an entirely one-sided fight. Team Cherry acquitted itself so well that the 2d Panzer Division commander reported a counterattack on his flank.

BASTOGNE

Continue on N 474 into Bastogne. Watch for signs to Mardasson at the eastern edge of the city. Turn northeast to Mardasson Memorial (10) and the Bastogne Historical Center (20).

The Mardasson Memorial commemorates the American dead of the Battle of the Bulge. This large edifice of white marble in the shape of a five-pointed star was dedicated in 1950. On top of the memorial at the tip of each point of the star is an orientation table.

Adjacent to the memorial is the Bastogne Historical Center—also known as the "Nuts" Museum. Open 0800–1900 in summer and the rest of the year 0900–1800; closed from mid-November to mid-March. Admission charge.

Return to the main road and turn west into Bastogne. You are now on the Grand Rue. At the large church, turn north, cross the railway overpass, and bear northwest onto Rue de la Roche. Pull off the road at the complex of red brick buildings across from the cemetery (21).

MAP 27

This is Caserne Heintz, the Belgian barracks where General McAuliffe maintained 101st Airborne divisional headquarters throughout the battle. The barracks is still used by the Belgian military and is not open to the public.

Return to the Grand Rue; turn west. Proceed to the traffic lights at the large square with the tank parked at the corner. Take the road to Assenois to the south for 2 km. Watch for the concrete pillbox on the east side of the road. Stop (22).

Late in the afternoon of 26 December, with night already falling, Lieutenant Charles Boggess at the head of a column of eight Sherman tanks approached this pillbox from the south. Three direct hits—still visible—from Boggess's tank killed the defenders. A hundred yards to the north Boggess made contact with an outpost of the 101st Airborne. For six days the Germans had encircled Bastogne. Boggess, followed by others of the 4th Armored, had forged a narrow corridor into the city. Although Bastogne would remain under siege until 12 January 1945, the Germans were never able to close the corridor.

Return to the main square in Bastogne and park (23).

The Bastogne square is named Place General McAuliffe in honor of the 101st's commander during the fighting. The tank at the southwest corner is a Sherman M 4 knocked out in a nearby engagement. It mounts a short-barrel 75-mm gun. Worth noting are the "grousers" attached to the tank tread, which gave a wider footprint and therefore greater flotation than the standard width, and the 50-mm machine gun mounted on the turret. The latter feature is rare among surviving examples of the M-4.

Staying on the west side of the square, walk north out of the square to the rue de Marche. In the middle of the block on the east side is the Hôtel Lebrun (24).

This hotel was headquarters for Colonel William Roberts, commander of CCB, 10th Armored. Roberts came under McAuliffe's command soon after the arrival of the 101st in Bastogne. Because of Roberts's special knowledge of armor, he played a significant role in the defense of Bastogne. Across the street is the garage where stragglers from units broken in the east were organized into Team Snafu.

> *Walk back to the tank. Cross the street and go down the Rue de Neufchâteau. In the middle of the block on the south side is a private museum (25). Admission charge.*
>
> *Retrieve your car. Drive southeast on the road to Arlon for two blocks. On the west side, beside a large parking lot, is a memorial to General George Patton (26).*

WILTZ

> *From the Arlon road, turn southeast onto the road to Wiltz—N 34. In 15 km, at Schumann, turn northeast on N 26 to Wiltz (27). Drive to the upper town.*

On the Grand Rue—N 12 to Ettelbruck—at the Place du Festival is the Museum of the Battle of the Bulge. Open 1000–1200 and 1300–1700 daily. Admission charge.

Major General Norman Cota's 28th Division headquarters was in Wiltz at the start of the offensive. From crossings at Vianden and other sites on the Our, Panzer Lehr and several infantry divisions struck for Wiltz. By midnight, 19 December, the Germans had captured the town. A little over a month later, on 21 January, the 26th U.S. Division reoccupied Wiltz, which brought the emergence of several GI's from the cellars where they had been hidden by friendly Luxembourgers.

ETTELBRUCK

Proceed on N 12 south out of Wiltz. At the intersection with N 15 turn south to Ettelbruck. In Ettelbruck (28), take N 7 toward Diekirch.

At the east edge of Ettelbruck, on the north side of the road, is a statue of Patton and a Sherman tank. There is also a memorial plaque to the general donated by his son, then Captain George S. Patton.

Reverse course; take N 7 west and south to Luxembourg City.

On 19 December, the 109th Infantry, 28th Division, withdrew from its positions along the Skyline Drive to the hills south of Ettelbruck. Units of the Seventh German Army occupied the city, but not for long. By Christmas Day, the 80th U.S. Division, as part of Patton's counteroffensive, was in Ettelbruck.

LUXEMBOURG CITY

In Luxembourg City, leave N 7 on N 2 to the east. Follow the signs to the airport. Watch for signs to the American military cemetery south of the airport (29).

Here lie buried 5,076 Americans, many of whom were casualties of the Ardennes fighting. At the head of the graves site is a chapel and two rectangular pylons. The pylons are faced with operations maps. Between the flagpoles overlooking the graves site is the grave of General George S. Patton, Jr. Originally Patton was buried among the other men. However, the numbers of people who came to visit his grave were so great that the surrounding grass was killed. The present site paved in front with stone solved the problem.

A German plane above Francorchamps provokes a response from 30th Division troopers. (*U.S. Army*)

75th Division infantrymen march through Bussorville, Belgium, on the tail of armor. (*U.S. Army*)

Patrols from the 84th Division, First Army, and 11th Armored, Third Army, meet near Houffalize to close the bulge. (*U.S. Army*)

Infantrymen of the 3d Armored Division advance under enemy fire in a small village near Houffalize, Belgium. (*U.S. Army*)

262

A congested street in Bastogne after the siege. (*U.S. Army*)

7

Through the West Wall to the Rhine

Aachen and the Huertgen Forest: An Overview

In its first 1945 issue, *Life* magazine compared the battle then being fought in the dark recesses of the Huertgen Forest with the American army's earlier battles in the Wilderness and the Argonne. As in those earlier fights, American soldiers were again learning how difficult it was to press the offense where wooded terrain favored the defense. Ernest Hemingway, who witnessed some of the fighting with Colonel Charles T. "Buck" Lanham's 22d Infantry, called it a "Passchendaele with tree bursts." By all accounts, it was one of the bitterest ordeals experienced by American fighting men in the campaign.

Before the almost three-month-long battle had run its tragic course, the Huertgen Forest had consumed five of the First Army's finest infantry divisions—the 1st, 4th, 8th, 9th, and 28th. Other units, including the 2d Ranger Battalion, Combat Command Reserve of the 5th Armored Division, and assorted smaller groups, were also ruined by the forest fighting. Of the 120,000 Americans who fought there, 33,000 became casualties. With those lives we bought a few kilometers of dense evergreen forest and 30,000 German casualties. It was a battle that should never have been fought.

Lieutenant General Courtney H. Hodges's First Army approached the West Wall across from the Aachen corridor because of Eisenhower's earlier insistence that it should swing north of the Ardennes Forest to support Montgomery's 21 Army Group in its drive through the Low Countries. The First Army's three corps reached the German border on a broad front without the offensive punch necessary to exploit their initial penetrations. As the battle to capture Aachen and open the way to the Rhine developed, Hodges believed that it was necessary to commit divisions piecemeal into the Huertgen area to protect his right flank. Almost totally ignored for months was the only strategic objective in the forest worth fighting for—the dams on the Roer River, which could flood the river downstream, thereby delaying any advance to the Rhine.

The first American unit to be committed to battle in the wooded area south of Aachen was the 9th Division. Ordered initially to cover the right flank of the VII Corps' advance through the Stolberg corridor south of Aachen, the 9th's battle soon took on a life of its own. Throughout the remainder of September and half of October the 39th and 60th regiments slugged it out against the German 89th and 12th Infantry divisions along the two ridge lines running northeast from Monschau. By mid-October, the 47th Infantry held Schevenhuette in the north, while the other two regiments had spent themselves. Casualties ran to some 4,500 men.

While the battle in the Huertgen Forest continued in this deadly and inconclusive fashion, the American High Command decided that the time was ripe to move on Aachen. Their plan called for the 30th Division (XIX Corps) to encircle the city from the north, while the 1st Division pushed north out of the Stolberg corridor. Once isolated, opposition in the city could then be systematically eliminated.

Although Bradley and Hodges did not know it at the time, Aachen had been theirs for the taking in September when the commander of the 116th Panzer Division garrisoning the city had been ready to surrender it without a fight. That commander

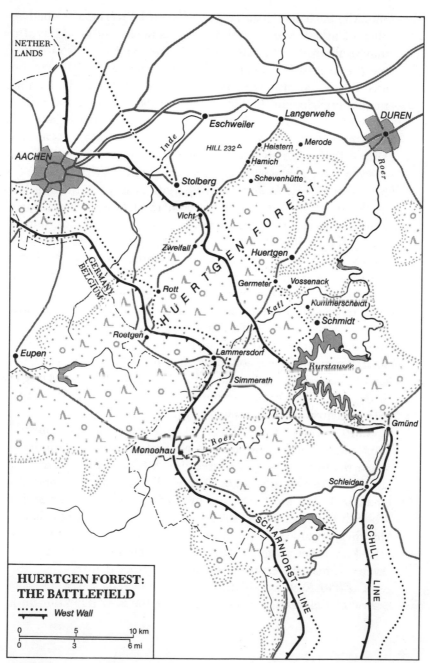

HUERTGEN FOREST:
THE BATTLEFIELD

········· West Wall

0 ——— 5 ——— 10 km
0 ——— 3 ——— 6 mi

MAP 28

was Major General Gerhard Graf von Schwerin, who had refused to attack with his 116th Panzers at the outset of the Mortain counteroffensive. He had been relieved of his command, then restored a few weeks later. His bizarre actions in October again cost him his command and a reprimand, but he escaped further punishment. Besides the 116th Panzers, first withdrawn, then returned to the city, Aachen's defense fell to the 246th Volksgrenadier Division, commanded by Colonel Gerhard Wilck. Hitler had given orders that Aachen, the probable birthplace of Charlemagne, founder of the First Reich, was to be defended at all cost. Wilck was prepared to carry out those orders.

The ring around Aachen closed on 16 October, when a patrol from the 30th Division reached the 1st Division's positions on Ravelsberg Hill east of the city. Throughout six days of fierce street fighting (with Germans counterattacking American squads from the sewer system), GI's of the 26th Infantry fought their way across the ruined city. Lieutenant Colonel John T. Corley, commanding the 3d Battalion, brought up 155-mm howitzers to blast the defenders from their positions. Near the end of the battle, Corley used one of his big guns to batter the huge four-story reinforced-concrete air-raid shelter on Rutscherstrasse where Wilck had moved his tactical headquarters. After a day of siege, Wilck surrendered his command post and the bloody battle for Aachen was over.

But the battle in the Huertgen Forest was merely entering a new phase with a new cast of characters. Still determined to clear the forest, Hodges ordered the 28th Division, a Pennsylvania National Guard unit commanded by Brigadier General Norman D. Cota, into the positions held by the exhausted men of the 9th Division. The 28th's assignment, one that Cota thought his division too weak to accomplish, was to fight its way across the Kall River gorge to the town of Schmidt, a position that would threaten German control of the Roer dams.

The 28th Division's attack was postponed on 1 November because of rain and fog, but jumped off the next day after an intense artillery barrage plastered German positions along the Germeter-Huertgen road. The 109th Infantry advanced down the road until stopped by the threat of German infiltration. At the same time the 110th and 112th regiments moved toward the Kall gorge. The 110th was unable to make any headway against an enemy fighting from log-covered bunkers, but the 112th quickly crossed the gorge and pushed through Kommerscheidt to Schmidt. The 112th's advance had been almost too easy. Un able to reinforce or adequately supply the positions across the gorge, Cota could do little when grenadiers of the 116th Panzers counterattacked in the morning of the fourth. By noon, GI's were fleeing Schmidt in disorder.

At Kommerscheidt their panic subsided. Strengthened by three Shermans brought across the Kall by Lieutenant Raymond E. Fleig, the men of the 112th held at Kommerscheidt, but they held for only four days. By 9 November the 28th Division had pulled back all units that had crossed the Kall. "Dutch" Cota's troops would fight on until the fifteenth without much determination. Charles B. MacDonald called the 28th Division's fight for Schmidt one of the most costly divisional actions in the war. Total casualties were 6,184; the 112th Infantry alone lost 2,093 men from all causes.

The next big push in the forest—in fact, the big push for the entire First Army—was assigned to the Big Red One, with the 9th Division's 47th Infantry attached, the 4th Division, reinforced by CCR of the 5th Armored, and the untested 104th Division. The plan of attack called for the 1st Division to attack toward Langerwehe, while the 104th protected its northern flank along the Stolberg corridor. The 4th Division was to take over the exhausted 28th Division's positions near Huertgen and attack toward that town.

After a week of postponements, the skies cleared on 16 November, allowing Operation Queen, as the preliminary bombing attack had been named, to go off as scheduled. In the war's largest air attack in support of a ground operation, some 1,200 heav-

ies of the Eighth Air Force pulverized targets ahead of the waiting American infantry. Before Queen was done, some four thousand aircraft had dropped 20 million pounds of bombs on
various German positions. Duren, Eschweiler, and Langerwehe
were destroyed, but due to the elaborate precautions to avoid
another short bombing, the German front lines were not hit. The
bombs were followed by a rain of shells from artillery, tanks, and
mortars. Despite the bombardment and a five-to-one American
numerical superiority, the enemy's 12th and 47th regiments
would not break. Not until 28 November, after days of slogging
through the cold, dank forest, dodging mines and tree bursts,
were the American 12th, 22d, and 121st regiments able to gain
the Germeter-Huertgen road.

Meanwhile, the 1st Division was pressing its attack north
from Hamich and Hill 232 toward Langerwehe. A battalion of
the 18th Infantry took Heistern on 21 November and held
through the night against a determined counterattack by a battalion of the 47th Volksgrenadier Division. Morning light on 22
November revealed the bodies of 250 German soldiers strewn
around the town; another 120 had surrendered.

By the twenty-eighth, the 16th Infantry had battled its way
into Langerwehe in the face of stiff opposition from the teen-
agers of the 3d Parachute Division. Two miles away, at Merode,
the 26th Infantry was not so lucky. Two companies of GI's managed to penetrate the stoutly defended town, but enemy fire
prevented their supporting tanks from following. Cut off, the
two companies were overrun by a counterattack. Despite this
setback, the 1st Division and attached units had fought their
way four miles to the northern edge of the forest, absorbing
4,600 battle casualties along the way. Their part in this battle
was over.

To the south, the 4th and 8th Infantry divisions and CCR of
the 5th Armored pressed their attack along the road from
Huertgen to Duren. By 8 December these divisions had moved
to the banks of the Roer River, but all were used up by the ef-

fort. They had been reduced by 11,252 casualties from all causes. Replacing them were the 9th and 83d Infantry divisions and the other two combat commands of the 5th Armored. Their combined attack jumped off on 10 December, followed in two days by that of two V Corps divisions, the 2d and 78th, pushing up the Monschau corridor toward Schmidt and the Roer dams. All these attacks ended on 16 December, when the Germans opened their strategic counteroffensive in the Ardennes.

Tour of Aachen and the Huertgen Forest

This tour begins in the ancient imperial city of Aachen, directs you to sites that were important in the struggle for that city, then moves south to Roetgen at the edge of the Huertgen Forest.

The name Huertgen Forest was that given by American GI's to the entire northern tip of the wooded Ardennes-Eifel upland. The ground fought over by the 28th Infantry Division in the fall of 1944 was cut by two major ridges running generally northeast from Monschau. The ridge tops were covered with open cultivated fields and pastures, with the local towns and villages strung out like beads along the major ridge-line roads. The valleys and lower ridges were heavily wooded. The terrain remains little changed since 1944, except that there is now a small reservoir on the Wehebach. Today, the area is shown on maps as being part of a Deutsch-Belgischer Naturpark.

The road net through the Huertgen Forest is not always well marked, and we found several secondary roads away from the ridge lines closed to vehicular traffic. Other than a German military cemetery and an occasional row of dragon's teeth, there is little to commemorate the long battle that was fought here. Today, the only soldiers one is likely to find in the Huertgen Forest are those from the Bundeswehr and the U.S. Army touring the battlefield in buses.

The tour is laid out to enable you to visit the positions held by

Brigadier General Norman D. Cota's 28th Division in the early November fighting and the Rurstausee Reservoir on the Roer River. Thus, we first direct you to the village of Huertgen, then backtrack to Vossenack. The route leaves Vossenack to cross the Kall gorge to Schmidt. We also include a side trip to the resort of Simonskall tucked away in the Kall gorge. From Schmidt, we take you to the Rurstausee. The tour then retraces the outward route back toward Aachen, dropping you off at the E 5 autobahn for good access to all points. The total round trip distance is approximately 170 kilometers.

Aachen

Aachen today is a bustling German city which shows few signs of its devastation forty years ago. There are, however, a few sites which figured prominently in the battle that may be visited today.

Quellenhof Hotel–Farwick Park Complex (1)*

You may reach this site, northeast of Aachen's center, by driving to Monheimsallee (the hotel is No. 52). Park in the public lot just south of the Spielcasino on Monheimsallee.

The Quellenhof Hotel became an objective of Lieutenant Colonel John T. Corley's 3d Battalion, 26th Infantry, attacking across the three hills which dominate the northern sector of the city. After losing a tank while trying to move down the Julich-strasse, Corley called up a 155-mm howitzer which he then proceeded to use in direct support of the advancing troops. News of Corley's devastating weapon convinced Colonel Gerhard Wilck, who was now commanding the 4,392-man garrison, to move his headquarters from the Hotel Quellenhof to a massive air-raid

* Bold numbers are keyed to Maps 29 and 30.

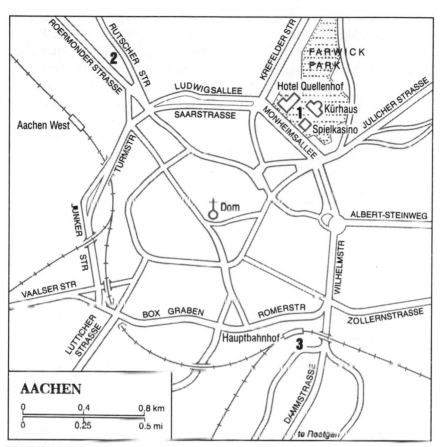

AACHEN

| 0 | 0.4 | 0.8 km |
| 0 | 0.25 | 0.5 mi |

MAP 29

shelter on Rutscherstrasse that was less directly in the path of the advancing Americans.

Unfortunately for the Americans, the Quellenhof position was reinforced during the night of 14 October by a battalion of SS troopers with eight assault guns. They were in position when the Americans struck the next day. The battle raged back and forth through Farwick Park, around the hotel and the nearby *Kurhaus*. At the end of the day, the SS held the hotel and *Kurhaus*, while the GI's clung to the perimeter of the park.

While both sides licked their wounds inside the city, to the east a decisive battle was being fought. By the seventeenth, the efforts of the 3d Panzer Grenadiers to relieve the city had been repulsed. Unknown to the American command at the time, the Germans had shot their bolt. For all of Wilck's bombast about defending the city to the last man, Aachen's fate had been decided.

On the eighteenth, reinforced by two battalions of the 3d Armored Division (Task Force Hogan), Corley's men began their final push. The battle for the Hotel Quellenhof was fierce. An American platoon, commanded by Lieutenant William D. Ratchford, stormed the lobby, tossing grenades into the basement where the SS troopers had retreated. When it was over, twenty-five of the defenders were dead.

The next day, two of the northern hills, the Salvatorberg and the Lousberg, fell to the 3d Battalion and Task Force Hogan. Meanwhile, Lieutenant Colonel Derrill M. Daniel's 2d Battalion, aided by the 110th Infantry of the 28th Division, had cleared the southern half of the city from Rothe Erde as far west as the *Hauptbahnhof*.

Rutscherstrasse Air-Raid Shelter (2)

The air-raid shelter, located at 348 Rutscherstrasse, can be reached from the Hotel Quellenhof by driving west on Saarstrasse until it intersects Roermonder Strasse. Turn right on Roermonder Strasse, then, in a block or so, bear right onto Rutscherstrasse. The shelter will be to your right. Park nearby.

The shell marks on the front of the building are those left by Corley's 155-mm gun. If you look closely, you can still see one of the rounds imbedded in the concrete.

By 21 October, Corley's men had surrounded the huge four-story shelter. For a day, division artillery had been pounding the nearby defenses and the building itself with point-blank fire. Wilck had already sent out two of his officers to surrender the bunker and the city; both had been shot down by trigger-happy GI's. Wilck now hit on the plan of sending out American prisoners under a white flag. Two GI's of the Big Red One volunteered and, after a harrowing moment under American fire, made their mission understood. By noon it was over. German POW's were herded into cages, while Wilck was driven off to begin a three-year stint behind bars. Aachen became the first major German city to fall to Allied arms.

AACHEN TO THE HUERTGEN FOREST

The West Wall

You can pick up the route out of Aachen by following Wilhelmstrasse (which becomes Dammstrasse) south from a point just east of the Hauptbahnhof (3). In 13 km this road intersects Highway 258 near Schmidthof. Follow 258 to Roetgen and park just inside the northern boundary of the town.

As you drive the above route, keep your eyes open for the dragon's teeth (4) in the pastures just before you reach the Schmidthof intersection. Hitler ordered the construction of the West Wall—of which these dragon's teeth represent the western cutting edge—in 1936 after he had reoccupied the Rhineland. Work was stepped up in 1938, with half a million

274

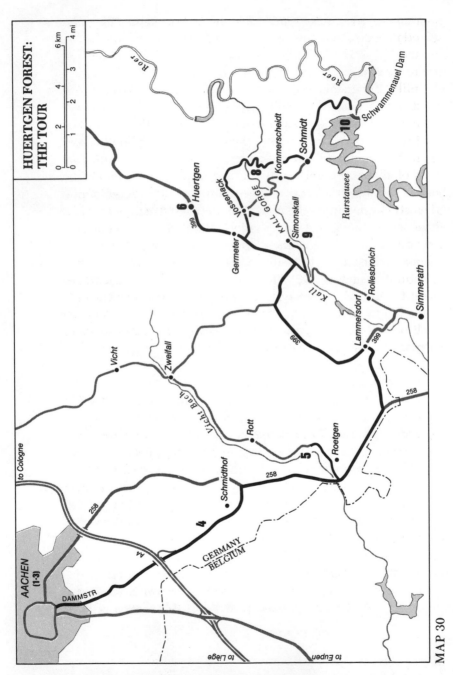

MAP 30

men employed in that year. After the Blitzkrieg of 1940, construction ceased and most of the weapons were removed. By late summer 1944, the West Wall housed neither guns nor the men to fire them.

Unlike the French Maginot Line with its massive forts, the West Wall (incorrectly called the "Siegfried Line" by Americans) consisted of a line of concrete pillboxes sited for interlocking fire and protected by a belt of anti-vehicle obstacles. Most often those obstacles took the form of dragon's teeth, four or five rows of truncated concrete pyramids ranging from one to 1.5 meters in height set in a continuous concrete slab. As ominous as they still loom today, the line of dragon's teeth was easily breached by the Allied armies in 1944, either by following roads they did not block, by blasting gaps, or by using a dirt fill. The pillboxes proved much more formidable. They were concrete structures with walls from three to seven feet thick, measuring about twenty-four by forty feet. Built by the Todt organization in the late 1930s to house the lighter weapons of that era, the small bunkers could not mount the machine guns and anti-tank weapons in service in 1944, greatly limiting their usefulness.

For all its weaknesses, the West Wall proved to be a formidable barrier to the exhausted Allied armies. It gave the equally exhausted Germans the time to begin that remarkable military recovery they would call the "Miracle of the West."

Because of Aachen's importance and location, the West Wall there consisted of two bands of fortifications passing east and west of the city and continuing for a considerable distance to the south. The western section of the wall, through which you have just passed, was known as the Scharnhorst Line. The eastern belt, where most of the Huertgen Forest fighting occurred, was the Schill Line.

Task Force Lovelady

Take the road north from Roetgen toward Rott. Almost any of the east-west streets in the northern section of Roet-

gen will funnel you in that direction. Some 3 km after you turn off Highway 258, just as you leave Roetgen, you will cross a belt of dragon's teeth (5), visible on your left. Just before you reach them, pull off onto the service road, also on your left. Warning: If you miss the turn onto the service road, you may have difficulty finding a spot to turn around short of Rott, some 8 km away.

This is the place where Task Force Lovelady crossed the Scharnhorst Line on 13 September. Commanded by Lieutenant Colonel William B. Lovelady, this task force of the 3d Armored's CCB found the road blocked by a huge crater which proved more of an obstacle than either the dragon's teeth or the thin line of pillboxes covering them. Engineers finally had to blow a gap through the teeth to facilitate movement. Halfway to Rott, Task Force Lovelady lost four tanks and a half-track to fire from a Panther and several anti-tank guns. By dark, Lovelady's command had moved barely two miles, enough to carry it through the first belt of German defenses.

Huertgen (6)

Retrace your route back through Roetgen to Highway 258. Drive south for 4 km, then turn east to Lammersdorf, where you can pick up Highway 399 headed north. Follow 399 along the open ridge top to Huertgen (16 km) and park.

The section of 399 you have just driven was the road the 9th and later the 28th Division fought so desperately to control in October and November. A good deal of that fighting took place in the heavily wooded valley of the Wehebach to your left (northwest). The town of Huertgen itself was not captured until 28 November after infantrymen of the 2d Battalion, 13th Infantry, stormed the town behind the charge of a company of Shermans. The Germans defended every house; two hundred surrendered late in the afternoon of the twenty-eighth. It would take another two weeks of hard fighting to bring the American advance the last six miles to the Roer plain.

Vossenack (7)

Retrace your route along 399 for 3.5 km. Just beyond Germeter, turn left (east) and drive through the town of Vossenack. Park near the church in the center of town.

Vossenack and the ridge on which it lies were held by the 2d Battalion of the 112th Infantry during the 28th Division's battle for Schmidt. The regiment was harassed the entire time by artillery and mortar fire. At dawn on 6 November, the men of Company G, in an exposed position where the road leaving town to the east makes its abrupt turn south before dropping off into the Kall gorge, broke under the strain. Their panic quickly spread to Company F south of the road. In a short time, both companies abandoned the eastern half of Vossenack. A thin defensive line was re-established just west of the church. The situation was saved by the tanks and tank destroyers in Vossenack and especially by the men of the 146th Engineer Combat Battalion, who entered the battle still wearing the hip boots they had donned to do road work. At dusk, the engineers held the church, but the Germans recaptured it during the night. Minus radios and hand grenades, the engineers of Company A retook the church on the morning of the seventh and, assisted by Company B, cleared most of Vossenack by the end of the day. During the night, the engineers were withdrawn as the 2d Battalion of the 100th Infantry took over their positions.

The Kall Gorge and Schmidt (8)

To cross the Kall gorge to Kommerscheidt and Schmidt, take the road which leaves Vossenack to the east.

This route best approximates the line of advance of the 1st and 3d battalions of the 112th Infantry. Note: If you wish to hike the Kall gorge trail, leave Vossenack by the road leading from the parking lot south of the church. Yet another route leaves 399 to the south just beyond the turn to Vossenack and winds its way down into the gorge to Simonskall (9), a small resort held

278 The March to Victory

during the battle by the 1st Battalion of the 110th Infantry. From Simonskall, you must either retrace your route to 399 or exit the gorge at Rollesbroich.

The 112th Infantry's attack jumped off in the cold, wet dawn of 2 November after the usual divisional artillery preparation. The 2d Battalion's objective was the town of Vossenack.

You have just driven the route of attack followed by the 1st and 3d battalions of the 112th Infantry on the morning of 3 November. While the infantry had no difficulty in crossing the Kall gorge, then moving on to Kommerscheidt and Schmidt, it remained to be seen if General Cota would be able to reinforce his exposed battalions.

His first efforts were not very promising. After the trail had been declared passable by tanks, Company A of the 707th Tank Battalion (supporting the 28th Division) attempted to cross, but turned back after the lead tank nearly slipped off the trail. During the night combat engineers pushed a wrecked weasel off the trail, then attempted to improve it. Around midnight on 3–4 November, three supply weasels managed to cross the gorge and reach Schmidt.

Just before daylight, the 1st Platoon of Company A, commanded by Lieutenant Raymond E. Fleig, tried its luck on the narrow, slippery trail. Fleig's tank had no more than begun the tortuous descent when it was disabled by a mine. The tankers managed to winch the second Sherman around the disabled one, and Fleig drove it across the river to Kommerscheidt. Three others also inched past the disabled tank and were able to negotiate a narrow turn a little further on.

A short time later three tanks of the 2d Platoon tried to cross, with disastrous results—all three either slipped off the trail or threw their tracks. Ahead of them on the trail, one of the three tanks following Fleig threw a track crossing the Kall. Thus, only three Shermans made it to Kommerscheidt; five had been disabled along the route. The four tanks of the 3d Platoon had yet to move out. Luckily for the infantrymen in Kommerscheidt, the firepower of Fleig's three Shermans proved just enough to save the day.

Elements of the German 89th Infantry and 116th Panzer divisions had counterattacked the 3d Battalion's perimeter defense at Schmidt just after dawn. With only machine guns, bazookas, and mortars to support the riflemen, the GI's were soon in trouble. Five panzers (Mark IVs and Panthers) appeared in support of the initial infantry probes. Shaking off bazooka rounds with ease, the panzers were soon pouring fire into the American foxholes. Artillery fire came too late to slow the German armor, and the continuing overcast prevented any close air support. Unable to stop the panzers, the men of the 3d Battalion broke, with men from some companies falling back into the wooded area to the southwest, while others retreated in disorder to Kommerscheidt. There, around 1000, the officers of Companies A and D attempted to quiet the panic, sometimes at gunpoint.

Flushed with their own success, the Germans quickly pressed on to Kommerscheidt. As they approached the village, they ran headlong into the stiffening American lines and Lieutenant Fleig's three Shermans. In short order, the Germans lost five tanks—four to fire from the Shermans, another to a well-placed bazooka round after it had been disabled by a P-47. At one point Fleig took on a Panther with high-explosive ammunition. After taking two hits, which apparently did no serious damage to the heavily armored tank, the German crew bailed out, giving Fleig time to rotate his turret to retrieve his armor-piercing rounds in the outside sponson rack. During the lull in the firing, the German crew reboarded their vehicle and got off one poorly aimed shot in Fleig's direction. Fleig fired back, his first shot severing the Panther's gun barrel, his next three taking the Panther apart.

That took the steam out of the German attack. Despite some brave talk about retaking Schmidt, the inability of Cota to get enough armor across the Kall or to prevent infiltration along the bottom of the gorge doomed the defense of Kommerscheidt. Neither Fleig's tanks nor the heroic efforts of two companies of

tank destroyers (the commander of one platoon, Lieutenant
Turney W. Leonard, won the Congressional Medal of Honor for
his actions here) could save the situation at Kommerscheidt. On
7 November, the Americans lost the town. The next day they
withdrew across the Kall. The 28th Division's battle for Schmidt
had ended in defeat.

The Roer Dams (10)

*Continue south from Schmidt. Follow the road as it drops
sharply to the marina on the Rurstausee, the large reservoir
behind the Schwammenauel Dam on the Roer River. Park
in the large lot and visit the marina.*

In 1944, there were seven dams on the Roer and its tribu-
taries, the most important being the Schwammenauel and the
Urft. The final attack to capture the dams did not begin until
February 1945, after several unsuccessful attempts to destroy
them from the air.

The idea of an aerial attack on German dams was not a new
idea. In October, planes of the XIX Tactical Air Command had
breached an eighteenth-century earthen dam on the Third
Army's front. In an even more famous operation in May 1943,
RAF bombers had struck at a string of dams on the Ruhr with
uneven results. Eleven of the nineteen bombers were lost and
the most important dam was untouched. (Note: There is a fascinating exhibit describing this operation at the RAF Museum in
Hendon, in Greater London. See our description in Appendix
A.)

Thus, the RAF was somewhat reluctant to have a go at the
Roer dams in December. The first attack aborted when the 190
bombers failed to find their target. A two-hundred-plane raid
the following day, the fourth, was almost as disappointing, since
fewer than thirty planes actually dropped their bombs. Following two more ineffective raids and two cancelled missions, Air
Chief Marshal Sir Arthur T. Harris persuaded Eisenhower to
call off the effort. The two dams had been only superficially
damaged.

As so often happened, it was again left up to the infantry—this time Major General Erwin P. Parker, Jr.'s, 78th Division attacking along the Monschau corridor—to finish the job. Pressed by Hodges's rather heavy-handed style of command and aided by the 9th Division's 60th Regiment, Parker's troops retook Kommerschcidt and Schmidt on the eighth and ninth of February. During the night of the ninth, the 1st Battalion of the 60th Infantry, accompanied by an engineer team, went for the Schwammenauel Dam. One group fought their way across the top of the dam to a tunnel entrance, only to find it blocked. They then rappeled down the sixty-five-meter dam face to locate the exit. But neither they nor a second group moving along the base of the dam located any explosive charges. Instead of blowing the dam, the Germans had merely destroyed the control machinery and valves. That action, along with water diverted from a higher reservoir, flooded the Roer downstream for two weeks.

Lieutenant General William H. Simpson's Ninth Army launched its assault crossing of the Roer on 23 February and after another week of hard fighting closed the Rhine at last.

Possibly the simplest way to extract yourself from the Huertgen Forest is to retrace your route to Aachen. Just south of the city you can pick up Autobahn E 5 which will take you either west to Liège for the start of the Battle of the Bulge tour or east toward the Rhine and Autobahn A 61 for the Rhine crossing tour. Liège is some 50 km from Aachen; Remagen is about 104 km.

The Lorraine Campaign: An Overview

Patton's Third Army, activated on 1 August 1944 following the breakout at Avranches, knew initially little but speedy advance. The enemy, disorganized and demoralized, streamed eastward, harried all the way by Allied fighter-bombers. Seldom did the Germans stand to fight. Le Mans, Orléans, Reims, and Verdun all fell in rapid succession. In just a month, the Third Army made 250 miles. As cap to this drive, the XX Corps seized a bridgehead over the Meuse at Verdun and the XII Corps another to the south near Commercy.

The Third Army stood poised on the banks of the Meuse for five days but unable to spring for want of gasoline. In late August and early September, supplies came through in a trickle. Faced with shortages all along the front, Eisenhower accorded priority to the campaigns waged north of the Ardennes by Montgomery's 21 Army Group and Hodges's First U.S. Army. This decision, much criticized later by Patton, had in fact insignificant practical consequence. Too little gasoline could be delivered to any of the armies in the field to sustain advance. At the time, the lull in operations did not dampen the optimism of the Third Army's commander.

Patton remained confident that, once sufficient supplies were provided, the Third Army could take Lorraine and breach the West Wall along the German border in a matter of days. When gasoline began to arrive again in large quantities after 4 September, he ordered attacks to and over the Moselle. On 7 September, with the offensive well under way, Patton directed the cavalry to cross the Moselle and "reconnoiter to the Rhine River." The virtually uncontested advance across France had made everything seem possible! It is a mere eighty miles from Verdun to Saarbrücken, and the Rhine lies only seventy miles beyond.

The Third Army would travel those eighty miles to Saarbrücken and the West Wall, but it took months not days. Not until the first week of December did American troops draw up to the Saar south of the Ardennes. The Rhine continued to beckon, but no American under Patton's command crossed the river until 22 March. Contrary, then, to Patton's expectations, and his preferences, the fighting in Lorraine turned out to be a slow, painful march characterized by prepared assaults and at-

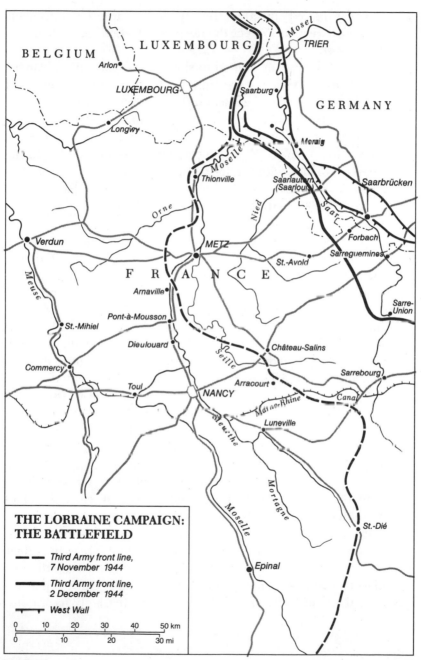

**THE LORRAINE CAMPAIGN:
THE BATTLEFIELD**

– – – Third Army front line,
7 November 1944

━━━ Third Army front line,
2 December 1944

┬─┬ West Wall

MAP 31

tacks for limited objectives. Rarely was the armor able to make the wide sweep and effect the deep penetration that it had during August.

Several things contributed to slowing the pace of the American offensive. All along the front September saw a stiffening of the enemy line. The logistical difficulties which forced a pause in Allied operations afforded German commanders time to reorganize and to bring forward a few fresh units. The line thrown up was thin in many places, but it was an organized line. In the chaos of August, with the foe in full flight, the Third Army had taken 65,000 prisoners. The following three and a half months yielded 75,000—only 10,000 more in a period over three times as long.

In Lorraine, the Germans fought on terrain which they knew well and which advantaged the defense. The Moselle and Saar rivers running south to north across the Third Army's axis of advance were significant obstacles. The large forests and stout stone villages of the region provided rallying points for delay and counterattack. In addition, the fortifications at Metz and Thionville, and those which made up the West Wall, although in disrepair and undermanned, proved more resistant to modern weapons than the Third Army commanders anticipated.

The weather conspired to deny full advantage to the Allied superiority in tanks and aircraft. Autumn usually brings rains of between 2.5 and 3.0 inches a month in Lorraine. More than twice that amount fell in 1944; November recorded almost seven inches. For the XIX Tactical Air Command the effect was to greatly reduce the number of sorties which could be flown in support of the troops on the ground. In August, clear skies had permitted 12,292 sorties. The onset of the rainy season reduced that number to 7,791 in September, 4,790 in October, 3,509 in November, and 2,563 in December. For the tankers the effect was to turn the Lorraine clay to mud. Although it was still possible to maneuver cross-country in September, any departure from the roads in later months became increasingly hazardous.

An effort was made to regain mobility for the armor by welding pieces of channel iron to the outer edges of the track connectors. These "grousers" or "duck-bills" improved flotation, but prudent tank commanders stuck to the roads.

The rain, of course, also made life even more miserable for the front-line infantry. Most of the combat troops had three blankets and an overcoat, which quickly became sodden in the continual rain. Waterproof tents and raincoats were in short supply, as were socks and woolen clothing. Rubber overshoes were, for some time, issued on the basis of one pair for every four men. These material shortcomings, combined with the practice of leaving units in the line for long periods, produced large numbers of non-battle casualties—trench foot, fatigue, and exposure were common.

As the campaign wore on, dropping temperatures changed the very locus of the fighting. In September and October the battle was for high ground and woods. In later months the combatants sought a roof over their heads in the villages.

After weeks of hard slogging, the Third Army finally drew up to the West Wall along the Saar in early December. It had suffered 55,182 casualties, including 6,657 dead. Non-battle casualties from exposure and disease ran nearly as high; official data give the figure of 42,088, which probably underreports actual incidence. German losses were much higher, although no precise figures exist. The number of captured alone substantially exceeded the American total. The Third Army had reduced the combat effectiveness of the First German Army, its antagonist throughout the Lorraine campaign, by more than half.

As his divisions prepared to launch a major offensive against the West Wall on 19 December, Patton received a telephone call from Bradley at 1030, 18 December, requesting that he come as soon as possible to 12th Group headquarters. At that meeting, and one the following day with Eisenhower, Patton learned that his scheduled offensive was to be halted and most of the Third Army's divisions shifted northward to meet the growing threat in the Ardennes.

Tour of the Lorraine Battlefield

The tour of the Lorraine battlefield begins at Saarbrücken near the Franco-German border and ends at Metz after a journey of 175 kilometers. There are no museums or monuments commemorating the Third Army's campaign in the area. Following a visit to the American military cemetery at St.-Avold, the tour swings south beyond Château-Salins to several battle sites of the September and November offensives. The tour then goes west to the Moselle above Nancy and follows the river north. Along the way you pass through the sites of bridgeheads secured in mid-September 1944. A drive through the western environs of Metz concludes the tour. Unfortunately, the ring of forts surrounding Metz are all on French military reservations and, as of the summer of 1984, closed to the public.

From Route 9 near Worms turn west on A 6/E 12 and go 109 km to Saarbrücken. The Autoroute becomes A 32 at the Franco-German border just beyond Saarbrücken. Proceed on A 32 toward St.-Avold.

This highway marks the boundary between XII and XX Corps during the last stages of the November 1944 offensive. The 5th Division, XX Corps, drove eastward on the north, and the 80th Division, XII Corps, on the south. At Forbach you cross the Third Army's front line as of 20 December 1944.

Turn south on N 3a toward St.-Avold. Stop at the American military cemetery on the east side of the road (1). *

---

* Bold numbers are keyed to Map 32.

287

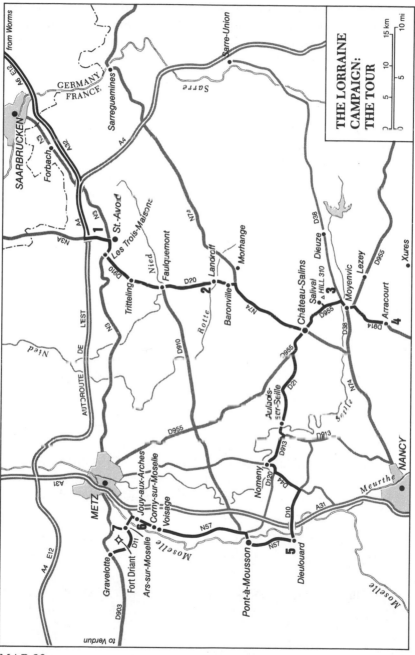

THE LORRAINE
CAMPAIGN:
THE TOUR

from Worms

GERMANY
FRANCE

SAARBRUCKEN

Forbach

Sarreguemines

Sarre-Union

Sarre

St-Avold

1

Les Trois-Maisons

Faulquemont

Nied

Tritteling

Lancroft

Morhange

2

Baronville

Château-Salins

Salival

HILL 310

Dieuze

Moyenvic

Lezey

Xures

Arracourt

3

4

Aulnois-
sur-Seille

Nomeny

NANCY

Meurthe

Jouy-aux-Arches

Corny-sur-Moselle

Voisage

METZ

Fort Driant

Ars-sur-Moselle

Gravelotte

6

Pont-à-Mousson

Dieulouard

5

Moselle

to Verdun

MAP 32

This is the largest American World War II cemetery in Europe. It contains the graves of 10,489 soldiers and airmen, most of whom died while fighting in Lorraine and Germany. There is a visitors' center, chapel, and memorial building. The cemetery is open daily 0800–1800 in the summer and 0800–1700 in the winter.

Continue south on N 3a to St.-Avold.

Troops of the 80th Division captured the town without resistance on 27 November 1944. The enemy had withdrawn but not before planting time bombs. At 1730, 3 December, the first explosion killed twenty-two men and injured thirty. Within an hour another four explosions occurred. All personnel had evacuated the buildings however, and no further casualties were sustained. Ironically, St.-Avold had been made a rest area for 80th Division.

Leave St.-Avold west on N 3. In 3 km, at Les 3 Maisons, turn south on D 910 toward Faulquemont.

The German line in late November ran northwest from Tritteling. Although based on Maginot Line fortifications, the Germans had little time to repair the neglected works or to familiarize themselves with its possibilities. On 25 November, the 80th Division, supported by elements of CCR, 6th Armored, attacked the 36th Volksgrenadier Division in its trenches and pillboxes. General August Wellm attributed the collapse of his division to the American artillery and to the intrepid infantrymen who advanced "with their weapons at the ready and cigarettes dangling from their lips."

Proceed to Faulquemont where you should take D 20 south to Landroff (2).

On the morning of 14 November, Team Davall of CCA, 6th Armored, advanced toward Landroff from the west along Rotte

Creek on D 76. German artillery shelled the road, but by late afternoon Landroff was in American hands. The small occupying force readied itself for the inevitable counterattack. It came from the north at dusk. One German self-propelled gun and supporting infantry reached the center of town only to be driven out. Around midnight artillery stopped the second assault at the town's edge. Still another attack at 0100 failed to gain the town's buildings. The final assault began at 0200. By this time a company of armored infantry had slipped into Landroff to reinforce its defenders. The first wave of German troops was permitted to come within three hundred yards before the artillery opened up. Suooooding waves of Germans pushed into the town. There followed a hand-to-hand fight for several hours. The arrival of a company of the 319th Infantry, 80th Division, permitted the Americans to drive the Germans out. Company A, 68th Tank Battalion, which had borne the main burden of the fighting, suffered ninety-seven casualties. More than one hundred German bodies were counted outside the town. Many of Landroff's buildings still bear the scars of the fighting.

Continue on D 20 south to Baronville. Pick up N 74 and drive the 16 km to Château-Salins.

Château-Salins fell within the 26th Division's zone on the right flank of the XII Corps during the November offensive. The town fell to the 104th Infantry on 9 November.

From Château-Salins go southeast for 8 km on D 955 toward Moyenvic. Due east of the intersection with the secondary road to Salival lies Hill 310 (3). The hill may be reached by a footpath from Salival.

The 101st Infantry, 26th Division, and troops of the 559th Volksgrenadier Division fought a four-day battle here. From positions to the south, the 101st jumped off at 0600, 8 November. The 2d Battalion soon seized Moyenvic and its bridge across the Seille River. Companies E and F advanced up the forward slope of Hill 310. About five hundred yards from the top, these men were pinned down by enemy fire. In the fusillade, Company E lost its commander plus a few men, and all of Company F's officers were casualties.

Despite the arrival of reinforcements, all efforts to press forward on the eighth were unavailing. The Germans on the hill, armed with six howitzers, mortars, and machine guns, and supported by artillery in Marsel, swept the slope with a deadly fire. The night brought cold and rain to add to the miseries of the riflemen huddled behind rocks and trees.

The 101st finally took Hill 310 on 11 November by double envelopment. The 3d Battalion had advanced up a ravine on the west to Salival, and the 1st Battalion had encircled on the east to the ridge behind the hill. The fight cost the 101st 478 dead and wounded.

Drive into Moyenvic. Take D 914 south for 8 km to Arracourt **(4).**

In the area bounded by Arracourt, Lezey, Xures, and Bathelemont the largest tank battles of the Lorraine campaign occurred, as the 4th Armored Division fought off a series of attacks by the LVIII Panzer Corps in the period 19–29 September. These attacks were part of a larger operation by Manteuffel's Fifth Panzer Army aimed at retaking Nancy and restoring the German line along the Moselle to the north.

Owing to the ever-present threat of Allied fighter-bombers and the serial arrival of tanks at the front, General Walter Krueger committed his panzers piecemeal in a series of jabs to create an opening in 4th Armored's defenses. From 19 to 22 September, CCA parried the German thrusts around Bezange, Rechicourt, and Arracourt and inflicted large losses on the German armor. On 25 September and for the next three days CCB met attacks along a line from Bathelemont to Rechicourt. The Germans made some local gains, but at the end of the counteroffensive remained far from their objectives. In the process the Fifth Panzer Army had lost over two hundred tanks and other armored vehicles. The losses of 4th Armored were relatively small; CCA lost twenty-five medium tanks and seven tank destroyers.

Most of the villages in this gently rolling countryside suffered some damage—still visible today—in these tank battles.

From Arracourt, take D 914 north. At Moyenvic turn north on D 955 and proceed 5 km beyond Château-Salins. Turn west on D 21 for 12 km to Aulnois-sur-Seille, where D 21 runs into D 45. In just over 1 km turn southwest on D 45a, which links up with D 913. Turn north. In Nomeny turn south on D 120 and then south again on D 44. At the junction with D 10 turn west and drive into Dieulouard (5).

On 12 September, against scant resistance, the 80th Division put five battalions across the Moselle at Dieulouard. These troops established a perimeter about a mile deep around the crossing sites. Engineers quickly put heavy bridging across the river and the parallel Obrion Canal, which permitted two tank companies and a battalion of 105-mm howitzers to join the infantry in the bridgehead.

About 0100, 13 September, the Germans launched a counterattack out of the hills and forests overlooking Dieulouard on the east. This attack overran American positions all along the line. Communications were destroyed and command posts overrun. Small units became isolated in their village outposts. As the infantry fought from the houses at close quarters, the tanks engaged at ranges of less than two hundred yards. By dawn the Germans had come within one hundred yards of the bridges, but were unable to push the attack home. With the coming of full light, they began to withdraw.

At this point CCA, 4th Armored, crossed into the bridgehead and, on its way east, cut into the retreating Germans. Infantry of the 80th Division following in the van of the tanks restored the original bridgehead perimeter. CCA continued on into the German rear, bagging over a thousand prisoners and leaving a path of destruction all the way to Arracourt, where in the evening of 14 September it coiled up to await further orders.

The 80th Division back in the bridgehead was left with its hands full in beating off persistent counterattacks. Four or five battalions of infantry with some forty tanks launched a major counterattack on 15 September and again the next day.

Meanwhile a task force made up of a battalion of infantry and a company of tanks under the command of Major C. L. Kimsey had left Arracourt in late afternoon of 15 September to return to Dieulouard. The task force fought its way west (along the road which you took) throughout the night. Kimsey's attack from the rear took the Germans by surprise. On the sixteenth, the tankers in support of 80th Division infantry pushed out the perimeter some four miles. The arrival of additional reinforcements that same day secured the bridgehead for good.

Drive north on N 57 to Pont-à-Mouson, where you recross the Moselle to the east bank. Continue north on N 57 toward Metz. In about 15 km you pass through the village of Voisage.

This village lies in the center of a bridgehead seized by troops of the 10th Infantry, 5th Division, in the early morning hours of 10 September. Supported by thirteen artillery battalions on the west bank and the fighter-bombers of the XIX Tactical Air Command, the infantry managed to fight off German counterattacks. However, until the engineers bridged the river, no breakout was possible. Under constant fire from the casement guns at Fort Driant to the north and from roving guns in the hills to the east, the engineers got a bridge in at midday on the twelfth. The tanks of CCB and CCR, 7th Armored, then crossed into the bridgehead in preparation for a drive to the northeast.

Continue north on N 57. Three km north of Corny-sur-Moselle pull off the road (6).

This was the site of the first crossing of the Moselle by the XX Corps and the scene of a valiant attempt by the 11th Infantry, 5th Division, to gain an American foothold on the east bank. Although strong German units still occupied both banks of the river to the north and south, the 11th Infantry passed to the river's edge through a narrow corridor created by CCB, 7th Armored. About 1045 on 8 September, Companies F and G began crossing. In late afternoon the two assault companies advanced out of the woods—which lie between the river and the road—and across the road toward two forts atop hills a mile to the east. They encountered little resistance until they gained the forts, where they were struck hard from both sides by an enemy battalion. It took the GI's three hours to crawl back to the woods through the hail of gunfire. The survivors joined Companies E and K, which had crossed in the afternoon.

The four infantry companies, reinforced by forty-eight men of the 23d Armored Infantry Battalion, dug foxholes at the woods' edge. Captain Jack Gerrie's men defended their tiny bridgehead—three hundred yards deep and two hundred yards wide—for three days. During this period elements of four German battalions launched some thirty-six separate attacks without breaking the American line. The toll among the enemy was high, at least six hundred dead and many more wounded, but American casualties were also high. Over three hundred, better than half of the force in the bridgehead, were killed or wounded.

The end came in the evening of 10 September. Two men swam the river to inform Gerrie that he and his men were to be withdrawn. Private Dale B. Rex of G Company, who had already distinguished himself as a machine-gunner in the bridgehead, swam the river four times to help bring back the wounded. He received the DSC for his heroism. By midnight the evacuation was completed.

Proceed north through Jouy-aux-Arches. Turn west on D 11 across the Moselle. On the western outskirts of Ars-sur-Moselle a narrow secondary road on the south winds up the hill to Fort Driant (7), the southern bastion in the Metz defenses.

For the Third Army, Metz commanded the most direct route to the Rhine. It had been a fortified city since the days of the Romans and had not fallen to assault since the fifth century. West of the Moselle the approaches to Metz are heavily wooded and cut by numerous draws and ravines. In the nineteenth century the French and then the Germans had reinforced these natural obstacles by constructing rings of forts around the city—Third Army maps showed more than twenty.

General Walton Walker, whose XX Corps faced Metz, knew little of the Germans' intentions, to hold or withdraw, perhaps after a delaying action, or of the condition of the fortifications. In any event, he and the Third Army's commander believed that modern firepower, in the air and on the ground, would make short work of the Metz defenses.

Cavalry squadrons of the 7th Armored Division first tested the enemy on 6 September, and the 2d Regiment of the 5th Division followed soon after. They found not a few dispirited troops and obsolete forts but many tough, zealous men who took full advantage of the terrain and the fieldworks. Moreover, the forts proved stubbornly resistant to artillery fire and aerial bombing. Although the fourteen thousand Germans who manned Metz were far fewer than the armies which had garrisoned the city in an earlier day, they were enough to stall the left wing of the Third Army for months.

Throughout September, the 5th and 90th divisions battered against the western defenses with inconclusive results. The 11th Infantry Regiment managed to get most of a battalion on the very top of Fort Driant, where once again Captain Jack Gerrie, one of the heroes of the Dornot bridgehead, found himself besieged. He and the others of the assault force were subjected to counterattacks by German infantry who emerged nightly from their underground shelters and to constant artillery fire from nearby batteries. After a week of this, Gerrie reported that "the situation is critical. We may be able to hold till dark, but if anything happens this afternoon I can make no predictions." Despite some bluster about never allowing an attack by his army to fail, Patton sensibly permitted the withdrawal of the decimated companies.

Patton and Walker returned to their original strategy for taking Metz by means of encirclement. The Germans in early September had been unable to prevent CCR, 7th Armored, and the 90th Division from closing on the river north of Metz or CCB and the 5th Division's 10th and 11th Infantry regiments from seizing bridgeheads south of the city. Thus began an envelopment which finally brought the fall of Metz in mid-November. The forts west of the river held out for several weeks more Fort Driant capitulated on 0 December and Fort Jeanne d'Arc, the last to go, on the thirteenth.

Your return to Paris can be made most quickly on the Autoroute de l'Est (A 4). If you wish, however, to visit the World War I battlefields at Verdun, take D 903 west at Gravelotte. You can then pick up A 4 west of Verdun. On the drive back to Paris, you might also wish to leave A 4 at Reims to see the site of the German capitulation. The Collège Moderne et Technique is located at 10 Rue Franklin Roosevelt. The rooms are marked by a plaque on the building's exterior and are open daily 1030–1200 and 1400–1800 except Tuesday.

The Rhine Crossings: An Overview

In late February and early March the Allied armies eliminated the last pockets of German resistance west of the Rhine. Only the river now stood as obstacle to the German heartland. However, "it will be realized," Eisenhower had said some weeks before, "that a crossing of the Rhine, particularly on the narrow frontages in which such crossings are possible, will be a tactical and engineering operation of the greatest magnitude." Thus he expected the Germans to destroy all the existing bridges and to sharply contest any Allied crossing. In this, Hitler's policies had much compromised the hand of his field commanders. His "hold at all costs" orders and the Ardennes counteroffensive had used up the German armies in the west. And his refusal to permit a timely and orderly withdrawal behind the Rhine denied his armies the opportunity to prepare a defense behind the river.

So rapidly did German units disintegrate in face of the American thrusts to the Rhine that the possibility developed for seizure of a bridge intact. Prospects seemed best for Lieutenant General William H. Simpson's Ninth Army, which had crossed the Roer on 23 February and closed on the Rhine in a rush. A regiment of the 83d Division made a stab at Neuss on 1 March but found all three bridges destroyed. The next day another regiment of the 83d gained the western end of the bridge at Oberkassel, opposite Düsseldorf, only to see it blown at the last moment. Several miles downstream at Uerdingen the remnants of a German parachute division held up elements of the 2d and 5th Armored and 84th Infantry divisions just long enough to permit German engineers to drop the Adolf Hitler Bridge into the river on the morning of 4 March. Still farther downstream the 95th and 84th divisions moved quickly against light resistance in a try for the bridges into Duisburg. There was nothing left to capture; all the bridges had been destroyed.

Thwarted in his efforts to get a bridge, Simpson then proposed to Montgomery that the Ninth Army immediately launch an assault crossing between Uerdingen and Düsseldorf. Given the large force available to Simpson and the porous German defenses, such a venture promised success. Nevertheless, Montgomery refused permission on the grounds that the Ninth Army would get bogged down in the urban morass of the Ruhr—an eventuality which Eisenhower also wished to avoid. Since

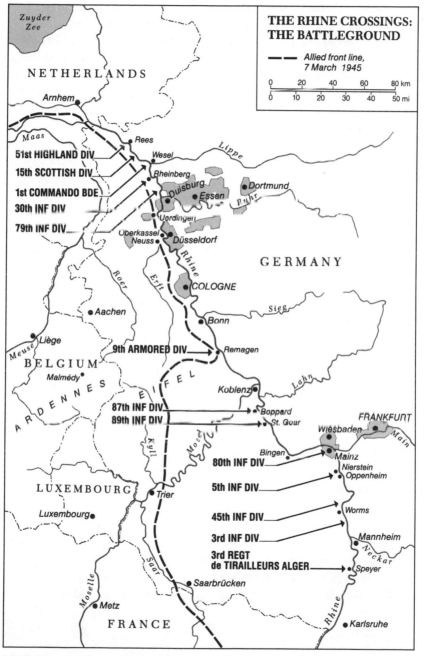

THE RHINE CROSSINGS: THE BATTLEGROUND

— — Allied front line, 7 March 1945

0   20   40   60   80 km
0 10 20 30 40 50 mi

MAP 33

Simpson's plan called for a drive north on the east bank, thus avoiding the Ruhr tangle, Ninth Army staff members concluded that Montgomery wanted no American crossing to detract from his own grand set-piece assault to be staged several weeks later. Quite by happenstance an American army put troops across the Rhine within the week.

Hopes for a bridge had all but faded when, shortly after noon on 7 March, an infantry platoon of the 9th Armored Division gained a bluff overlooking the river town of Remagen ten miles south of Bonn. Below them, the infantrymen could see German troops streaming in retreat across the still standing Ludendorff Bridge. Major General John Leonard, commander of the 9th Armored, had directed only a small task force from Combat Command B toward Remagen. The bulk of the division was pushing southeastward west of the Rhine to join the Third Army coming from the southwest in a maneuver designed to entrap the remnants of the Fifteenth German Army in the Eifel. Seizure of the Ludendorff Bridge was not in the plans, for no one expected it to be standing.

In the early afternoon, the commander of CCB, Brigadier General William Hoge (of St.-Vith fame), arrived on the scene and ordered a platoon of tanks to support the infantry already advancing on the bridge. As the Americans approached, an explosion opened up a large crater at the western end. Moments later, another explosion rocked the bridge but failed to demolish it. In a wild dash, machine-gun fire spattering around them, Lieutenant Karl Timmerman and his company of armored infantry crossed to the east bank. The First Army had a bridge.

As the news traveled up the chain of command, Leonard, Hodges, Bradley, and Eisenhower all expressed surprise and delight. Although Eisenhower remained committed to a main effort in the north by Montgomery's 21 Army Group, he immediately authorized the use of five divisions to hold the bridgehead. By late afternoon of the next day, some eight thousand men, including several tank and artillery units, had crossed the Rhine.

The German response was tardy and ineffectual. In the first days after seizure of the bridge, when the bridgehead was most vulnerable, German commanders sought in vain for a force large enough to repel the Americans. Unable to fashion anything more than a piecemeal defense, they struck at the bridge itself. In addition to artillery fire from the hills east of the river, the Luftwaffe attempted, without result, to bomb the bridge. A giant howitzer firing a 4,400-pound shell got off a few rounds, then had to be withdrawn for repairs. Eleven V-2 rockets were fired from sites in the Netherlands in the only tactical use made of these weapons during the war. The closest hit wiped out a house three hundred yards from the bridge. Colonel Otto Skorzeny organized a small group of underwater swimmers who attempted to emplace plastic explosives. All were captured.

What the Germans were unable to do at a stroke, the accumulation of shocks and strains finally accomplished. The Ludendorff Bridge collapsed on 17 March, just ten days after Timmerman's company had raced across. Its loss little affected operations. The divisions in the bridgehead continued to slowly push out the perimeter as the First Army awaited authority from Eisenhower to break out. On 19 March, the order came. Hodges was to increase the number of divisions across the Rhine to nine and to prepare for a drive to the southeast sometime after the twenty-third.

After the American coup at Remagen, attention shifted to the north, where, seemingly, the stage was set for Montgomery's crossing, scheduled for 23 March. Patton, however, had other ideas. As his divisions drew up to the Rhine on 20–21 March, he could not resist the chance to beat his old rival across. Ever since the dash across France in August, he had carefully accumulated bridging equipment and assault boats for an attack across the Rhine. He had also put his staff to work on plans for such an attack some three months earlier. So although the Third Army crossed on the run, it had prepared for the leap.

Unannounced by any artillery bombardment, two battalions of the 5th Division slipped into the river at Nierstein and Op-

penheim late on the evening of 22 March. Against scant resistance they made the opposite shore and fanned out. By midnight, the whole 11th Infantry was across, at a cost of twenty
casualties. Buildup in the bridgehead proceeded rapidly, aided
by a treadway bridge which engineers completed on the
twenty-third. That morning Bradley told the press that "without
benefit of aerial bombing, ground smoke, artillery preparation,
and airborne assistance, the Third Army at 2200 hours, Thursday evening, 22 March, crossed the Rhine River."

Monty may have been upstaged but he still had an audience.
Churchill and Eisenhower were both in attendance to see the
start of the 21 Army Group's assault. The focal point was Wesel,
a small industrial city on the lower Rhine which stood at the
center of road, rail, and canal networks. The plan called for
multiple crossings along a twenty-two-mile front by units of the
First Canadian Army, the Second British Army, and the Ninth
U.S. Army, and an airborne attack by the First Allied Airborne. Once bridgeheads were secured, the Canadians were to
swing north to the sea to trap the remaining German troops in
the Netherlands, the British were to drive eastward across the
northern German plain in the direction of Berlin, and the
Americans were to skirt the Ruhr as the northern arm of a pincers to join with the Third Army east of the Ruhr.

At 1800, 5,500 artillery pieces began a bombardment of hor-
rendous intensity. Ninth Army guns alone fired 65,261 rounds in
an hour at the peak. The Scots of the 51st Highland Division,
XXX Corps, jumped off first at 2100. An hour later, a British
commando brigade crossed at Wesel. The 15th Scottish Division, 30th U.S., and 79th U.S. divisions followed in the early
hours of the twenty-fourth. Nowhere were the crossings contested. The two American divisions suffered only thirty-one casualties in the assault. Against slight resistance, the Ninth Army
quickly moved out of the crossing sites. Only at the extreme left
of the Allied front were the Germans able to hold up advance,
but after two days of hard fighting, this resistance too was over-

come. By 28 March, the 21 Army Group had a bridgehead thirty-five miles wide and up to twelve miles deep with twelve bridges across the river.

With the British, Canadian, and American armies across the Rhine—the Third Army had crossed again at St. Goar on 25 March, at Mainz on 27 March, and the Seventh Army at Worms on 26 March—De Gaulle cabled his field commander General de Lattre de Tassigny: "My dear General, you must cross the Rhine, even if the Americans do not agree and even if you have to cross it in rowboats. It is a matter of the greatest national interest." De Lattre already had clearance to cross, but receipt of this telegram on 29 March inspired an improvised assault on the thirty-first. Before dawn, an Algerian division using four rubber boats shuttled across ten men at a time. That same day a division of Moroccans established a tiny bridgehead farther north against determined resistance.

These two French crossings near Speyer put all the Allied armies on the east bank of the Rhine. Little more than a month later, German commanders signed papers of capitulation at Reims on 7 May 1945. The surrender went into effect at 2301, 8 May—V-E Day. The march to victory was done.

Tour of the Rhine Crossing

None of the bridges put in by Allied engineers remains, and with two exceptions there are no memorials or relics marking the sites of the assaults across the Rhine. The stone towers of the Ludendorff Bridge at Remagen still stand. Atop those on the west side the flags of the United States and the Federal Republic fly, and on the wall facing the river is a small plaque. A stone memorial on the riverbank just south of Speyer marks the spot where the French launched their crossing.

A tour of the Rhine crossing sites can be made in one long sweep by driving along the river. On the west bank Route 9 runs virtually the whole length. Bridges and ferries permit you to

302

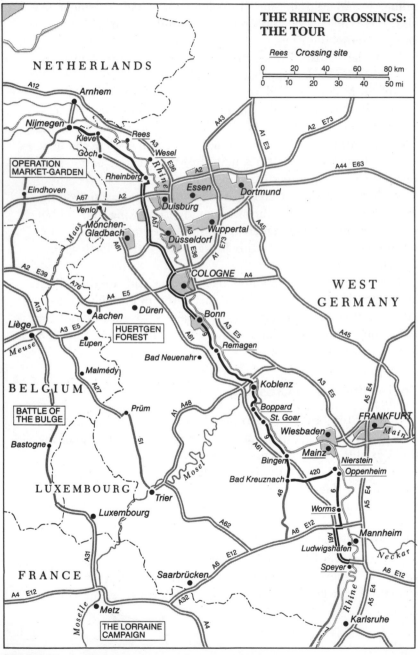

THE RHINE CROSSINGS:
THE TOUR

Rees Crossing site

0   20   40   60   80 km
0   10   20   30   40   50 mi

NETHERLANDS

A12   Arnhem

Nijmegen
Kleve   Rees
Goch   Wesel

OPERATION
MARKET-GARDEN   Rheinberg

Eindhoven   A67   A2
Venlo

Mönchen-
Gladbach
Düsseldorf

Essen   Dortmund
Duisburg
Wuppertal

COLOGNE   A4

WEST
GERMANY

A2 E39   A76

A4 E5

Liège   A3 E5   Aachen   Düren   Bonn
Meuse   Eupen   HUERTGEN
FOREST   Remagen
Malmédy   Bad Neuenahr

BELGIUM   Prüm   Koblenz

BATTLE OF
THE BULGE   Boppard
St. Goar

Bastogne   Wiesbaden   FRANKFURT
Main

Bingen   Mainz
LUXEMBOURG   Bad Kreuznach   Niérstein
Trier   Oppenheim

Luxembourg   Worms

Mannheim
Ludwigshafen   Neckar

FRANCE   Saarbrücken   Speyer

A4 E12   Metz   Karlsruhe

THE LORRAINE
CAMPAIGN

MAP 34

cross to the other side at many places. North of Cologne the Rhine valley is densely populated and heavily industrialized. South of Cologne the rainy weather often encountered along the Rhine is more than relieved by the picturesque villages and the views of vineyards and castles perched high on the adjacent bluffs. The distance from Rees to Speyer is about 350 kilometers.

You may choose to visit these sites in several sallies from the battlefields to the west. The northern crossings are readily accessible from Nijmegen. Thus, after touring the Market-Garden battlefield, you could drive east from Nijmegen on Route 9 to Kleve and then southeast on Route 57. The crossing sites near Rees, Wesel, and Rheinberg are just off Route 57 and all are within 50 kilometers of Kleve.

A visit to Remagen and the other southern crossings might follow the Huertgen Forest or Ardennes tour. Aachen to Remagen is 130 kilometers via E 5 and A 61. Further south on Route 9 are Boppard (54 kilometers) and St. Goar. Oppenheim and Nierstein lie another 100 kilometers south of St. Goar.

REMAGEN

From Aachen take E 5 toward Cologne (Köln). At the junction with A 61 turn southeast. Leave A 61 at the exit for Bad Neuenahr. In that town go east on Route 266, which runs into Route 9. Turn north and drive into Remagen. Watch for Allwetterbad Strasse on the river side and then follow the signs to the "Brücke von Remagen." There is a ferry at Sinzig-Linz just south of Remagen which allows yuo to visit the east side of the crossing site.

BOPPARD–ST. GOAR

Continue south on Route 9 to Boppard and St. Goar. At the latter is a ferry to St. Goarhausen across the river.

OPPENHEIM-NIERSTEIN

Proceed south on Route 9 to Bingen. Turn south on Route 48 and then southeast on Route 424—this routes you around Mainz, which is a maze. At the junction with Route 420 turn east to Route 9. Nierstein lies just north of this intersection and Oppenheim just to the south.

WORMS-SPEYER

Continue south on Route 9 for 27 km to Worms. Should you go on to Speyer, avoid Ludwigshafen by taking A 6 west and then A 61 south to join Route 9 a few km north of Speyer.

M-10 tank destroyers of the 3d Armored negotiate a muddy track in
the Huertgen Forest. (*U.S. Army*)

Two GIs from the 102d Division enjoy Thanksgiving dinner near
Wauruchen, Germany. (*U.S. Army*)

Two GIs wearing newly issued snow capes patrol near Vossenack in early January 1945. (*U.S. Army*)

5th Division infantrymen carry a boat down to the Moselle at Dornot, France. (*U.S. Army*)

Troops of the 319th Infantry, 80th Division, take shelter near Faulquemont against the incessant rain. (*U.S. Army*)

DUKWs carry supplies across the Rhine in support of First Army's Remagen bridgehead. (*U.S. Army*)

APPENDIX A

Museums

Belgium

Bastogne: Bastogne Historical Center. Located northeast of Bastogne off N 474.

This is the major museum for the Battle of the Bulge. All the holdings of the former Museé de l'Offensive des Ardennes at Spa are now exhibited here. Most remarkable in the large and varied collection is film footage shot during the battle. There are also dioramas, an extensive display of American and German uniforms, and many vehicles.

There is a large shop and bookstore. Open 0800–1900 daily during the summer, and 0900–1800 the rest of the year; closed mid-November to mid-March. Admission charge.

Museum. Located at 20 Rue de Neufchâteau in the center of town.

This is a small private museum which collects battlefield remains ranging from mess kits to small arms. Most of the articles are for sale

No opening times were posted. Admission charge.

La Gleize: Musée. Located in the café Echo des Campagnes on the square in front of the post office.

This small private museum collects battlefield remains. No opening times were posted. Admission charge.

Another museum was scheduled to open in La Gleize in the summer of 1984. Inquire locally.

Malmédy: Musée. Located at the Baugnez crossroads—N 32/N 23—four kilometers southeast of Malmédy.

This small private museum contains a few uniforms, weapons, photographs, and contemporary newspapers.

No opening times were posted. Inquire at the café. Donations asked.

England

Aldershot: Museum of Airborne Forces. Located on Queens Avenue in Aldershot, Hampshire.

The museum traces the history of British airborne forces. The original briefing terrain models for operations at Pegasus Bridge, Arnhem, and other objectives can be seen. Much airborne equipment, including a motorcycle, and a jeep prepared for drop, and the cockpit of a Horsa glider, is displayed. Small arms occupy a separate room. This is a well-organized museum with a large and interesting collection.

There is a small shop and bookstore. Open Monday through Friday 0900–1230 and 1400–1630; 0930–1230 and 1400–1630 Saturday; and 1000–1230 and 1400–1630 Sunday. Admission charge.

Bovington Camp: Royal Armoured Corps Tank Museum. Located northwest of Wool near Wareham, Dorset.

The museum contains over 150 tanks and armored cars which exemplify development from "Little Willie," the first World War I tank, to post–World War II models. Many World War II tanks from around the world are displayed, including a number of Sherman variants. Film footage of tanks in battle is shown in a special viewing room. The facility is a bit congested, but this is one of the two best armored museums in the world.

There is a large shop and bookstore and a restaurant. Open Monday through Friday 1000–1230 and 1400–1645; 0915–1230 and 1400–1600 on Saturdays, Sundays, and bank holidays. Admission charge.

Duxford: Imperial War Museum. Located off the M 11 south of Cambridge, Cambridgeshire.

The Imperial War Museum has converted this former RAF and Eighth Air Force fighter base into a museum. The hangars are used to display and restore the more than seventy aircraft in the collection—among them, a B-29 Superfortress, B-17, P-51, and P-47. The sheds house some fifty military vehicles, including tanks, transports, and a Jagdpanther tank destroyer. The airfield is still in use. On special days historic aircraft put on demonstration flights. On a more regular basis, the military vehicles are driven about the grounds. For a fee you can take a short flight in a P-51 Mustang.

There is a restaurant. Open 1030–1730 daily from March to November. Admission charge.

London: Hendon Air Museums. Located in northwest London. Nearest Underground station is Colindale on the Northern Line.

Hendon comprises three museums—the RAF Museum, the Battle of Britain Museum, and the Bomber Command Museum. The RAF Museum displays aircraft flown by the RAF from its beginnings early in the twentieth century to the present. The Battle of Britain Museum is the most complete collection of the aircraft which figured in the battle. There are also reconstructions of the 11 Group Operations Room, an anti-aircraft battery, and an air-raid shelter, among other things. The recently opened (April 1983) Bomber Command Museum is dedicated to the pilots and crews of the USAAF and RAF who lost their lives in the bomber offensive. It displays bombers built for service in World War II and to the present, including a B-17, a B-25 Mitchell, a Mosquito, and a Lancaster All the museums are exceptionally well done. The buildings are spacious and well lighted, and the collections are well displayed.

There is a large shop and bookstore at the entrance to the RAF and Bomber Command museums and a restaurant adjacent to the Battle of Britain Museum. Open 1000–1800 every day. Admission charge to each museum.

HMS *Belfast.* Moored on the south bank of the Thames opposite the Tower of London. Nearest Underground station is London Bridge on the Northern Line. You can also reach HMS *Belfast* by ferry from the Tower.

This 11,900 ton cruiser provided fire support at Juno Beach on D Day. She was launched in 1938 and served on active duty until 1963. Most of the ship is open to public inspection. There are many special exhibits, including one on Operation Overlord. The displays are well done, and the ship is fascinating.

Open 1100–1750 daily in the summer; 1100–1630 in the winter; closed holidays. Admission charge.

Imperial War Museum. Located south of the Thames on Lambeth Road. Nearest Underground station is Lambeth North on the Bakerloo Line.

This museum is devoted to all conflicts involving British forces since 1914. Special exhibits are a regular feature. The collection is large and includes a Spitfire, German V-1 and V-2 rockets, and Montgomery's campaign trailers. The museum is congested, but there is much here to reward the visitor.

There is a large shop and bookstore. Open Monday through Saturday 1000–1750 and Sunday 1400–1750; closed holidays. Admission is free.

National Army Museum. Located on Royal Hospital Road in Chelsea. Nearest Underground station is Sloane Square on the Circle or the District Line.

This museum traces the history of the British army through five centuries up to 1900.

Open 1000–1730 Monday–Saturday and 1400–1730 Sunday; closed holidays. Admission charge.

Portsmouth: D-Day Museum. Located off Clarence Esplanade near Southsea Castle in the Portsmouth suburb of Southsea.

The museum contains exhibits and simulations dealing with all aspects of the invasion. The relative absence of hardware is made up for by an excellent slide show which runs every half-hour. Also on permanent display is the Overlord Embroidery, the modern counterpart of the Bayeux Tapestry, which commemorates the invasion. This is the best of the D Day museums.

There is a shop and bookstore. Open 1030–1900 weekdays and 1030–2100 weekends. Admission charge.

Yeovilton: Fleet Air Arm Museum. Located off the A 303 near Ilchester, Somerset.

Over fifty aircraft are displayed. There are many dioramas and model aircraft and ships. A large exhibit is devoted to the Falkland Islands campaign. The museum does not emphasize World War II aircraft.

There is a shop and bookstore and a restaurant. Open 1000–1730 daily except 24–25 December. Admission charge.

France

Normandy, Arromanches-les-Bains: Exposition Permanente du Débarquement. Located near the seawall in the small port of Arromanches.

Displays include a diorama of the landing beaches which uses lights and commentary to explain D Day operations, a British film showing the construction of the Mulberry, and a magnificent model of Mulberry B. The remains of the real Mulberry can be seen through the panoramic window running the length of the building. In addition there are cases with mementos, weapons, and photographs. Along with some fieldpieces, an LCA sits on the sand on the museum's south side. The museum is said to be crowded most of the time—it was in June 1984—so be prepared for a wait. This fine museum is definitely worth visiting.

Bayeux: Musée Mémorial de la Bataille de Normandie. Located on the Boulevard General Fabian Ware near the British military cemetery.

This museum, opened in 1982, houses an extensive collection of weapons, mementos, and uniforms. Over one hundred manikins dressed in the uniforms and carrying the weapons of the multitude of units (German as well as Allied) which fought in Normandy line the walls. Outside are an American M-10 tank destroyer, a British Churchill Mark VII Crocodile, and a German "Hetzer" Jagdpanzer (tank destroyer). Do not miss it when you are in Bayeux.

Bénouville: Musée des Troupes Aéroportées. Located adjacent to the Pegasus Bridge.

The exhibits of this small museum are devoted to retelling the story of the British airborne assault. On display are mementos donated by participants, including some donated by General Humfrey Gale, a relief map of the area, and the bagpipes carried by Bill Millin.

Open April through September 1000–1230 and 1430–1700. Admission charge.

Cherbourg: Musée de la Libération au "Fort du Roule." Located adjacent to the Fort du Roule on the bluff overlooking the town from the south.

The museum's collection of weapons, flags, and uniforms— some of the latter donated by the U.S. Military Academy—has now been sadly depleted by the six burglaries since 1954.

Merville: Musée de la Batterie de Merville. Located east of the Orne River just outside the town of Merville-Franceville.

One of the original casemates of the Merville Battery has been converted into a small museum which concentrates on the British attack. The museum, which opened in 1982, contains various models and exhibits which are explained by a recorded narration.

Open June through August 1030–1230 and 1400–1730; closed
Tuesdays. Admission charge.

Ouistreham-Riva-Bella: Musée du Commando No. 4. Located on the
Boulevard du 6 Juin near the Riva-Bella beach.

This small private museum contains displays of weapons and
memorabilia focused on the commandos of the 1st Special Service Brigade. There are some interesting photographs of the casino before and after the invasion and of a number of General
Hobart's specialized armored vehicles. A "Goliath," a small German remote-controlled tank, is one of the more unusual exhibits.
Photography is strictly forbidden.

Open June to 15 September 0900–1200 and 1400–1830. Admission charge.

Ste.-Marie-du-Mont–La Madeleine: Musée du Débarquement à Utah
Beach. Located where D 913 reaches the beach at La Madeleine.

A German bunker (W5) on the beach sector where the 8th Infantry was scheduled to land has been converted into a small museum devoted to telling the story of the landings. Displays
include weapons and mementos. There are two slide shows, one
with commentary in French, the other in English, with the
French version much better done. Upstairs is a terrain board
using lights and models to recreate the landing sequence. The
commentary is in rapid-fire French. Handsets provide an English
translation, but they do not work well near the board. On the
sand dunes outside there are various pieces of equipment, including a Sherman tank and two Alligators.

Ste.-Mère-Eglise: Musée des Troupes Aéroportées. Located just off the
town square in Ste.-Mère-Eglise.

This interesting museum, opened in 1964, focuses on the
American airborne assault in the early hours of D Day. The cor-
nerstone of the building—the roof of which is fluted like a parachute canopy—was dedicated by Lieutenant General James
Gavin, deputy commander of the 82d Airborne Division on D
Day. You enter the museum through the body of a Waco glider.
The collection itself is composed of weapons, mementos, photographs, and documents concerning the night drop. Behind the
museum is an annex housing one of the C-47s of the 92d Squadron, 439th Troop Carrier Group, which actually flew missions on
D Day. A well-preserved Sherman (an Easy Eight) and a 90-mm
anti-aircraft gun are parked on the museum grounds. This is a
museum you should make every effort to see while in Normandy.

Open Easter through October 0900-1200 and 1400-1900; open on Sundays and bank holidays during winter. Admission charge.
Surrain: Musée de la Libération de Normandie. Located in the village of Surrain some 12 kilometers west of Bayeux on N 13.

This exposition consists of a private collection of World War II memorabilia, including helmets, insignia, rations, and other equipment; some, if not all, is for sale.

Opens at 0900 from Easter to September. Admission charge.
Tilly-sur-Seulles: Musée de la Bataille de Tilly. Located in a lovely romanesque chapel near the center of the village.

The exhibits in this municipal exposition are concerned with the weeks of fierce fighting in the vicinity as the 50th British Division sought to outflank Caen.

Open June through August on selected days (every day in July and August) 1430-1900; open Saturdays and Sundays in September 1430-1900.
Vierville-sur-Mer: Exposition Omaha, 6 Juin 1944. Located in a Nissen hut just outside Vierville on D 514.

This private collection is devoted mainly to the American landing on Omaha Beach.

Open Easter to September 1000-1200 and 1400-1700. Admission charge.

In addition to these museums, several small expositions based on private collections could be seen during the summer of 1984. Two of the more interesting were found in Garvus, southwest of Caen, and in Falaise. It is unlikely that these collections will be on display in subsequent years. There is also a small municipal museum located in L'Aigle, on N 26, 54 kilometers east of Argentan. Open April through October 1000-1200 and 1400-18.30; closed Mondays in winter.
Paris. Musée de l Armée. Located in the Hôtel des Invalides. Metro stop: Invalides.

The collection of the Army Museum is one of the world's finest. Although most exhibits predate the twentieth century, there are several galleries devoted to World War I and World War II arms and memorabilia. World War II exhibits occupy a large gallery on the second floor, west. Through photographs, mementos, and documents, the visitor is led through the war years, from the debacle of 1940 to the triumph of Allied arms in 1945. French military activity is emphasized. Films on both world wars are shown in a theater on the ground floor, east side. Your admission ticket is also valid for two days for the Museum of Relief Maps and Plans (an exhibit of fortress models) and the Dome Church, where Napoleon is buried.

Since there is a cafeteria in the building, you may plan to spend the day. Open April through September 1000–1800 (to 1700 in winter); closed 1 January, 1 May, 1 November, and 25 December. Admission charge.

Musée de l'Ordre de la Libération. Located west of the Hôtel des Invalides on the Boulevard Latour-Maubourg. Metro stop: Invalides.

De Gaulle formed the Order of the Liberation in 1940 and closed its membership in 1946. Enrolled were those who made outstanding contributions to the liberation of France. This small museum is devoted to the memory of those individuals, thereby preserving the history of the resistance and liberation. Displays include the mementos and personal effects of Leclerc, Jean Moulin, De Gaulle, Eisenhower, and many others. One wing is given over to the heroes of the Free French forces; the other is devoted to the memory of the members of the resistance. All signs and captions are in French.

Open September through July 1400–1700; closed Sundays and holidays. Admission charge.

Musée de l'Air. Located at Le Bourget Airport just north of Paris on Autoroute A 1.

This outstanding air museum contains a number of World War II aircraft, including a FW-190, Bf 109, Ju 52, and many others. A model of the *Spirit of Saint Louis* commemorates Charles Lindbergh's landing at Le Bourget after his 1927 solo flight across the Atlantic. We would rank this museum just behind those at Hendon and Duxford in England.

There is a bookstore and shop. Open May through October 1000–1800; in winter to 1700. Closed Mondays, 25 December, and 1 January.

Musée de la Marine. Located in the Chaillot Palace. Metro stop: Trocadéro.

The Musée de la Marine is one of the world's truly great naval and maritime museums. Unfortunately, the exhibits pertaining to the World War II era are confined to a few ship models and a few paintings of the D Day landings. Still, it is worth the trip just to see the graceful barge built for Napoleon in 1811. Almost half the museum is devoted to non-military French maritime history.

There is a bookstore and shop. Open year round 1000–1800; closed Tuesdays and holidays. Admission charge.

Saumur: Musée des Blindés. Located on the western side of the city, inside the Cavalry School grounds. Saumur itself is in the Loire valley 63 kilometers west of Tours, some 300 kilometers southwest of Paris.

The French army's tank museum contains an impressive collection of World War II tanks, armored vehicles, and weapons, German as well as Allied. The total collection runs over 120 items. On display are several modifications of the American M-4 (Sherman) and the Russian T-34. It is worth the trip just to browse through the museum's back lot, where you can examine unrestored military vehicles (and their parts), some of which date back to the pre-World War II era.

There is a bookstall inside the museum. Open daily 0900–1130 and 1400–1730. Admission charge.

Luxembourg

Clervaux: Battle of the Bulge Museum. Located in the château at the east end of the ridge above the Place de la Libération.

The collection includes many small arms and uniforms. Its outstanding feature is the extensive display of before and after the battle photographs. The latter alone makes a visit worthwhile. The château also houses the original Stieglitz Family of Man, which should provide some relief from the record of human discord.

Open 1000–1700 daily. Admission charge.

Wiltz: Museum of the Battle of the Bulge. Located in the upper town on the Grand Rue (N 15).

This small museum has on display a number of small arms and uniforms and a set of before and after the battle photographs. Nearby is one of the ubiquitous Shermans.

Open 1000–1200 and 1300–1700 daily. Admission charge.

The Netherlands

Oosterbeek: Airborne Museum. Located at 232 Utrechtseweg in the Arnhem suburb of Oosterbeek.

The museum occupies the former Hartenstein Hotel, which was General Urquhart's 1st Airborne Division headquarters during the battle of Arnhem. Several field guns and a Firefly are situated on the grounds. Inside one can see a diorama with commentary which describes the course of the battle. Many contemporary photographs, weapons, and uniforms are displayed. The emphasis is on 1st Airborne operations at Arnhem, but some space is given to the 82d and 101st as well. This is a fine museum with a large and interesting collection.

There is a shop and bookstore. Open weekdays 1100–1700 and 1200–1700 Sundays. Admission charge.

Overloon: Oorlogsmuseum. Located north of Venray and east of the village of Overloon, province of Noord Brabant.

Situated in a park of thirty-five acres, this museum contains a large number of military vehicles and guns set along its outdoor trails. Among others, you can see a German *Nebelwerfer* (a multi-barrel rocket launcher), a Mark V Panther, a Sherman V Flail, a DUKW, and a Weasel. A documentation center houses a small-arms collection, uniforms and other equipment, and many maps and photographs which tell the story of the Dutch people from 1940 to 1945. A special exhibit chronicles the treatment meted out to Dutch Jews during the Nazi occupation. This is a first-rate museum.

There is a shop and bookstore. Open 0900–1900 daily; closed 24–26 and 31 December and New Year's Day. Admission charge.

Select Bibliography

General

The most extensive treatments of operations in Europe are the various official histories. For the U.S. army, see the multi-volume series written by the Office of the Chief of Military History, Department of the Army, *United States Army in World War II: The European Theater of Operations*. The British story is found in L. F. Ellis, *Victory in the West* (2 vols., 1962, 1968), and that of the Canadians in C. P. Stacey, *The Victory Campaign* (1960). W. F. Craven and J. L. Cate edited *The Army Air Forces in World War II* (7 vols., 1948–58). Sir Charles Webster and Noble Frankland, *The Strategic Air Offensive Against Germany, 1939–1945* (4 vols., 1961) records the efforts of Bomber Command.

Among the shorter and more accessible histories, Charles B. MacDonald's *The Mighty Endeavor* (1969) is the best general introduction, although half the book is devoted to the Mediterranean campaigns. He is evenhanded in his treatment of the controversies which marked the Allied effort. Chester Wilmot in *The Struggle for Europe* (1951) takes the British side in those controversies. This work, as dated and argumentative as it is, remains important. Russell F. Weigley, *Eisenhower's Lieutenants* (1981) is less about the commanders than it is a close account of operations from D Day through the final victory. Weigley has come close to providing a condensation of the official histories. In a lengthy bibliography, he identifies the memoirs of the commanders and the unit histories.

The German point of view is reported in B. H. Liddell Hart, *The Other Side of the Hill* (2d ed., 1973); H. A. Jacobsen and J. Rohwer, eds., *The*

Decisive Battles of World War II: The German Side (1965); and Cajus Becker, *The Luftwaffe War Diaries* (1968).

Time-Life Books has a series entitled *World War II*, with individual volume titles. Some volumes are devoted to operations in northern Europe. All are excellent pictorial histories.

A small group of World War II buffs in England publish *After the Battle*, a magazine quarterly. Each issue (there are now over forty) features stories, illustrated with "then and now" photographs, which deal with various phases of the war. Many back issues contain invaluable information for anyone wishing to explore World War II sites.

Duane Denfeld, *World War II Museums and Relics of Europe* (1980) is a country-by-country listing of the museums, sites, and monuments. Russia is not included, but many Eastern European countries are. Because Denfeld attempted so much, he missed much. Nonetheless, his work is helpful.

The war also inspired the writing of many fictional works. A few of these which you might enjoy are John Hersey, *The War Lover* (1959); Irwin Shaw, *The Young Lions* (1948); Beirne Lay, Jr., and Sy Bartlett, *Twelve O'Clock High* (1948); and Len Deighton, *Goodbye, Mickey Mouse* (1982).

Two books which elude our categories but which ought not to escape attention are Bill Mauldin, *Up Front* (1945) and Keith Mallory and Arvid Ottar, *The Architecture of War* (1973).

Battle of Britain and the Bomber Offensive

The best short introduction to the Battle of Britain is Len Deighton, *Battle of Britain* (1980). Many excellent photographs illustrate the text. In *Fighter: The True Story of the Battle of Britain* (1978), Deighton expands on the ideas presented in his later work and provides a day-by-day analysis.

Among the "few" who wrote accounts of their experiences, see Alan C. Deere, *Nine Lives* (1969); John Kent, *One of the Few* (1971); and Peter Townsend, *Duel of Eagles* (1971). George Goldsmith-Carter, *The Battle of Britain: The Home Front* (1974), describes how Britons reacted to the Blitz.

A good introduction to the strategic bomber offensive is Alfred Price, *Battle over the Reich* (1973). Price concentrates on Bomber Command and should be supplemented by Roger A. Freeman, *The Mighty Eighth* (1970). Anthony Verrier, *The Bomber Offensive* (1968), is highly critical of the strategy and tactics of Bomber Command and the USAAF.

Several American participants have written interesting, and often moving, books. Elmer Bendiner, a perceptive and sensitive observer, wrote *The Fall of Fortresses* (1980) from the perspective of a B-17 navigator. Bert Stiles, a B-17 pilot, contributed *Serenade to the Big Bird* (1952); and Robert Johnson, the second-leading ace in the ETO, wrote *Thunderbolt* (1958).

In their fine tribute to the Eighth Air Force, Philip Kaplan and Alan Smith, *One Last Look: A Sentimental Journey to the Eighth Air Force Heavy Bomber Bases of World War II in England* (1983), describe the life lived by the aircrews on base and in the air. There are many photographs of the bases then and now. Roger A. Freeman, *Airfields of the Eighth* (1978), more systematically describes the bases.

The Battle of Normandy and the Pursuit Across France

Just after the war the Army Historical Division published battle studies on Omaha Beach and St.-Lô which remain the most detailed accounts of those battles yet written. The naval side of the landings is told by Samuel Eliot Morison, *The Invasion of France and Germany, 1944–1945* (1957).

Because of the movie *The Longest Day*, which starred virtually every Hollywood actor who was anybody in 1964, Cornelius Ryan's book of the same name, published in 1959, is justly famous. By focusing on individuals' experiences, Ryan was able to bring real drama to the events of 5 and 6 June 1944.

Less well known are S. L. A. Marshall's *Night Drop* (1962), a detailed account of the American airborne assault, and "First Wave at Omaha Beach" in *Battle at Best* (1963), which recounts the travails of Company A of the 116th Infantry. Both works are based on Marshall's patented after-action interview techniques. Marshall also left a hilarious account of his liberation of Paris in "When Papa Took Paris," *American Heritage* 13 (1962), 4–7, 92–101, also in *Battle at Best* and *Bringing Up the Rear* (1979).

More recently, a spate of books on the Normandy campaign have appeared. Easily the most readable is John Keegan's *Six Armies in Normandy* (1982). By focusing on the experiences of the six national armies which fought in Normandy, Keegan moves the action from the American airborne drop zones to Paris, providing a wealth of information about those armies along the way. The following year, retired U.S. Army Colonel Carlo D'Este published *Decision in Normandy* (1983) in which he sifts judiciously through the controversies that have grown up around the Allied commanders and their command decisions, especially Montgomery's execution of his master plan. Less useful is Max Hasting's *Overlord: D-Day and the Battle for Normandy* (1984), which attempts to combine the narrative technique of a Cornelius Ryan with an argument for the superiority of German weapons and training.

The Battle of the Falaise Pocket has been treated by Eddy Florentin, *The Battle of the Falaise Gap* (1967); James Lucas and James Barker, *The Killing Ground* (1978); and more recently by Richard Rohmer, *Patton's Gap* (1981). None really explains why the pocket was not tightly closed, a question that S. L. A. Marshall said "would go forever unanswered."

The trail of the Third Army breakout can be followed in Robert S. Allen's *Lucky Forward* (1947) and Charles R. Codman's *Drive* (1957).

The events surrounding the liberation of Paris are skillfully recreated in Larry Collins and Dominique Lapierre, *Is Paris Burning?* (1965).

Finally, there is a priceless memoir written by a former private in the 506th Parachute Infantry—Donald R. Burgett's *Currahee!* (1967). Burgett makes immediate the experiences of a young paratrooper making that night jump into the Cotentin.

The oldest guide to the Normandy beaches is Patrice Boussel, *D-Day Beaches Revisited* (1966), which is quite comprehensive, therefore bulky, and now somewhat dated. It presumes that you have a great deal of time to spend touring the landing beaches and nearby areas. More useful is Tonie and Valmai Holt, *Holt's Battlefield Guides: Normandy-Overlord* (1983). Major Holt and his wife, who have been conducting battlefield tours for years, produced this handy pocket-sized guide for the do-it-yourself traveler in time for the 1984 anniversary. It is quite comprehensive—the user may become lost in the wealth of detail—and is focused primarily on the landing beaches. The Holts do a better job of describing British and Canadian operations than they do the American. Ted Humes's *A Guide to the Atlantic Wall and D-Day Beaches* (1984) is unique in that it includes Atlantic Wall sites from Calais south, through Boulogne and Dieppe, to Le Havre. Unfortunately, it is marred by occasional errors of fact and omission.

Available in Europe are four additional guides of varying quality: Jean-Pierre Benamou, *The Landing Beaches* (1982); Philippe Jutras, *A Guide for Sainte Mere Eglise* . . . (1976); Raymond Ruffin, *Guide des Maquis et Hauts-lieux de la Resistance Normandie* (1984); and Joel Tanter and Maurice Chauvet, *A Guide to the Normandy Museums* (1983).

Market-Garden

Cornelius Ryan wrote the most vivid account in *A Bridge Too Far* (1974), upon which the movie was based. Christopher Hibbert, *The Battle of Arnhem* (1962), is also excellent. S. L. A. Marshall describes the trial of the 502d Parachute Infantry in the Zonsche Forest in a chapter of his *Battle at Best* (1963).

In addition to the memoirs of the commanders, firsthand accounts of particular interest are those of Colonel John Frost, *A Drop Too Many* (1980), and Ross S. Carter, *Those Devils in Baggy Pants* (1951).

Visitors to the battlefield should consult Tonic and Valmai Holt, *Holt's Battlefield Guides: Market-Garden Corridor* (1984).

Battle of the Bulge

Charles B. MacDonald's *Time for Trumpets* (1984) is a well-written, detailed narrative by this former captain in the 2d Infantry Division who fought in front of Rockerath and Krinkelt in December 1944. MacDonald joined the staff of the Office of the Chief of Military History after the war and wrote several volumes in the official series. He also wrote *Company Commander* (1947), which describes events at the level of the men at the front.

John Toland in *Battle: The Story of the Bulge* (1959) focuses on individuals in this day-by-day account. By drawing on his after-the-battle interviews with participants, S. L. A. Marshall in *Bastogne: The Story of the First Eight Days* (1946) explains what happened, and why, during the siege of Bastogne. Janice Holt Giles, *The Damned Engineers* (1970), relates the exploits of the combat engineers who did so much to impede the German advance.

Through the West Wall to the Rhine

The battle for Aachen is refought, street by street, in Charles Whiting's *Bloody Aachen* (1976). Charles B. MacDonald's *The Battle of the Huertgen Forest* (1963) captures the frustration and futility of that three-month-long battle.

There is little on the Lorraine campaign specifically outside the official sources and the unit histories. One notable exception is Anthony Kemp, *The Unknown Battle: Metz, 1944* (1980).

The crossing of the Rhine has received more attention. Ken Hechler,

The Bridge at Remagen (1957), is a well-done book based on the author's research for the Office of the Chief of Military History. John Toland in *The Last 100 Days* (1965) describes the Rhine crossings as well as other military operations at the close of the war.

Index

332